THE COMICS JOURNAL

#305

2020

COVER: HTML Flowers

TITLE PAGE: From *Dancing after TEN*, a Georgia
Webber and Vivian Chong collaboration.

THIS SPREAD: From Patrick Dean's sketchbook.

BACK COVER: Rebecca Kirby

Contributors

Fantagraphics Books, Inc.
7563 Lake City Way NE
Seattle, WA 98115
Fantagraphics.com
Facebook.com/fantagraphics
Twitter: @fantagraphics

First Printing: March 2020
ISBN: 978-1-68396-277-9
LOC Control Number: 2018949537
Printed in: Korea

Editor in Chief: Gary Groth

Managing Editors: RJ Casey and Kristy Valenti

Consulting Editor: Michael Dean

Designer: Justin Allan-Spencer

Production: Paul Baresh and Christina Hwang

Promotion: Jacq Cohen

Editorial Assistance: Jasmin Davis, Sora Hong, Alyson Podesta and Katherine Thomas

Advertising: Matt Silvie

Special thanks to Dr. Ann Casey and Pat Thomas.

For advertising information, email silvie@fantagraphics.com

For more thoughtful criticism and reviews, visit tcj.com

Alec Berry is a poet, novelist and journalist living in West Virgina. He has covered comics for Comic Book Resources and tcj.com.

Alece Birnbach is an illustrator and art director. Birnbach founded the Graphic Recording Studio, for which she creates live drawings for conferences, workshops and trade shows. She lives in California.

MK Czerwiec is a registered nurse, educator and the artist-in-residence at Northwestern University's Feinberg School of Medicine. Czerwiec is the author of 2017's *Taking Turns: Stories from HIV/AIDS Care Unit 371* and the co-author of the Eisner Award-nominated *Graphic Medicine Manifesto.*

Patrick Dean is a cartoonist from Athens, Georgia. He has had comics published in *Vice* and *Oxford American*, and is an organizer of the annual FLUKE Mini-Comics & Zine Festival.

In 1968, **Aaron Dixon** became a founder and first captain of the Seattle chapter of the Black Panther Party. Dixon formed the nonprofit Central House in 2002 to provide education and shelter for homeless youth in Seattle. He campaigned for the United States Senate with the Green Party in 2006. *My People are Rising*, his memoir, was published in 2012. Dixon continues to be an anti-war, civil rights and health care activist from his home in New Mexico.

Kayla E. lives in North Carolina and is a cartoonist, designer and editor-in-chief of *Nat. Brut* magazine. She has been profiled on NPR Illustration, and *American Illustration* has featured her work. Currently, she is on the board of directors of the illustration conference ICON.

Kim Jooha is a writer living in Toronto. In 2017, Jooha was nominated for the Best Online Comics Studies Scholarship Award.

Sloane Leong is a cartoonist, colorist and writer who has been published by Image, DC and tcj.com. She has been nominated for an Ignatz Award, and her graphic novel, *A Map to the Sun*, will be released by First Second in 2020.

Eisner Award-nominated cartoonist **Noah Van Sciver** has had his work appear in publications like *Mad* magazine and *Best American Comics*. A collection of Van Sciver's *Fante Bukowski* series is slated for 2020, and he is currently at work on a graphic novel covering the Grateful Dead from his home in South Carolina.

Editors' Note

COMICS AND HEALTH CARE have long been bound together; for example, the Baltimore City Medical Society published a 1950 Will Eisner studio comic about the "horrors" of socialized medicine ("The Sad Case of Waiting Room Willie," reprinted in *TCJ* #267) and Joyce Sutton and Lyn Chevli tackle women's medical rights in their 1973 underground comic *Abortion Eve.* Issue #305 focuses on how the post-2006 rise of the graphic memoir is tied to the graphic medicine genre, and how today's cartoonists are using the medium to examine and critique our system, communicate their experiences as fully as possible and, to some extent, destigmatize and deromanticize disability and illness. From stories about giving shape to the hopes of health care professionals, blackly humorous hospital high jinks, to cautionary tales about how infirmity comes for us all eventually, our authors and their works create a snapshot of 2020 life.

This issue also features a zine about voting rights that is as timely today as it was in 1967; an homage to one of the funniest cartoonists born in the 19th century by one of the funniest born in the 20th; and an appreciation of Little Lulu. The creators and communities of the past are reaching forward, handing tools to us in the present. What can we build with them in the future?

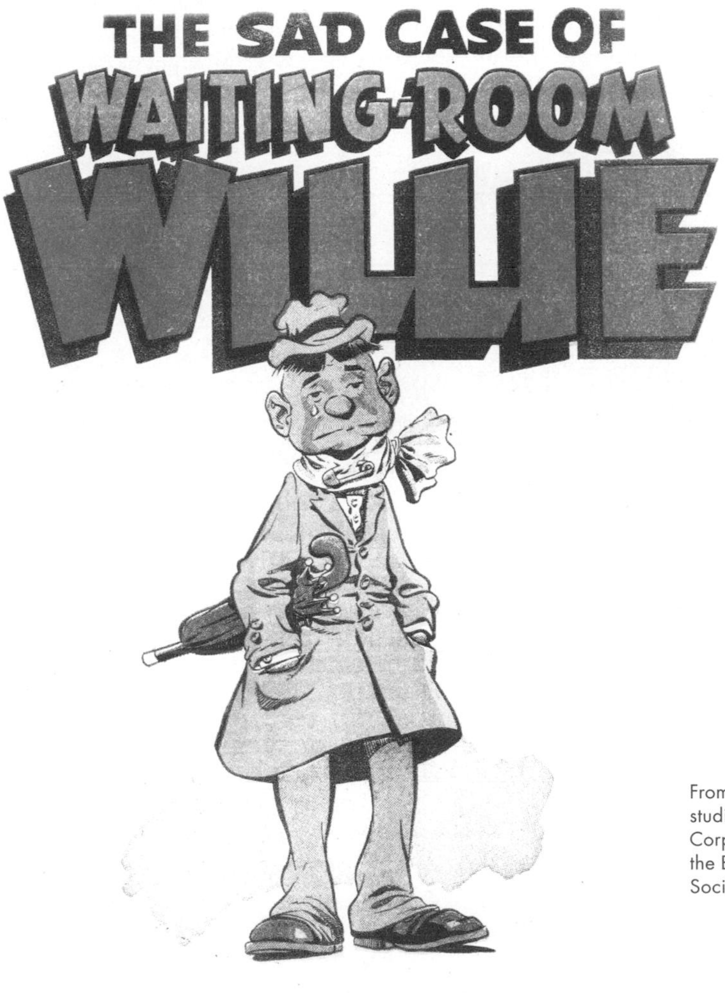
THE SAD CASE OF
WAITING-ROOM
WILLIE

From a comic by Will Eisner's studio, American Visuals Corporation, distributed by the Baltimore City Medical Society, 1950.

BLOOD & THUNDER

In this issue, we reached out to cartoonists across the medium and asked: "How do you approach physical movement and anatomy when creating comics?"

Illustrations by Ben Nadler

SINCE I'M PRIMARILY DRAWING PEOPLE smashing their bodies together, I put a lot of importance on understanding anatomy. Starting from the initial gesture drawing, I make sure the action is readable even in silhouette. As for motion, I try to apply the animation principles of "squash and stretch" while looking for unique ways to apply those drawings to comics. I make it a habit!

Lin Visel

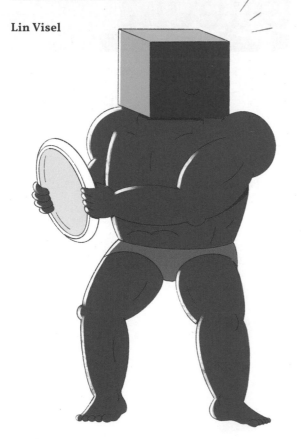

DRAWING THE FIGURE has become a cathartic practice for me. I have a tendency toward restraint with my own physicality, almost to the point of stoicism, which I consider to be a personal flaw. Drawing a writhing figure in a still moment of physical confusion is a way for me to process violent reactions to stress. I have not punched a wall since I was a boy, but I have related countless moments of physical distress in my work. Cartoonists are a big influence on the way I approach anatomy. I do use tropes from classic cartooning in my work, but I also like to push the design of my figures beyond what is considered a classic cartoon figure. For instance, I may leave out an arm because I can't find a way to make two arms work together as a design. If the emotion is there in the drawing, and I've captured how the figures are feeling, anatomy becomes a secondary concern.

Jason Murphy

- I don't know if comics will break your heart, but they will most likely give you carpal tunnel, so it's not a stretch to say that my approach has been informed in no small part by physical limitations. Drawing for more than an hour or two is painful and exhausting, especially in the slashy-stabby manner that I've developed in my attempts to reduce every body I draw into a single gesture, both for efficiency and aesthetics.

- I never use photo references, although I often rummage through my memory banks and act things out (within reason).

- I tend to obsess about wrists, and I can spend hours redrawing a single hand, and often I go through hundreds of decent drawings until I find one that has the right feeling — this quality has nothing to do with beauty or storytelling, it is the same search for the thingness of the thing that makes me shuffle synonyms for months until the writing behind the words becomes invisible.

- I look for gestures that say everything and nothing at once, that seem to contradict each other. Certainty is depressing.

- I have noticed that all the sentences above begin with "I."

Roman Muradov

I USE THE CLASSIC "armature" technique (I don't actually know what this approach is called. If it has a name, someone please tell me), which I learned from *How to Draw the Marvel Way* and *Drawing the Head and Figure* by Jack Hamm, where you start out with a proportional stick figure moving through space, and then you construct the flesh and clothing over it. It's not really a stick figure — it's made of forms, which change depending in whether or not the figure is facing forwards or sideways. I love the Marvel philosophy of making movement as dynamic as humanly possible, and I mention John Stanley whenever I get a chance, and Dan DeCarlo as well, because the kinetic energy of their figures is so infectious. Also — I learned this technique from watching a documentary about William Kentridge — I work with a mirror by my desk. Two full-length mirrors, actually — one in front of me and one off to the side, both salvaged from the trash. I use them when I'm having particular difficulty drawing a pose, and I use myself as reference when I need to.

Anya Davidson

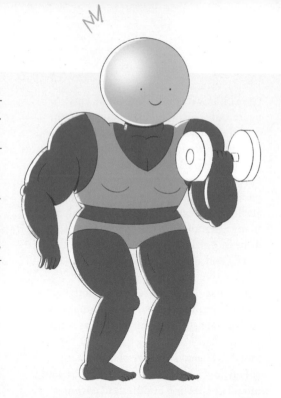

BEFORE I STUDIED VISUAL ART, my early sketchbooks were filled with ideas for choreographies. The notation of sequences was text-based — tiny stories, grouped into the corners of the page signifying their location on the stage or their relation to a musical phrase. These microstories indicated what moving a certain way reminded me of. However, as soon as I taught those movements to my peers, or performed them as part of a larger sequence, especially if an audience was involved, the movement broke loose of the original imagery and grew more and more abstract as it was absorbed by the muscles.

Nowadays, my sketchbooks don't disclose the fact that I have migrated into a new medium. They still consist of microstory clumps which I translate into movement, record myself dancing and draw the movement from the reference photos. Although I initially write stories in my sketchbook intending them to be published as such and carried to their completion, during the course of a day's work on a 30-by-20-inch page, I become hypnotized by the physical act of drawing. I obsessively fill an area with intricate patterns or swirl my arms around to create negative spaces. The drawing process also includes dance breaks to relieve back and shoulder tension and imagining the existence of an audience reading over my shoulder and making sure I am always sitting in an interesting pose.

The following day, in order to move on to the next image, I have to reinhabit the movement on the page in front of me and rewrite it as the beginning of a new story. I then look up reference books, research the subject matter associated with it, become lost in the mark-making again and repeat the process. The final stage of composing a book, is arranging all the images as abstract sequences on the floor. I look for harmonies, motifs or contrasts in the motion and sever the threads of their original inspiration. I then write an entire new set of "lyrics," accenting the movement as content. My stories are mostly about the consequences of obsessive rituals and the deconstruction of space through dysfunctions of the body and emotion. The characters are always interchangeable, their relationships are hallucinated or suspended in dream, their eyelids closed and their faces generic and expressionless in order to highlight the gesture as the force driving them through the narrative, and not the other way around — a misplaced or reversed "expression." Those lyrics are printed in the book as the narrating voice, but the words only indicate the specific moment in a particular performance of the images. I leave negative spaces in order to return to those images with a new story. Sometimes I even handwrite in already-printed books, adding and crossing out words. The book becomes a potential score for a live performance at a convention or a reading, and will change every time I inhabit the movements I had assigned my protagonists. I think of this in the way a person's inner monologue may change, though they go about the same routine every day, or the way different dancers will interpret the same choreography of *Les Sylphides* and inhabit a seemingly invisible space in which they move the way that particular moment in time feels like. It is also a coping mechanism to ensure I will always have worlds to escape to, even when physical space is binding or "set."

Keren Katz

MOVEMENT AND ANATOMY are crucial comics storytelling for me. It's two of the first things that got hammered into my brain once I decided to actually *learn* how to draw them. Y'know, *after* you're done tracing your favorite *Alpha Flight* cover.

Anatomy is the first thing somebody looking at a first-time artist will point out. Studying it allows you to trick the mind into believing that the figures you're drawing exist. Knowing the rules of anatomy allow you to play and stylize them as well. I don't draw a purely naturalistic figure when I make a comic. I want to play with shape and form and make something that appeals to me. As long as I do it consistently, I'm OK. Consistency is key.

I used to try to have something always moving in a panel. I don't anymore, mostly because I fell in love with facial expressions and acting.

Mike Norton

WHEN I AM DRAWING, I tend to feel the most confident in the gestures of the figure. The movement of their hand, the expression on their face and the weight of their step are all things I get almost giddy to draw. I find that I contort my own face to be like theirs and hold on tight to the gestural lines of the initial sketches when inking rather than a tighter pencil line. I don't want to lose the fluidity of that first thought, and I only want to draw what is necessary for the reader to see what the character is feeling and doing. I echo that drawing further by having it affect the background — the repeated shapes in the figure, or even the angle of a thru-line, gets reused elsewhere to the point of abstraction. I probably do this because I don't feel so sure about drawing anything else!

Molly Mendoza

FROM THE TRENCHES

Graphic Medicine

MK Czerwiec, RN

COMICS AND PUBLIC HEALTH have enjoyed — and continue to enjoy — a long and productive relationship. It's a medium that effectively delivers critical health information to the people who need it — especially when they are experiencing stress, as is often the case when dealing with an existing or threatening illness. In the past 10 years, cartoonists have employed the efficiency and immediacy of comics to encompass health, illness, caregiving and disability. Thanks to UK physician and comics artist Ian Williams (*The Bad Doctor, The Lady Doctor*) this genre has a name: graphic medicine.

In his explanation of why he used the art form for his influential 2006 graphic memoir *Mom's Cancer,*

NOW WE WAIT AND LET THE POISONS WORK.
MOM FALLS INTO AN ODD, DEFEATED FUNK.
MAYBE BECAUSE SHE FINALLY HAS NOTHING TO DO BUT THINK.
MAYBE DEPRESSION IS THE PRECISELY APPROPRIATE RESPONSE.
AFTER A WEEK SHE'S MUCH WORSE INSTEAD OF BETTER.
A SORE OPENS ON HER NECK WHERE THE RADIATION SPLIT HER SKIN LIKE A SAUSAGE IN A MICROWAVE.
HER HANDS TINGLE PAINFULLY. EVERY BREATH IS A BATTLE CLIMAXED BY A COUGH.
WE CALL MOM'S ONCOLOGIST.

Brian Fies wrote, "Comics were the right medium for the story I wanted to tell. They meld words and pictures to convey an idea with more economy and grace than either could alone." *Mom's Cancer* was, in many ways, a catalyst for the expansion of graphic medicine we are witnessing today. When I first encountered Fies' book, I was in graduate school studying medical humanities and bioethics. My intention was to inform the comics I had started making — about my experiences as a nurse during the AIDS crisis in Chicago — with critical theory. Fies' book made me ask two wider questions. First, I wondered if there were more books like his — nonfiction comics aimed primarily at adults, created by the very people experiencing a health crisis — either their own or that of someone in their immediate circle. And it turns out there were. I eagerly started reading as many of them as I could get my hands on: *Cancer Vixen* by Marisa Acocella Marchetto, *Years of the Elephant* by Willy Linthout, *Epileptic* by David B, *Psychiatric Tales* by Darryl Cunningham. Many, many more have appeared since. These books were important. I believed then (and I do today) in what my peers and I articulated some years later, in the panel below from the *Graphic Medicine Manifesto*:

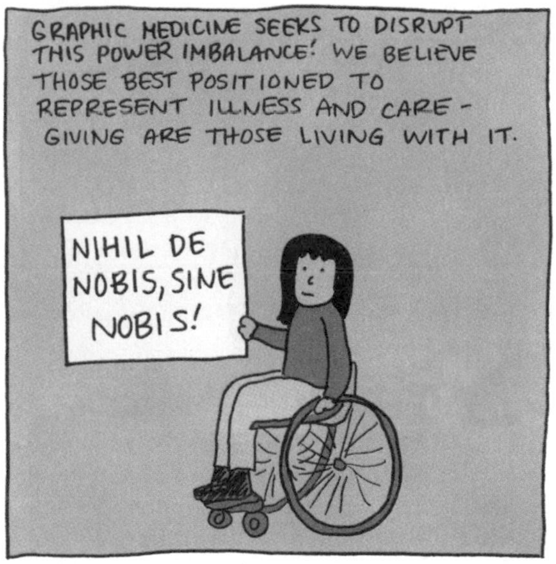
GRAPHIC MEDICINE SEEKS TO DISRUPT THIS POWER IMBALANCE! WE BELIEVE THOSE BEST POSITIONED TO REPRESENT ILLNESS AND CARE-GIVING ARE THOSE LIVING WITH IT.
NIHIL DE NOBIS, SINE NOBIS!

OPPOSITE: A page from the webcomic *Mom's Cancer* by Brian Fies, collected as a book in 2006.

ABOVE: A panel created by MK Czerwiec and Ian Williams for 2015's *Graphic Medicine Manifesto.*

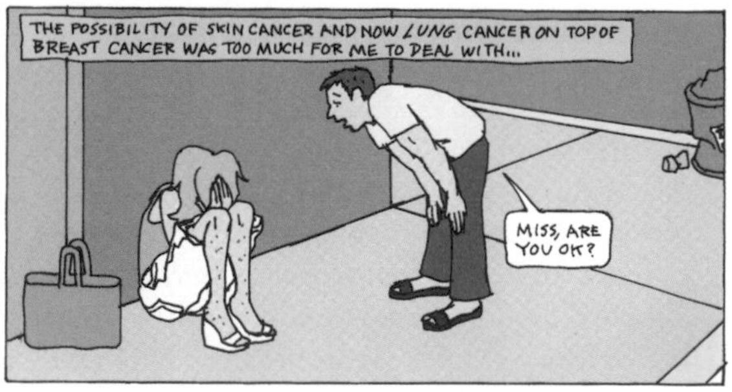
THE POSSIBILITY OF SKIN CANCER AND NOW LUNG CANCER ON TOP OF BREAST CANCER WAS TOO MUCH FOR ME TO DEAL WITH...
MISS, ARE YOU OK?

From *Cancer Vixen* by Marisa Acocella Marchetto, 2006.

The other question Fies' book inspired (and I formalized this query in my graduate schoolwork) was: "Could comics play a serious role in the discourse of health, illness, caregiving and disability?" The answer, as we know now, is yes. Absolutely. In London, in 2010, Ian Williams convened the first conference on the intersections of comics and health; Brian Fies was one of the keynote speakers. Annual conferences followed, and people who had been working in isolation gathered and began to form a vibrant community. Many of them described this as "finally finding a home." Irrespective of their jobs, people seemed to cherish sharing the common bond of having one foot in health care and the other in comics: collaborations and new projects were born. Today the intersection of comics and health is populated by people from around the world, working in many languages and styles. The Graphicmedicine.org website now has a Spanish-language sister site, Medicina Gráfica, and a Japanese-language site is in development. We are researchers, scholars, comics artists, health care practitioners. And, we are all auditioning for the part we all ultimately play at one point or another — to paraphrase Susan Sontag, users of that other passport:

> Everyone who is born holds dual citizenship, in the kingdom of the well and in the kingdom of the sick. Although we all prefer to use the good passport, sooner or later each of us is obliged, at least for a spell, to identify ourselves as citizens of that other place. (*Illness as Metaphor*, 1978)

Traditional health information outlets have taken notice, if not joined the movement. In launching the National Library of Medicine's new collection and traveling exhibit of graphic medicine, curated by Ellen Forney (*Marbles, Rock Steady*), NLM Director Patricia Brennan stated that, "Without graphic medicine we were incomplete … it addresses an unaddressed dimension of health and it provides us a way to archive these expressions of that dimension."

The medical journal *Annals of Internal Medicine*, originally founded in 1927 and previously the exclusive territory of physicians, began a special online comics section, titled "Annals of Graphic Medicine," in 2013. This is a unique place where health care providers, caregivers and people living with illness and disability are all on equal footing. This alone is a huge milestone! *Annals* only requires that if the comic contains medical information, it needs to be represented accurately and fairly.

What are the goals of graphic medicine? They are as diverse as its practitioners. Comics are created and read to:

- Help everyone better understand the lived experiences of illness and caregiving by providing a very unique window into those experiences.

- Provide a space, opportunity and format for how to process complex experiences with health, illness, caregiving and finite bodies.

- Assist people experiencing post-traumatic stress disorder to potentially reclaim some agency over their traumatic experiences.

- Help students of medicine, nursing and allied health professions reflect on their practice and more deeply understand the experiences of their patients.

- Conduct research. Comics are being used as the educational intervention whose effectiveness is being measured as a means to monitor health attitudes and outcomes, and as a translational tool with which complex research outcomes can be more easily understood.

- Expose implicit and explicit bias in medicine and advocacy for justice in the practice of and access to health care.

- Allow space for conscious and unconscious issues to surface and be addressed.

- Bring to light and bear witness to (and sometimes, helpfully show the humor in) topics which have been marginalized and stigmatized, such as natural death, assisted death, etc. as well as the difficult — often traumatizing — work of personal and professional caregiving.

- Help people contemplate what they prioritize in their care should they no longer be able to speak for themselves (also known as advance care planning).

The medium of comics itself has unique tools and conventions that make all of the work mentioned above — and more — possible. We can't see inside our bodies, and no one else can feel our pain. Because of this, we use metaphors to describe our experiences. Comics can make those metaphors visual, literal, seen. Consider the representation of receiving a devastating diagnosis in Peter Dunlap-Shohl's *My Degeneration*.

Consider, also, the comics convention of the speech bubble and the thought bubble. When applied to an encounter between a care provider and a patient, they become powerful tools. What is a doctor thinking, perhaps worried about, but not saying? What is a patient or family caregiver thinking, worried about, but not saying? Comics have the power to expose all of this in plain view. When patients or care providers are encouraged, in a supportive environment, to draw their encounters, they are able, with the tools available via comics, to express the previously unsaid, and imagine what the other participants in the encounter may have also left unsaid, as in the image drawn by a medical student enrolled in a graphic medicine elective seminar.

This is why I'm interested in the intersection of comics and health. As I mentioned, I started making comics to reflect on and sort out my experiences as a nurse, but I continue working in this area because I believe comics have the potential to help make things better for every person — that's everyone — whose human body sometimes performs less-than-optimally. Nurses see a lot of things go wrong in health care, and I'm not referring to clinical error; I'm referring to errors in communication. The kinds of comics

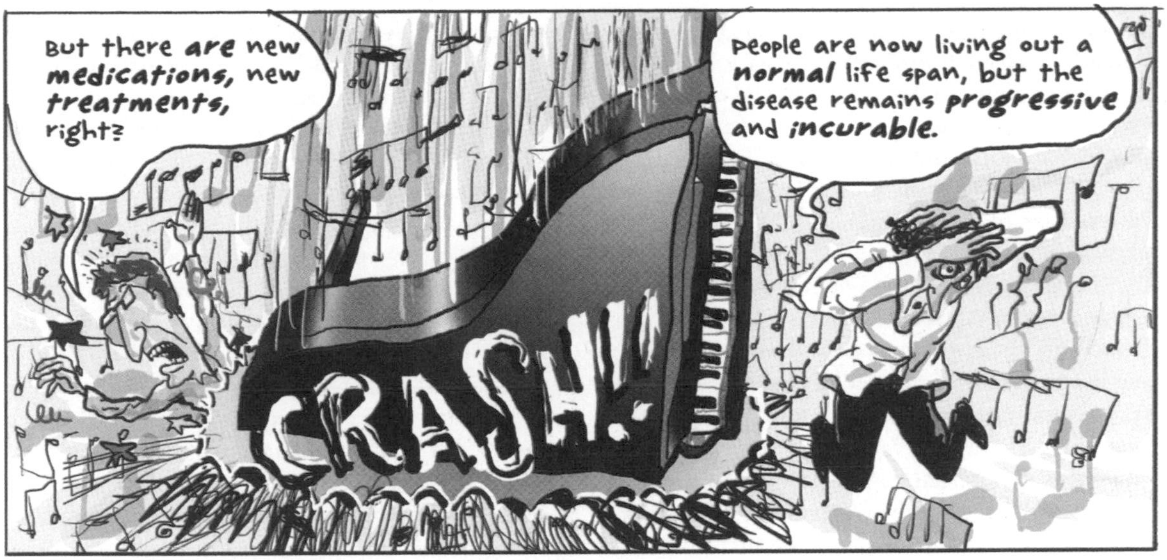
But there are new medications, new treatments, right?
People are now living out a normal life span, but the disease remains progressive and incurable.
CRASH!

From *My Degeneration: A Journey Through Parkinson's* by Peter Dunlap-Shohl, 2015.

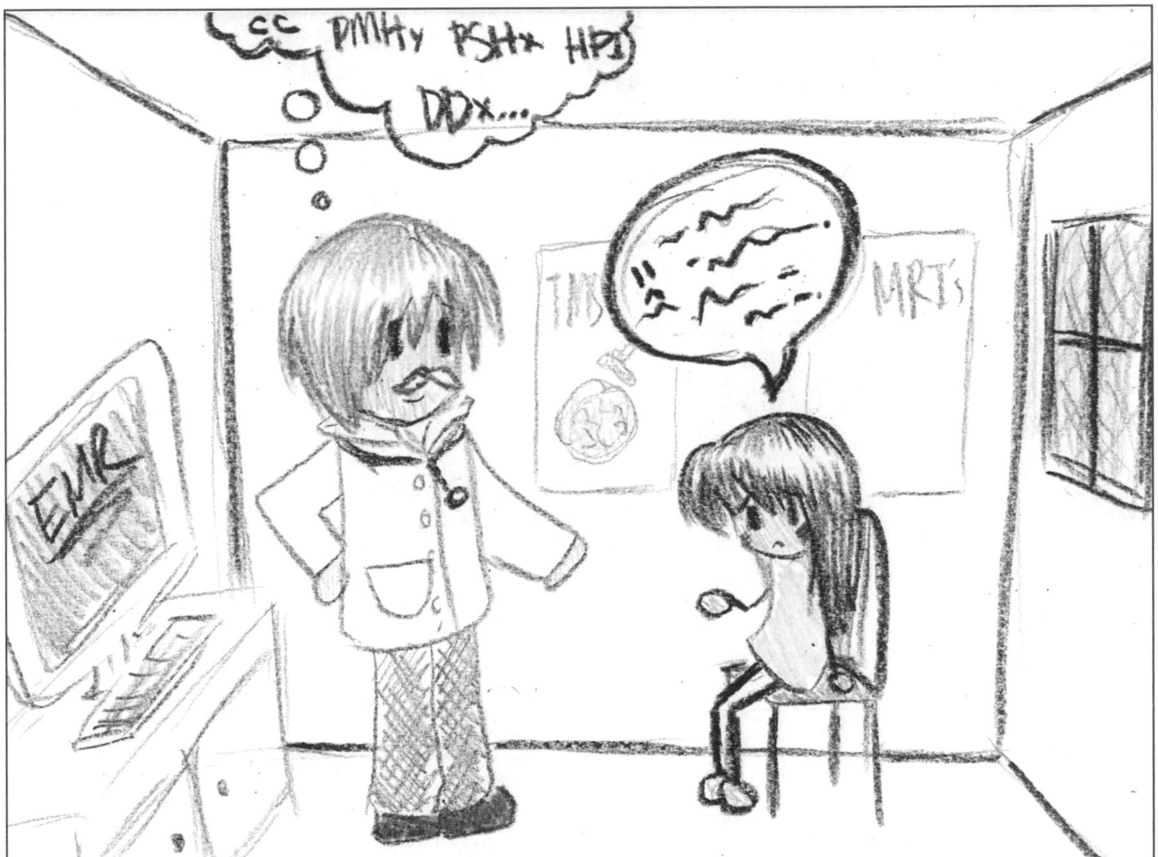
CC PMHx PSHx HPI DDx...
TMS
MRI's
EMR

Drawn by one of Czerwiec's students, Melanie Zhang, in 2015.

I'm describing can be a first step toward deepening empathy, to begin to bridge those often-wide chasms between family members, patients and care providers, communities, as well as persons and the society in which they live and depend on for their care.

Those of us working for the last 10 years at the intersection of comics and health have proven that graphic medicine is a legitimate pursuit. Now we are faced with the challenges of doing better. We need to expand representation, tell stories that are not being heard and include populations who may still be living in the shadows. We need to be sure to avoid the trap of creating and contributing to master narratives that narrowly capture familiar experiences, rather than seeking alternative perspectives. We need to highlight the challenges that various populations face, raise the issue of access to care, justice and the disparities that disadvantage particular communities while advantaging others, preventing health equity. We need to expand access to comics about health, as well as the tools and instruction for making and publishing new work.

As my colleague, University of Chicago physician and graphic medicine activist Brian Callender, points out, medicine is becoming increasingly complex and technologically driven. As this happens, access to care and the health literacy gap are likely to widen further. How can comics be most effectively used to minimize this gap? How can we best support the publicly available outlets for these comics? For example, *The Nib* is a website that has been an enormously useful resource for graphic medicine. (See work on the site by Whit Taylor, Aubrey Hirsch and many more.) *The Nib* recently announced that they had lost their underwriting funding. Those of us who care about the kind of applied, nonfiction cartooning that *The Nib* is providing to the public can step up and support their work by becoming members if we are able. (This is an honest, conflict-free and unsolicited endorsement.)

In *Comics & Sequential Art* (1985) Will Eisner wrote that, "Unless comics address subjects of greater moment how can they hope for serious intellectual review? ... The future of the graphic novel lies in the choice of worthwhile themes and the innovation of exposition." I think the work of graphic medicine has answered Eisner's call. Here's to taking that work even further.

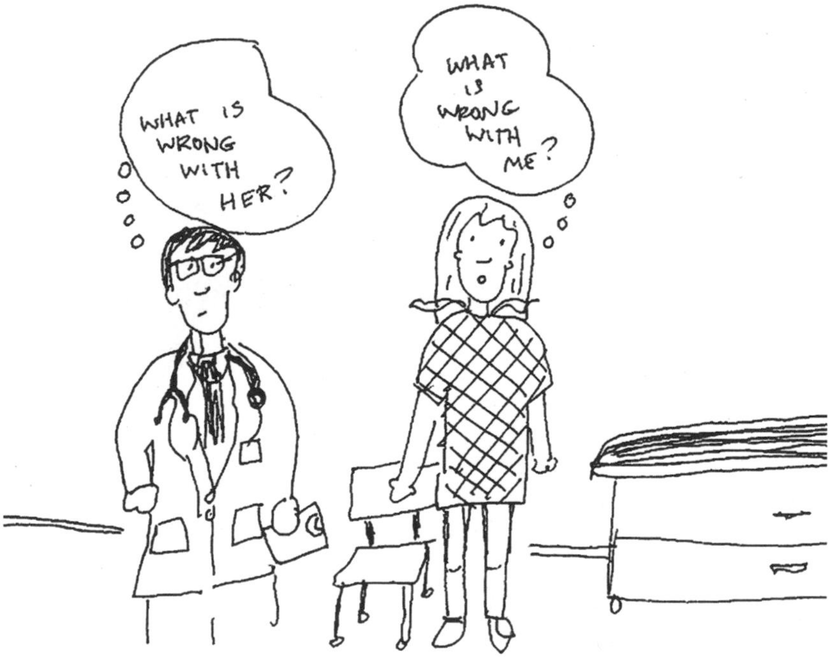
WHAT IS WRONG WITH HER?
WHAT IS WRONG WITH ME?

From *What's Wrong* by MK Czerwiec, 2012.

FANTAGRAPHICS

INTERNATIONAL SENSATIONS!

Around the World With The Greatest Contemporary Cartoonists

Portrait
of a
Drunk
Ruppert & Mulot
O. Schrauwen

Portrait of a Drunk

By Olivier Schrauwen,
Ruppert and Mulot

COW
BOY
RIKKE
VILLADSEN

Cowboy

By Rikke Villadsen

GOBLIN GIRL
MOA ROMANOVA

Goblin Girl

By Moa Romanova

VOLUME TWO
DEMENTIA 21
KAGO

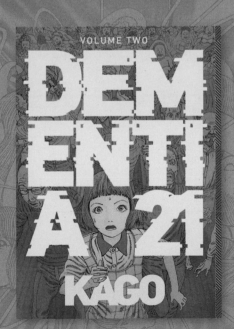

Dementia 21 Vol. 2

By Kago

INTERVIEW

They Are Escaping the Hospital and Are Going to Kill Their Captors

A Conversation with Rebecca Kirby and HTML Flowers

Moderated by RJ Casey

HTML FLOWERS (who goes by Grant Jonathon in real life) creates illustrations, music (he was nominated for the Australian Music Prize in 2017) and zines from his home in Melbourne. They are full of harrowing artifacts of a life spent in and out of the hospital with cystic fibrosis — plastic bracelet fragments, manuals for medical devices, prescription slips — along with poetry and, of course, comics. These comics, mostly serialized in the self-published, one-person-anthology *No Visitors*, feature HTML Flowers' thin line and grimly witty dialogue as they tell the tales of the artist's stand-in, Little.

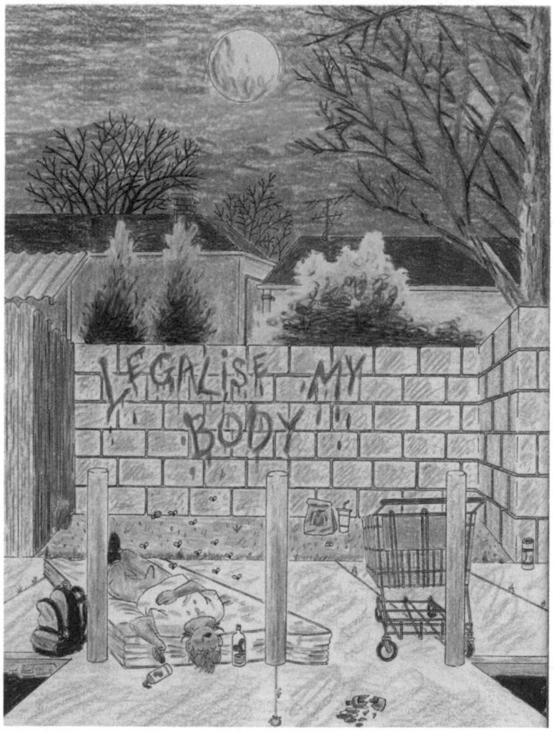
LEGALISE MY BODY

HTML Flowers' back cover illustration for *No Visitors* #3, 2018.

There's a story in the second issue of *No Visitors* that I believe wholly encapsulates the work of HTML Flowers. It takes place immediately after Little is diagnosed with prediabetes. Little takes off to the nearest food court, heads to the bakery and proceeds to order "one of everything" and "two of everything with custard." He takes his bounty to a nearby table and morosely thinks, "Last supper," before a group of dudes across the court start throwing insults and slurs his way. Little gets up, pulls the bloody IV implant out of his wrist and throws it at one of the perpetrators' heads. It bounces off into one of their

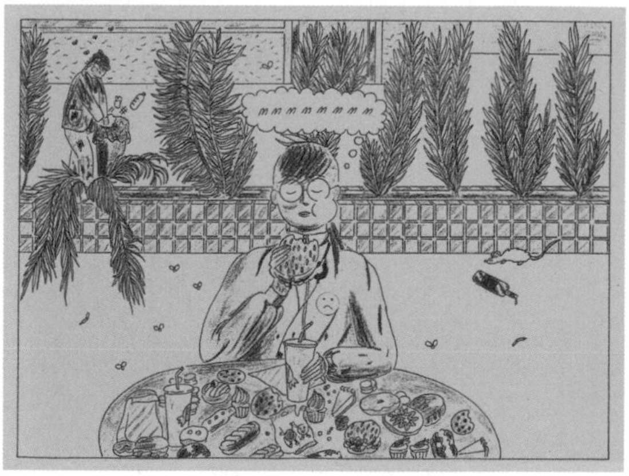

From *No Visitors* #2 by HTML Flowers, 2016.

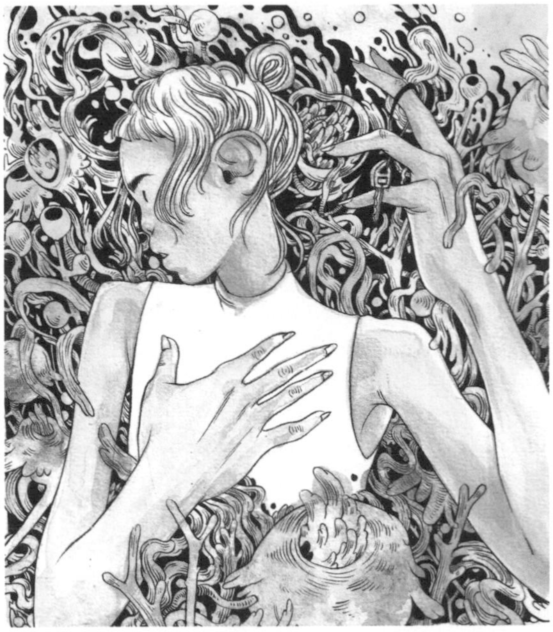

From the title page from Rebecca Kirby's story "Waves," which ran in *Now: The New Comics Anthology* #4, 2018.

sodas, with a "plop." As they flee, Little incorporates their abandoned fast food into his feast. He makes a cheeseburger donut sandwich while thinking, "I should be a nurse." There you have it — melancholic death wish meets "fuck you" merriment.

Incidentally, as I learned later, the raw veracity and body horror (naturally) of HTML Flowers' comics have inspired Rebecca Kirby. Kirby's art was once all luminous undulations of massive hands and eyes, flowing attractively throughout her pages and pinups for publishers like Image, Silver Sprocket and Fantagraphics' *Now* anthology. But seemingly, for Kirby, that wasn't enough — and, luckily, now readers are able to see a cartoonist find her artistic voice in real time. Over the last year or so, Rebecca Kirby's comics have become less serious but markedly more mature and affecting, as she has taken on the singular pangs of personal guilt and acceptance of someone living with chronic illness.

Biopsy (2018), self-published and then serialized on Vice.com, shows Kirby at her best — vulnerable and over-the-top — as she undergoes surgery and awaits what may be a fatal diagnosis. Her style — big panels with pink, blue and yellow gouache — and sense of humor is uniquely suited to take on the anesthesia-induced roller-coaster ride of waiting for what could be the worst news of her life. How can she contemplate mortality when her "books haven't even come out yet," or what if she dies "before [she] evolve[s] into a hot, middle-aged fashion icon?" The medical verdict is positive — at least relatively so — but the true kicker of the story comes when Kirby can't recall what the doctor told her over the phone because she's too stoned to remember.

HTML Flowers and Rebecca Kirby make comics that are undeniably funny and brutishly truthful, but most of all, they feel truly rebellious. When I learned that they communicate frequently and have just started collaborating on a project, I knew I had to speak to both of them.

* * *

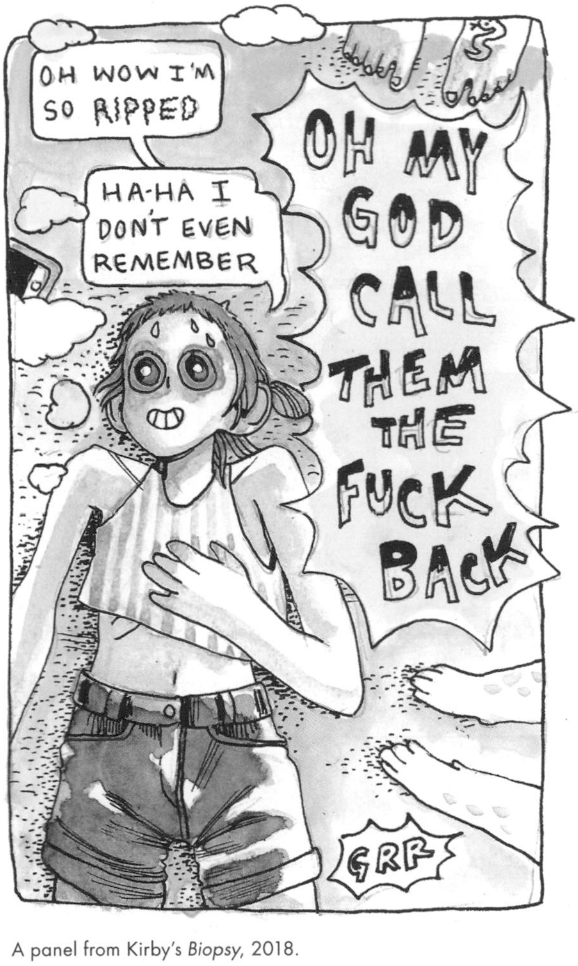
OH WOW I'M SO RIPPED
HA-HA I DON'T EVEN REMEMBER
OH MY GOD CALL THEM THE FUCK BACK
GRR

A panel from Kirby's *Biopsy*, 2018.

PUBLIC ORIGIN STORIES

RJ CASEY: I'm trying to tackle a big theme here. I want to focus on health, in general, and health care, in particular, and how it relates to art and comics.

REBECCA KIRBY: Nice. Wait, I'm going to get a book. [*Goes to shelf and pulls a book.*]

HTML FLOWERS: [*Laughs.*] Kirby's got this new book about the American health care system.

***The History and Evolution of Health Care in America*. Is that an easy read?**

KIRBY: It's *so* boring. [*Laughter.*] And it sucks. But I feel like I'm obligated —

HTML FLOWERS: Like you must know more.

KIRBY: If I'm going to complain in a comic format about how much this sucks, I at least want to be able to say, "In 1927 is when it got very bad and I know this for a fact. I've read it!" [*HTML Flowers laughs.*]

That's for research rather than a pleasure read.

KIRBY: I'm going to write it off.

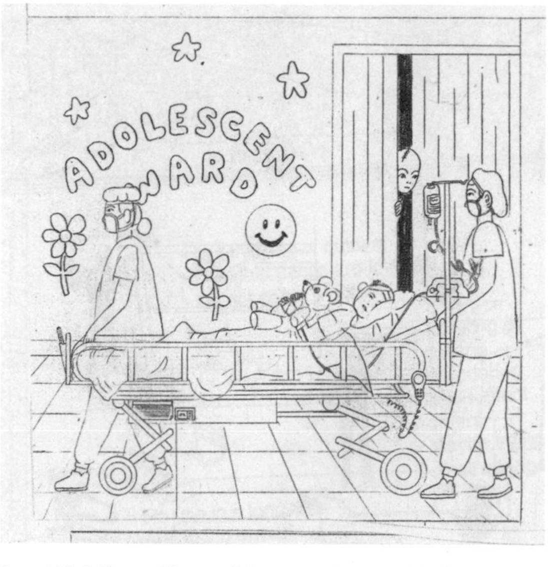
ADOLESCENT WARD

From HTML Flowers' hospital diary zine *Incision*, 2017.

Grant, where were you born in Illinois?

HTML FLOWERS: I was born in a tiny town called Carbondale. Then I moved just a little bit up the way to Lincoln, which is where my family lived. My mom had moved to Carbondale and bought a treehouse off an incarcerated pot dealer.

KIRBY: Shit!

HTML FLOWERS: For like 15 or 20 grand or something. She was like, "You'll have money when you get out."

When you say "treehouse," what do you mean?

HTML FLOWERS: A house built into a tree.

KIRBY: That's the sickest thing I've ever heard in my life. Thank you.

HTML FLOWERS: I think you can still see it online. I can ask my mom to send you a photo. She found it a while ago and was like, "They changed it a little bit, but it's basically how it was."

KIRBY: I just started watching a TV show called *Treehouse Masters*. They talk about treehouses and maybe it's on there.

HTML FLOWERS: So, this guy — Mandelbaum was his name — he inherited it from his family. Mom bought it while he was in jail. Then I got sick and she had to sell it. We had to move to go stay with family members in Lincoln. From there, my mom just ended up staying in Lincoln and had family there. It was easier to survive there than it would have been living alone in Carbondale.

How old were you at the time?

HTML FLOWERS: I was probably just near a year old. When I was born, I spent six months in the hospital. The local hospital didn't know how to handle my issues and they referred us to someone in St. Louis. So, we went up to St. Louis and I ended up staying at a hospital there. They were like, basically, "Your son needs a lot of care." My mom and I lived there for about six months. It destroyed her financially.

KIRBY: Damn.

HTML FLOWERS: At the end of the stay, my health care costs half a million dollars.

By the time you were a 1-year-old?

HTML FLOWERS: Yeah, because I was hospitalized for months and it was specialized care. The bill for that was insane. I lived in the hospital for months as a kid. A brand-new baby. My mom had to declare bankruptcy because she couldn't pay the bills. She had to sell the house. Anything she had in her name was repossessed. She ended up moving back to Lincoln and worked cash-in-hand for like 10 years. Just had a bunch of different jobs and was always paid in cash. She would rent a house under someone else's name and stuff, because that's all she could do. A lot of the time we were just living with family members and friends of hers.

When were you officially diagnosed? That early on?

HTML FLOWERS: I think a bunch of doctors couldn't figure out what was wrong with me. Then one doctor was like, "That seems like cystic fibrosis. We should get him tested. Send him to St. Louis." When they realized it was CF, they were like, "His condition is really bad. He has had no medicine for it up to this point, so we'll have to keep him for a while." It just took them months to stabilize me.

Can you explain how you got to Australia, then? What's that timeline look like?

HTML FLOWERS: So, after 10 years of my mom struggling to get basic health care for me using all the tricks in the book — appealing to the kindness of nurses and doctors and shit, collaborating with any health care professional who would tell her the secret ways that you can game the system so that you can get some assistance — she was fucking tired. She was like, "I can't do this forever. He's going to have a shit life here." And the town where I came from, there weren't a lot of success stories. She wanted better for me and my brother. My brother's family had a particularly bad reputation and it was hard for them to get work. His

dad was a con. So, she was like, "I don't want either one of my boys growing up here, sick or not."

She started to look into English-speaking countries that had better health care. She thought about Canada. She did some reading and didn't find it that much better. She thought about London, but England has one of the worst standards of living in the English-speaking countries. It's just impossible to get work and a house there. She read about Australia and was like, "Shit, maybe Australia is the one. Health care seems to be one of the better ones, overall. It's English-speaking." She was on a forum — she was just thinking about this and was like, "I have to get out of here." She was on this forum for Hunter S. Thompson, and started talking to this Australian guy.

A Hunter S. Thompson forum?

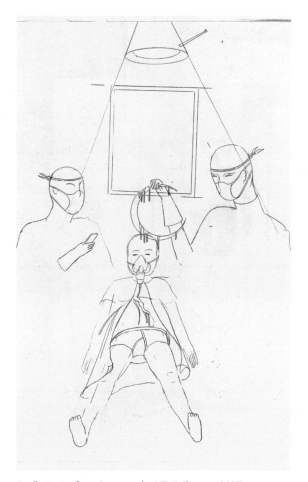

An illustration from *Sonogram* by HTML Flowers, 2017.

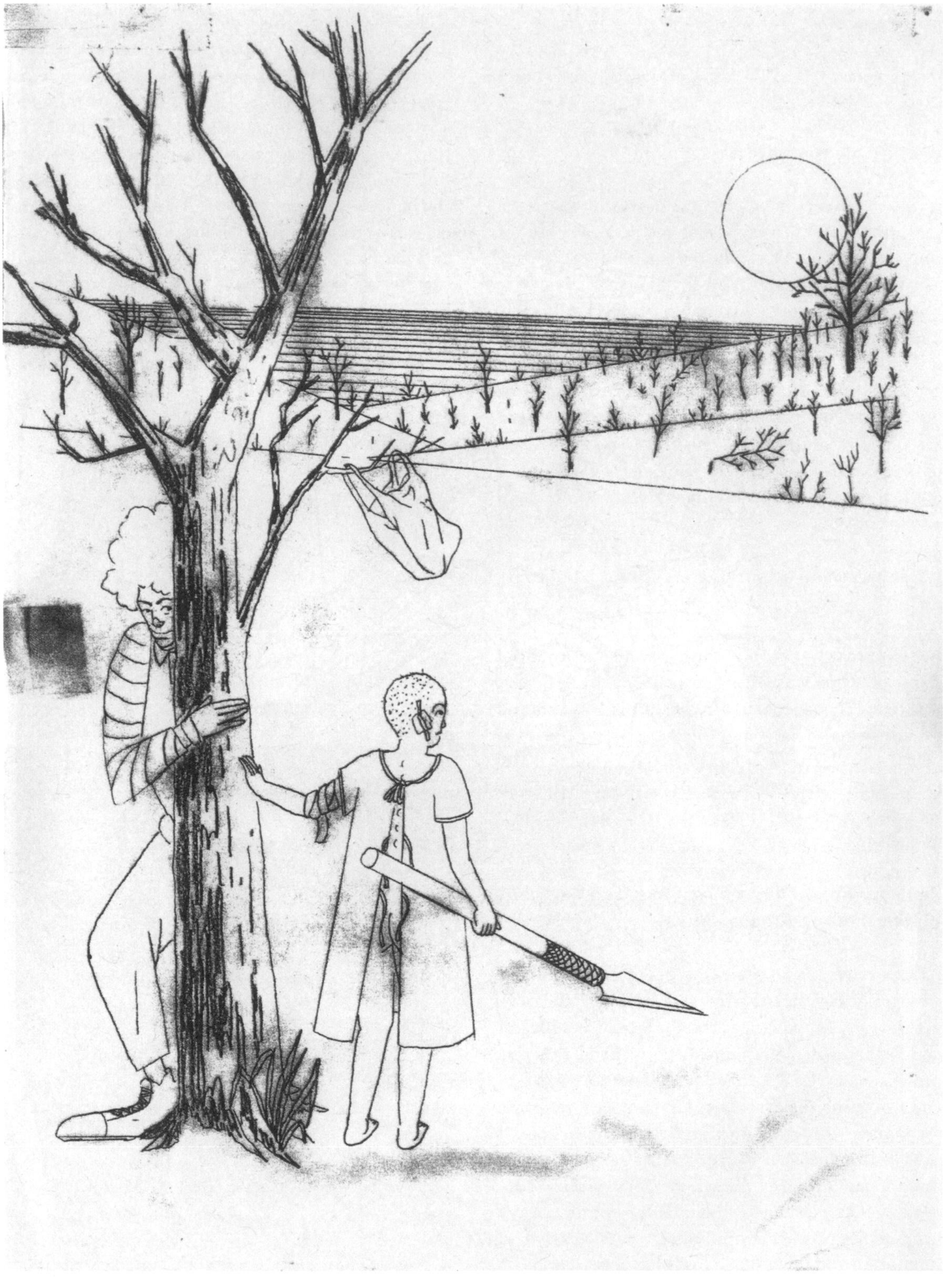

HTML FLOWERS: She's a big fan. She was like, "This Australian guy … Mmmm." [*Laughter.*] I think she very much liked him at first and they had a legitimate connection. But he quickly became a fuckwit and she just persevered with him because she knew she had to get us over here. It took us 13 years to become citizens.

How old were you when you moved?

HTML FLOWERS: I was 10.

Does that coincide with when you started to make art or draw at all?

HTML FLOWERS: I was already making art and drawing. My mom wanted me to be a painter. I would come home from school and she'd give me paper and paint. She was always obsessed. She wanted to be a painter before she had me, then had to give her life away to look after me. "I want him to go for the dreams that I never got to have," I guess. I think I had an interest in it. I don't know, this could all be her fault. [*Laughter.*] I was always making stuff. When I was about 12, I think I really started writing. Writing became a serious passion for me.

What were you doing at that time?

HTML FLOWERS: Short stories and poetry. The short stories were really fleshed out. I would write 50-page novels or whatever. I was obsessed with this Magnus Crowe character I created. I used to write about him. He was this boy with four hearts. It was easier for him to die, but he was more powerful because of it as well. He could get shot in the heart more. So weird.

KIRBY: That's a really interesting concept of superheroism. He could get shot a bit more.

HTML FLOWERS: My brother was a huge fan. Because I was playing *Final Fantasy VII* at the time, Magnus Crowe carried around a huge, flat sword. I would do drawings of him. My brother is only three years younger than me, and he'd be like, "What happens next with Magnus Crowe?! I gotta know! When are

OPPOSITE: From *Sonogram* by HTML Flowers, 2017.

you writing the next book?" [*Laughter.*] It was very cute. Very encouraging for me.

KIRBY: Does he like your comics now?

HTML FLOWERS: He's always been a big supporter of mine. He reads my comics and collects my music. He's a beautiful boy and I love him.

Those types of long swords come back all the time in your comics, even today. You make them scalpels now, though.

HTML FLOWERS: That's true. I'm obsessed with the idea of extremely elongated, super-pointy scalpels. It looks creepy.

KIRBY: It looks cool. It's like when you look at old arms and armor. Those swords are always the coolest-looking shit you will ever see.

HTML FLOWERS: Everyone's got little bitch scalpels these days. I see the ones they use in the doctor's office all the time. [*Laughter.*] It's like a bit of plastic with a tiny little knife at the top.

KIRBY: It's pathetic. When you cut us, make it look cool at least. [*Laughter.*]

HTML FLOWERS: Cut me with a real knife, you fuck.

You always draw the sick characters, like your main character, Little, with the scalpels, rather than the doctors. Are they weaponizing it, or weaponizing their illness somehow?

HTML FLOWERS: They are escaping the hospital and are going to kill their captors. In my fantasies … It's true, though. Drug companies and hospitals mutually benefit off their parasitic attitudes.

KIRBY: Yeah.

Rebecca, you live in Philadelphia. Is that where you're originally from?

KIRBY: I am from Delaware County, Pennsylvania, which is 20 minutes away.

What part of the state is that?

KIRBY: The southeast corner, right by Jersey. I've lived within 20 minutes of where I am presently almost my entire life. I've been in the same neighborhood, even, for 10 years.

You might have to correct my pronunciation, but you are diagnosed with gastroparesis?

KIRBY: You nailed it!

HTML FLOWERS: Nice one, RJ. Somebody's done his homework. [*Laughter.*]

Well, I got the name right, but I'm not sure what it really means.

KIRBY: Gastroparesis is the result of a larger diagnosis that we're trying to find now. But gastroparesis is essentially a gut motility issue. If you're a normal, healthy person, your stomach will contract every couple minutes — to allow food to go out of your belly and into other parts. If you have gastroparesis, that doesn't happen so much. Food just sits there, or you puke it up, or it hurts or nothing works right. It's just in there forever. It's gross. [*Laughs.*]

When did you start having symptoms of this?

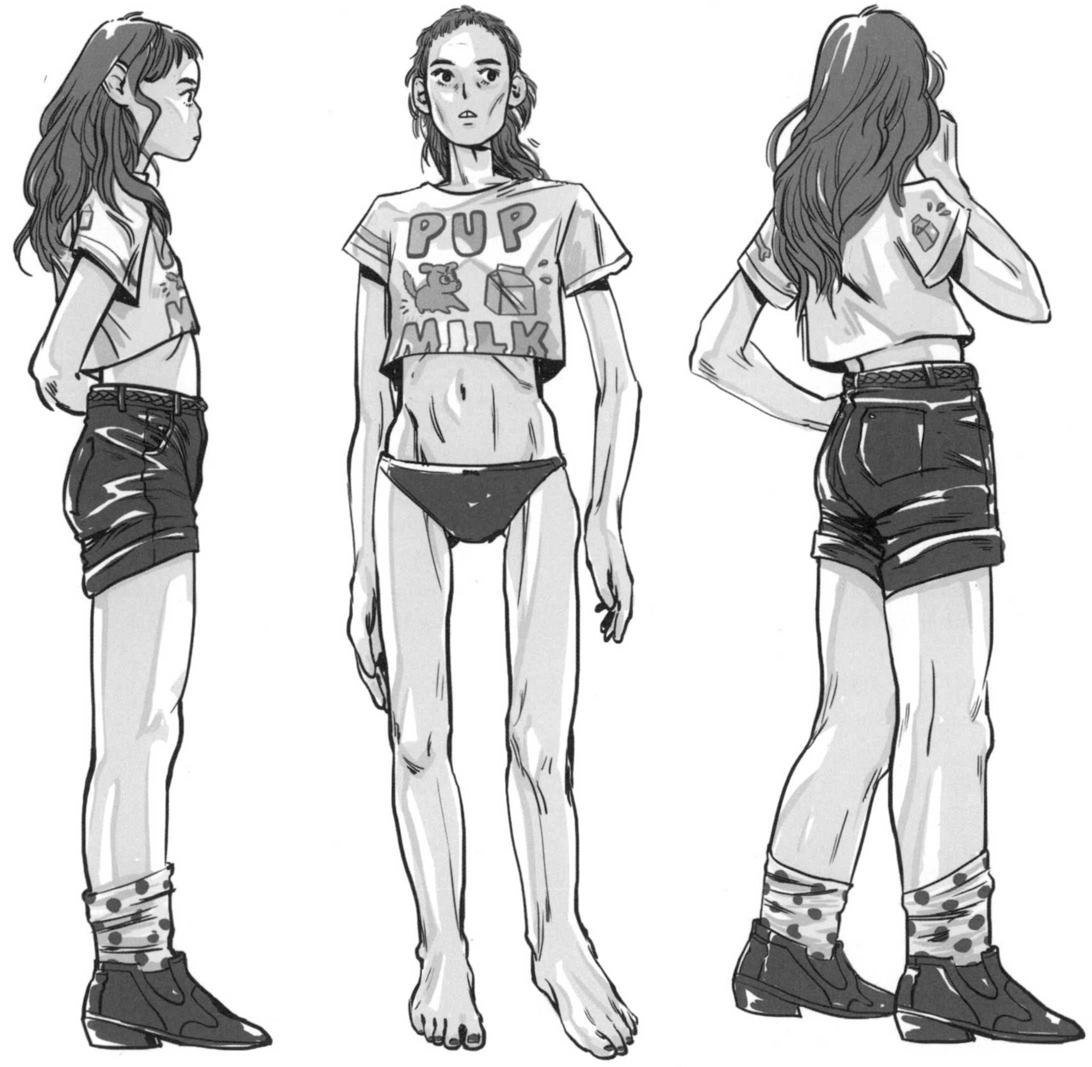
PUP
MILK

KIRBY: Forever. Definitely since childhood. It started getting real bad about a decade ago. That's when I started seeking specialty care for this. It took a long time to diagnose. A lot of personal research and fighting with specialists and everything. Doing my own research and coming in and being like, "Maybe you should test for gastroparesis." The fucking test is they make you eat an egg sandwich that has radioactive dye in it. Then you have to stand in front of an X-ray machine forever. They see if goes anywhere. It if doesn't, then you got it. [*Laughter.*] That's what happens.

Why an egg sandwich?

KIRBY: I don't know! You would really think that with all the disgusting options they can feed you, they would pick maybe the second-to-last-most-disgusting option. But no. It's an egg sandwich with perfectly round disks of egg. Disgusting.

How does this affect your day-to-day?

KIRBY: It makes eating very difficult. I'll frequently have issues that then happen as a result of not being able to eat right or very much at all. The food restrictions are extensive. The consequences of not adhering to all of the rules are pretty large and pretty painful. I also have a large number of other gastrointestinal issues like enterocele and gastric polyps. They compound everything. A lot of the times treatment for the upper GI system will impact the lower GI system. If you have an issue with both ... The enterocole is a herniated part of your pelvic floor. All my guts are out of order in here. There's no room for anything. If I eat stuff, it hurts so much. I recently got medication that's life-changing, called Ondansetron. It's like no-puke meds. The best thing I've ever experienced in my life. It's what they give chemo patients if they can't stop vomiting. It's the best shit on earth, ever. This is an ad now for Ondansetron.

Over the last year or two, your comics have become increasingly more confessional.

KIRBY: Yes. [*Laughs.*]

OPPOSITE: Rebecca Kirby self-portraits, 2018.

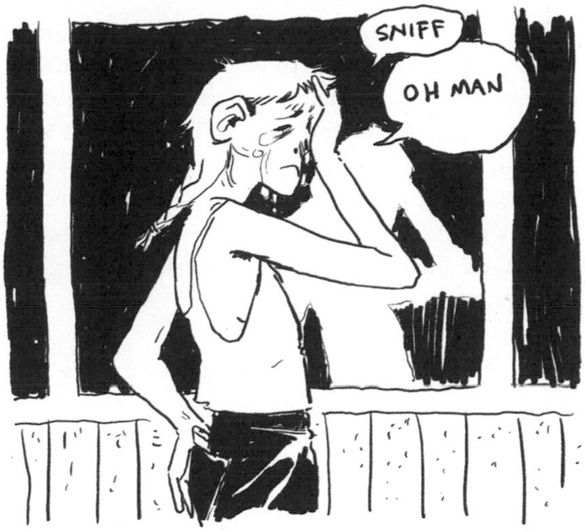
SNIFF
OH MAN

From a Kirby comic posted to Instagram, 2019.

You've been more open about everything. Did you consciously make a decision to work towards that or was it something you fell into?

KIRBY: I think that I'm getting lazier — I don't know if that's the right word. I can't be bothered to make an effort to conceal what the real driving purpose is behind anything I do anymore. Last year I sort of started freaking out. Part of that was realizing that my work couldn't grow into doing what I wanted it to unless I started fucking up. It's made sense that the next step was opening up the avenue to the possibility of fucking up *all the time*. I had to start telling things as they actually were. That's what I've been trying to do even though it's consistently embarrassing.

HTML FLOWERS: It's good work, though.

> *"I lived in the hospital for months as a kid. A brand-new baby. My mom had to declare bankruptcy because she couldn't pay the bills. She had to sell the house."*

KIRBY: I do feel like that's been helping me figure out how I want to tell stories and what I want to focus on. The opportunity to focus on illness has made it a lot easier to prioritize what I think is important about making comics for myself and for anybody else.

And, Grant, your comics have always been confessional in that way. You're both honest about everything.

HTML FLOWERS: Since people started paying attention, definitely. [*Laughs.*] No one gave a shit when I was writing weird fantasy comics, and that's a good thing, because I should have stopped that way before I did.

I haven't seen those.

HTML FLOWERS: You don't need to. [*Laughter.*] One time a partner's dad told me, "I like your comics. I like the work you make. It's *good*." He had a thick Polish accent. "But no one cares about your fantasies. You are a sick person. You need to write about your sickness and pain." I was like, "Suck my dick!" [*Laughter.*] "Get out of my face, telling me what to write." But that always stuck with me. Then I wrote this confessional book about a week in the hospital where I thought I was going to die. It felt really good. It was probably my most well-received work up to that point. I thought that maybe I should start making some comics too. That was literally just writing.

Whatever I do in comics, Simon [Hanselmann, *Megg and Mogg* cartoonist] is insanely supportive of everything I do. When I started writing about illness, Simon was like, "This is your best work yet. This is the most enthralling thing you've done. You can tell a story about anything, but this is incredible." Having Simon's support with that really helped me feel like it was the right place to go towards. It was something that had been brewing for such a long time. My partner's dad told me that shit in like 2012.

I didn't really start writing about Little until 2013 or 2014. I sat with it for a long time before I was like, "What the fuck? Maybe I should try this." And when I did, it felt so good and everyone responded to it so well. I've always done some kind of confessional thing about being sick, but once I took that step and felt I was good enough at drawing comics and had enough chops to actually do the story justice, that was a big part of it. For ages, I was like, "I don't even know how to do perspective!" [*Laughter.*] "In the fantasy comics, no one really minds if things are out of whack." I started working on doing more comics that take place in a room and I had to draw that room 12 times, you know?

Simon really helped me develop my skills through that. He's the most supportive person. He's never not supported me. I've gotten him in trouble before and he'll just tell whoever's mad at us, "He's one of the best comic artists in Australia. You can't say shit." Simon's the most loyal friend I've ever had, and if it weren't for him, I don't know if I would have gone this far into comics. Our friendship brought me here.

KIRBY: And I had *you*.

HTML FLOWERS: That's sweet.

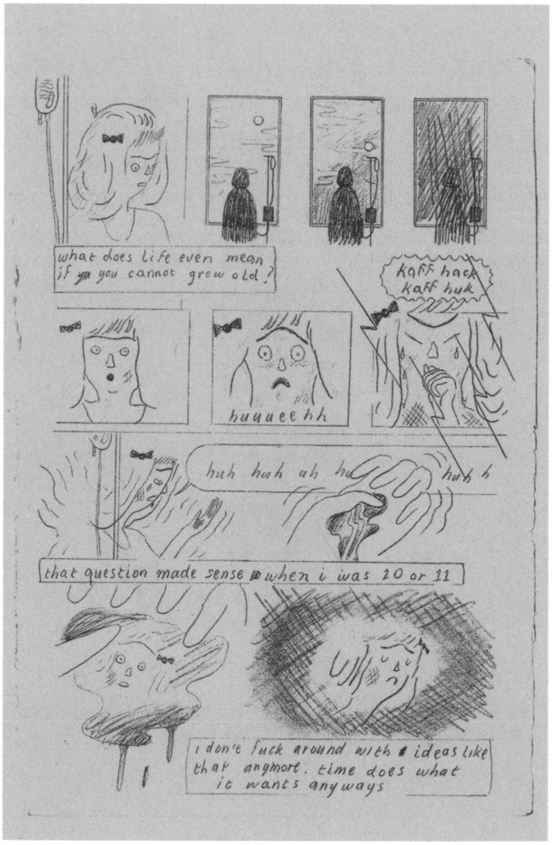

what does life even mean if you cannot grow old?
kaff hack kaff huk
huuueehh
huh huh uh hu
huh h
that question made sense when i was 10 or 11
i don't fuck around with ideas like that anymore. time does what it wants anyways

An HTML Flowers page from *No Visitors* #1, 2015.

KIRBY: You were my influence here. Or, at least, you gave me permission to do it. That was a big deal.

HTML FLOWERS: I didn't give you permission.

KIRBY: I needed to seek out and receive permission. I hadn't thought about it at all. I knew that I could make stuff about the dumb shit I think about, but in terms of real, tangible experience with absolutely no bars holding it ... No poetry to gently conceal what I think might not go so good. You don't do that. We had been talking for a while and I bought your comics before that. That made me realize, "You can do this."

HTML FLOWERS: That is a thing — not feeling like you can tell your story as a sick person.

KIRBY: Yeah.

HTML FLOWERS: "Who wants to hear that? Don't bring it to the cocktail party."

KIRBY: I couldn't even talk to my ex-boyfriend about why I was going to the hospital because it was about my butthole. He was not into hearing about it. Also, I'm a girl, so I was raised with the whole, "You don't have a butthole and you don't have a vagina. There's no part of you that actually exists, really."

You couldn't share why you were going into the hospital or going to get tests at all?

KIRBY: No, no.

HTML FLOWERS: That is a bitch-ass boyfriend.

KIRBY: His health issues eclipsed mine for a long time. This is my ex, by the way. My current partner is great. At the time, he made it very clear that he didn't want to hear why I was on the bathroom floor a lot. So, I just didn't tell him about it. It was such a point of pride for me, for a couple years, to not have anything wrong with me, at least in ways that I didn't have tell anybody what was wrong. That's stupid and fucked up, but I was like, "Oooh, I'm doing normal. That's awesome." I didn't want to ruin that streak.

HTML FLOWERS: Yeah.

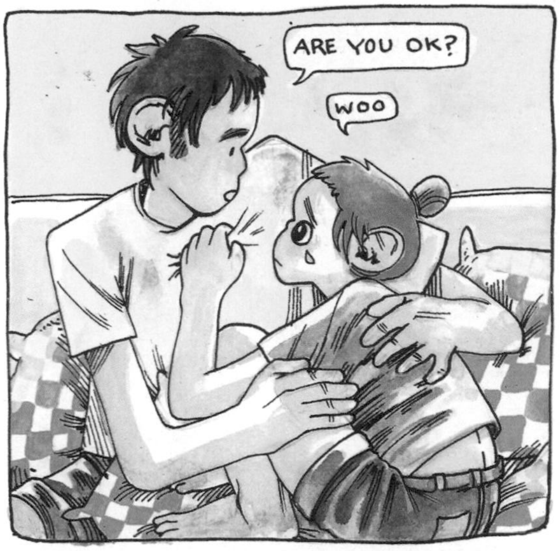
ARE YOU OK?
WOO

From Kirby's *Biopsy*, 2018.

KIRBY: Then it started getting too bad to be able to do that. There was a weird balance of who to tell and when. [*Long pause.*] Never and nobody. [*Laughter.*] It's like a safety valve now. It's all going to fucking come out. I have no choice now.

I can imagine taking care of your health can be a solitary task.

KIRBY: Yeah.

So can cartooning.

KIRBY: Those things are made to be married. I'm sick all of the time, anyway. I'd rather not go to another basement show in beautiful Philadelphia and sit at home. It's what I'd rather be doing. They both sort of excuse each other. [*Laughs.*] Not that I need an excuse, but I often feel like I do.

THE BRIAN ENO RULE

When I think of medical settings, which your stories often take place in, I think of drab whites and grays. Sanitized everything. But with Grant's covers, especially, and Rebecca, your whole catalog of work, they are full of bright, vibrant colors.

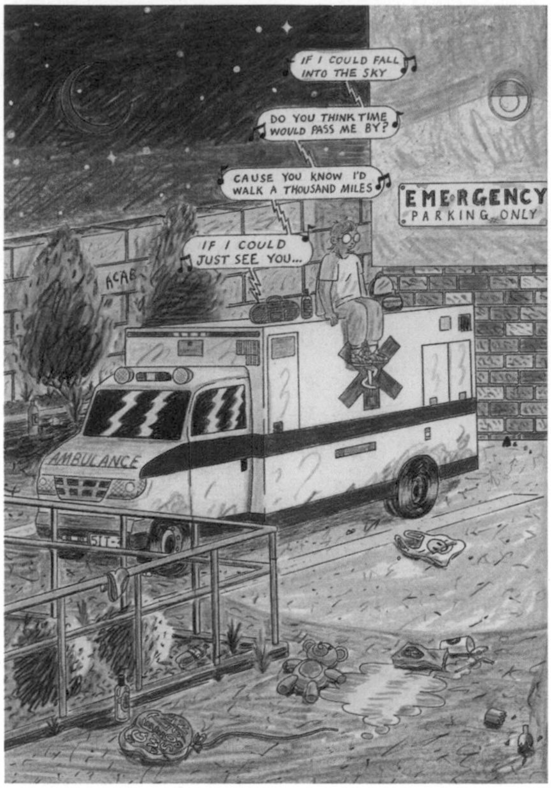
IF I COULD FALL INTO THE SKY
DO YOU THINK TIME WOULD PASS ME BY?
CAUSE YOU KNOW I'D WALK A THOUSAND MILES
IF I COULD JUST SEE YOU...
EMERGENCY
PARKING ONLY
ACAB
AMBULANCE

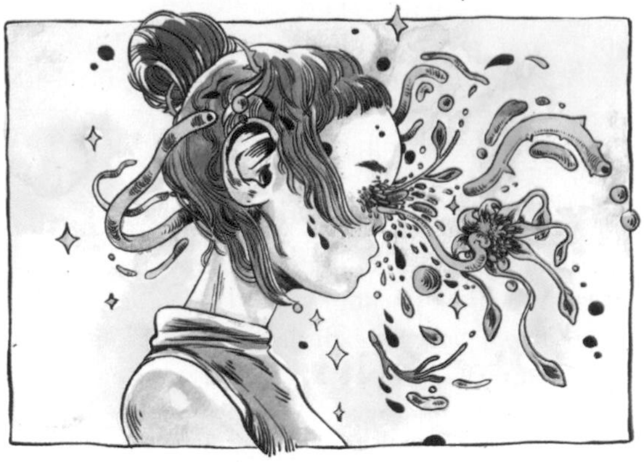

LEFT: *No Visitors* #4 back cover by HTML Flowers, 2018.

ABOVE: From *Now: The New Comics Anthology* #4, by Kirby, 2018.

KIRBY: Yeaaaaah! Grant, your colors! Talk about your colors. [*Laughter.*]

Do your color choices just come naturally or are you pushing back against that gray nothingness you are exposed to constantly?

HTML FLOWERS: I guess I could make my comics look like gray garbage.

KIRBY: We have to look at that all the time. Who wants to look at that a second time?

HTML FLOWERS: I think the colors of a hospital become really detectable to you when you're sick. You're in this room for days, weeks, and you become well-acquainted with the varying shades of teal and beige to the point where they feel quite right. You're always under those fluorescent lights. And, another thing, I'm just shit at painting. There's a pretty limited range to the color pencils I have, so ... [*Laughter.*]

KIRBY: Same!

HTML FLOWERS: I've got 48 colors to choose from. Also, I just love color. My comics became colorful just by need, you know? It's what I had around and how I started drawing. After the fact, the stuff that people liked the most of mine was very colorful. I'm happy I continued that.

KIRBY: You're living by the Brian Eno rule, dude.

What's the Brian Eno rule?

KIRBY: I hope I'm getting this right. It's like, rather than have a full box of crayons, it's better to have three.

HTML FLOWERS: Yeah, yeah.

KIRBY: Being forced to be limited is better. So, congrats on your small package of colored pencils. You're doing all right.

HTML FLOWERS: That's true. Your limitations become your trademark after a while.

KIRBY: Oh, yeah.

HTML FLOWERS: Brian Eno had this fucking sick quote that I love as well. He talks about the work you want to make. He thinks that people get too wrapped up in the point. He says you should always shoot the arrow then paint the bullseye around it. Yes, bitch!

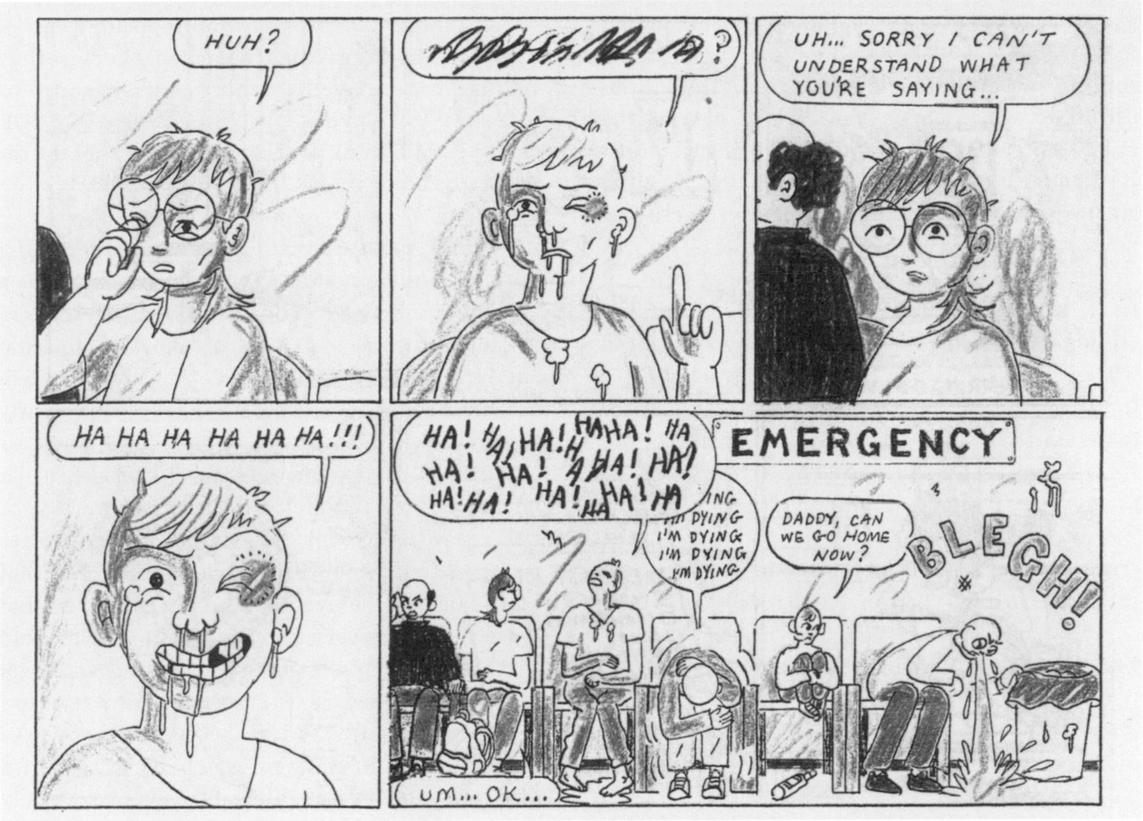
HUH?
UH... SORRY I CAN'T UNDERSTAND WHAT YOU'RE SAYING...
HA HA HA HA HA HA!!!
EMERGENCY
DADDY, CAN WE GO HOME NOW?
BLEGH!
UM... OK...
A sequence in *No Visitors* #4 by HTML Flowers, 2018.

That's what I've been doing my whole life. [*Laughter.*] Take your shot and it justifies itself after a while.

KIRBY: That's true. People seeking justification for everything they make I think end up in limiting situations.

HTML FLOWERS: It's so sad. You probably get this more than me because of your audience, but heaps of people who are younger kids —

KIRBY: Little babies.

HTML FLOWERS: And people trying to start illustration and stuff always write, "How do I be an artist?" We get questions like that. I either roast them or give them genuine advice, depending on the day. [*Laughter.*] It's usually a form of both. The whole thing is, like, stop thinking about being an artist and what it means. Honestly start working. You'll define yourself and it will just come out.

KIRBY: That same need for justification, why they're going to make comics, is the same need for justification they struggle with in storytelling too. "OK, if this person goes to the store, *why* did they go to the store?"

HTML FLOWERS: "Why did *they* go to the store?"

KIRBY: "Why do they have red hair? We have to know why their hair is red." Every single detail for them has to be accounted for.

HTML FLOWERS: "In my cinematic universe, when was this building cobbled together?" [*Laughter.*]

KIRBY: Yeah! Who the fuck cares?

HTML FLOWERS: "Is this a 1920s building? What year was it built?"

KIRBY: People don't care that much about their own fucking lives. I don't know why everyone thinks that suddenly everyone else is going to care. The only justification you need for any fantasy story ever is, "This is set 1,000 years in the future and it always works." If someone can do that every single time for every single story, you can just not explain anything. It does not matter.

HTML FLOWERS: One of the members of Fugazi was talking about feeling stressed out about making music when he was younger. A friend of his explained that, "In 100 years, no one will remember your contribution to the arts, so you should just do what you want to do."

KIRBY: They'll remember mine! [*Laughter.*]

HTML FLOWERS: I remember reading that when I was 18, and I was like, "Oh my God, that's so cool."

KIRBY: It's another excuse to make stuff, though.

HTML FLOWERS: Nobody gives a shit, and that's the most freeing thing. RJ's the only one who cares.

Do you think both of you are so open about this and are able to say, "Fuck it, it's freeing," because you are both dealing with real-life, serious shit? Your health, health care. A lot more than most people.

KIRBY: Yes.

HTML FLOWERS: Absolutely.

HTML FLOWERS: I'm trying to apply for a lung transplant and there's a real possibility I might not get it because I'm just not very good at looking after myself. That's such a constant fear for me, so I don't feel very stressed when I think about drawing. Come on. I go to the hospital all the time and there are fucking people dying in rooms next to me. I see the same guy in the hall, there's the lady who's always in the cafeteria.

KIRBY: The regulars, man.

HTML FLOWERS: The regulars. They're me and I am them. We look at each other like, "Yup, back again." People asking you, "Are you a young doctor who's —" then stop halfway through the sentence because they see that you're dressed like shit. I couldn't be a doctor. [*Laughter.*] "No, I'm just a patient." They're like, "Oh, sorry." I say, "I think as you become more of a doctor, you'll stop doing that."

KIRBY: The pressure that comes with maintaining normalcy and maintaining the highest standards a lot of people were fed early on fall away when you're literally incapable of performing those. I think that similarly carries over to a lot of other endeavors like drawing a comic book. Whether or not you knew early on that you were going to be unable to fulfill whatever picture of normalcy you were fed, or if you learned it later on and it was difficult to acknowledge or accept, either way the outcome is the same. There's going to be losses that come with that. It's the mindset that you adjust to when you're chronically ill. Not that these things are very important, but we were told that they were. You've got to get a house, you've got to get financial security, a career, you have to have a family, whatever the fuck else. Knowing that you've got to figure out a different way to do things and a different way to value things transfers very easily over to writing a fucking comic book, where there are no consequences anyway. It's a good carryover. If I'm going to be all silver-lining with this shit, that is one of them.

HTML FLOWERS: I'm glad I don't give a shit.

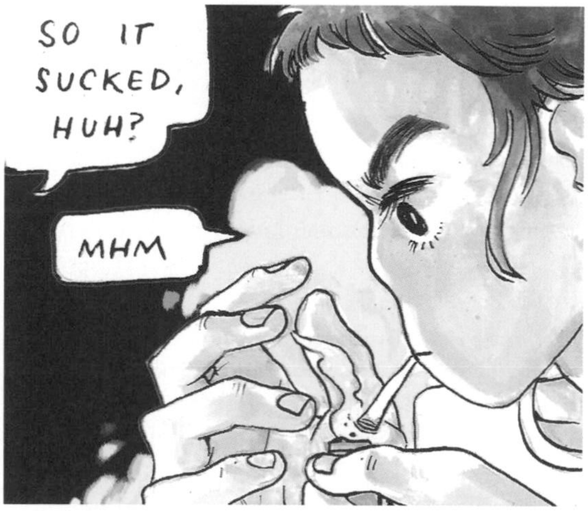
SO IT SUCKED, HUH?
MHM

From a *Sick Day* comic, posted online in 2019, by Kirby.

ILLNESS-WORK BALANCE

Rebecca, you once wrote, "There's a dangerously fine line between staying on top of things and pushing myself to a physical breaking point."

KIRBY: [*Laughs.*] Yeah!

Is it difficult to manage the overall pressures of art making — putting out new material, getting social media posts up, selling your work — and staying healthy at the same time?

KIRBY: Oh, my God, yeah. You can't do all of them together. Right now, there's a shitload going on in my personal life and I took on too many jobs because I can't say no to anything ever. I know what's coming, you know? It's going to be bad, and I'm going to shit blood and it's going to be disgusting. But I'll have slightly more money and maybe that's good. [*HTML Flowers laughs.*] You get obsessive. It feels good to finish things. If I had my choice, I'd just be working all the time.

But when symptoms get bad ... You can't see this, but I'm sitting like a frog. I can't sit like a normal person. But I can't draw like this either. One thing will eventually give way for the other thing. Either I can push myself really hard and get something done and feel good about that, but then I'll be very sick for an indeterminable amount of time. Or I can take really good care of myself physically and never get any art done and feel like a worthless piece of shit. So, I work really weird hours and try to drink my juice and that's what happens, but a lot of time I fail. One of the two things just doesn't happen.

THE JUICE, IT HEALS MY BONES
THANK YOU- FOR WHATEVER SMALL THING THAT MAY BE.
DELIGHTFUL
YES

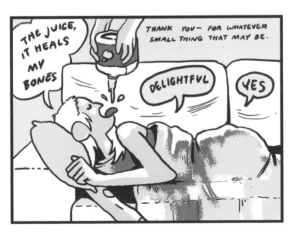

A panel from Kirby's *Sick Day*, 2019.

Your juice?

KIRBY: My juice is literally apple juice. I drink it because I'm not allowed to drink anything but water. I'm so bored. Now I drink juice all the time. It's probably not good, but I do it. It's my beautiful juice.

HTML FLOWERS: The juice-drinker has logged on. [*Laughter.*]

KIRBY: It's me!

Do you make work when you're in the hospital?

HTML FLOWERS: Yes, I probably work harder in the hospital than outside. I don't like to have visitors — *No Visitors*. Because there are people helping me in the hospital, and people will come by like, "Hey, it's time to do your physio," and most of the time I'm like, "Nice. Let's get it," unless I'm depressed and then I'm like, "Get the fuck out of here. How dare you!" [*Kirby laughs.*] No, I try to be nice to the physios.

KIRBY: Good to clarify.

HTML FLOWERS: Because of the isolation aspect and because of how minimal the environment is — like you were saying earlier, it's drab, it's gray, it's restrictive — it's actually the best place to write in. I have no distractions. The only thing that distracts you are the cries of pain from the other patients.

KIRBY: "Stop it! Shut the fuck up!" [*Laughter.*]

HTML FLOWERS: It doesn't hurt that the stuff I write about is very much about the experience that I'm having currently. So, I kind of get more work done in the hospital, because when I'm out, similarly to what Kirby was talking about, it's really hard to stay on top of my treatments and my work. It's been shit because up until 2015 or 2016, I had a pretty decent run with my health. I was sicker than your average person, but I was able to go for long periods without hospitalization and the repercussions wouldn't be that bad.

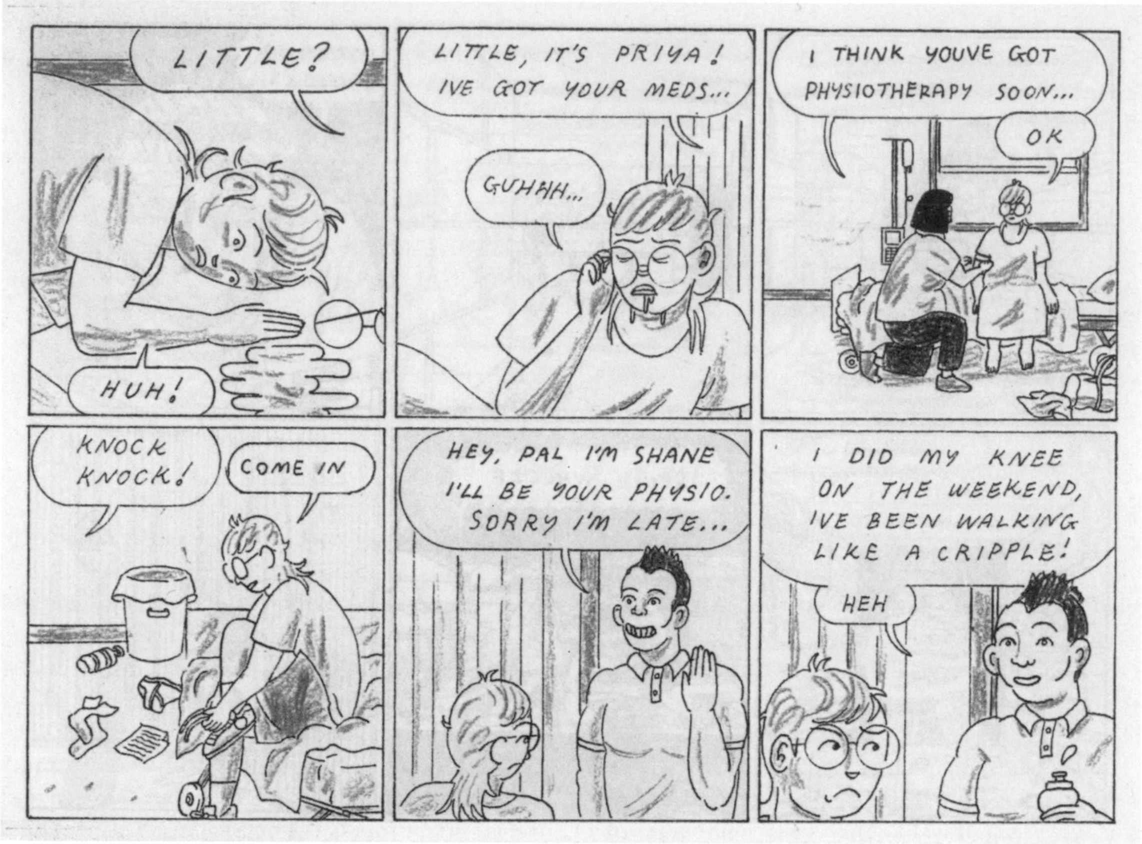
LITTLE?
HUH!
LITTLE, IT'S PRIYA! IVE GOT YOUR MEDS...
GUHHH...
I THINK YOUVE GOT PHYSIOTHERAPY SOON...
OK
KNOCK KNOCK!
COME IN
HEY, PAL I'M SHANE I'LL BE YOUR PHYSIO. SORRY I'M LATE...
I DID MY KNEE ON THE WEEKEND, IVE BEEN WALKING LIKE A CRIPPLE!
HEH

An HTML Flowers sequence from *No Visitors* #3, 2018.

That's changed drastically. Now I get fucked up very easily and have to go to the hospital. I've had to seriously dial back how much I work, which is a shame because I didn't really find my purpose until I started making comics about illness. I have a book in mind and I'm really working on it, but ... I look at it as the most important thing I've worked on. It's just such a fucking shame that I only started to commit to it once my health [*fart noise*] was declining.

KIRBY: Are those related?

HTML FLOWERS: Probably.

KIRBY: Is it just a coincidence?

HTML FLOWERS: I was thinking about it before then. It just took a long time. Like I said, I just didn't feel like I was ready to do it and had enough chops at drawing comics. If you read the early *No Visitors*, like the first one, there isn't a narrative comic in it really. There are a couple of scraps. There's the first comic with Little in it in there. It's like a one-page comic. In issue #2, there's some scrappy comics. Some of the stuff in there is really good. There's this other comic about Little getting fucked by his therapist. It's such a weird comic. I look back at it and I am like, "Why did I print that?" Simon was like, "You gotta do it. It's hilarious." Little got a haircut. He looks completely different in issue #3 and #4.

No more bowl cut.

HTML FLOWERS: I approached those issues like, "It's time to build this. Let's do some fucking work." But it took me ages to get those out because I was sick. In a day, if I do the treatments that I'm supposed to do, I never have the energy to draw. If I draw for too many days without doing treatments, I get really sick and

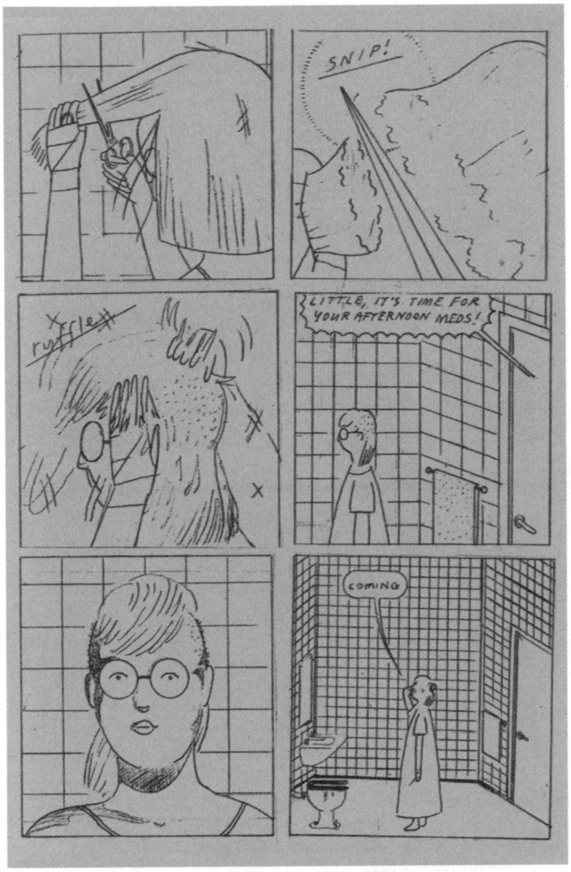
SNIP!
ruffle
LITTLE, IT'S TIME FOR YOUR AFTERNOON MEDS!
COMING

Little's haircut: from HTML Flowers' *No Visitors* #1, 2015.

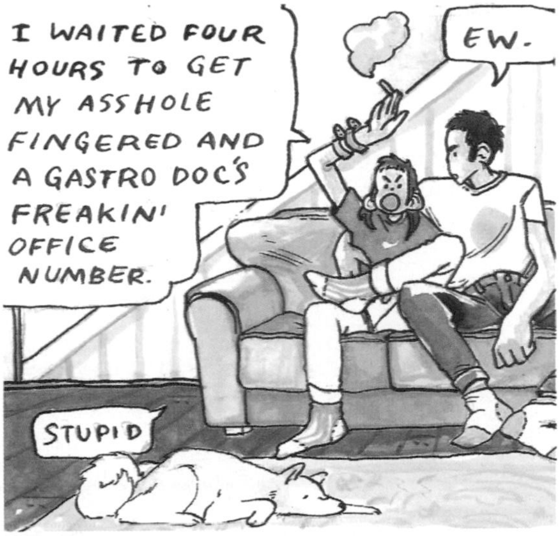
I WAITED FOUR HOURS TO GET MY ASSHOLE FINGERED AND A GASTRO DOC'S FREAKIN' OFFICE NUMBER.
EW.
STUPID

From a *Sick Day* comic by Rebecca Kirby, 2019.

the hospital starts to become a potential. So, I have to stop drawing and do the treatments, you know? It's a pendulum of bullshit, bro! [*Burps, Kirby laughs.*]

Is the frequent use of humor in your comics a way to lessen the weight of these heavy topics?

KIRBY: No, it's just factually funny.

HTML FLOWERS: It's such a funny lifestyle.

KIRBY: It just is funny. I know it's all "very tragic" or whatever, but half the reason any media that exists that centers on or acknowledges a chronically ill person, their story either has to be super tragic — it's so bad and it keeps getting worse — and we feel really bad for them and that's our only emotional connection. Or they are fighting against the odds and fighting against their illness. They're overcoming that with the help of an able-bodied person or just through their own moxie. They achieve something greater than any average person could because they overcame the circumstance of their illness. It's really a two-dimensional and fucking insulting depiction. How fucking stupid is it to think anybody with a shitty circumstance is going to be a flat, unhappy sack of shit that has no personality? Their only personality is that they got a tube up their rectum yesterday. It's two-dimensional and stupid. Our comics are funny because we're both funny and because our circumstances are funny.

There is an absurdity to it all.

KIRBY: Yeah. Things can be two things at once, you know? Our circumstances can be both really upsetting and also very funny. Some things, maybe a year or two later, after it's less fucked. [*HTML Flowers laughs.*] I was telling Grant about some of the tests that I've had done. If I were to tell you verbally what it was, first of all, you wouldn't believe me. Second of all, it sounds like a build up to a joke. It's fucking ridiculous. I had two doctors insert a balloon into my butthole and then inflate the butthole balloon. Then they gave me a test to figure out the strength of my butthole, apparently, where I had to set a timer and see how long it would take for me to eject said balloon from my butthole. And that is an actual test I had to take. You're welcome. If that's not funny —

See, I don't know if I'm supposed to laugh at that or not though.

KIRBY: Please laugh! It's funny. [*Laughter.*] It's fucked and invasive and disgusting and unnecessary. It did not accomplish anything. And also, it *is* funny. It can be two things. Most of the things that are really funny are usually not just that on their face. Tons of comedy is based off the expense of someone's dignity. It also extends to this experience.

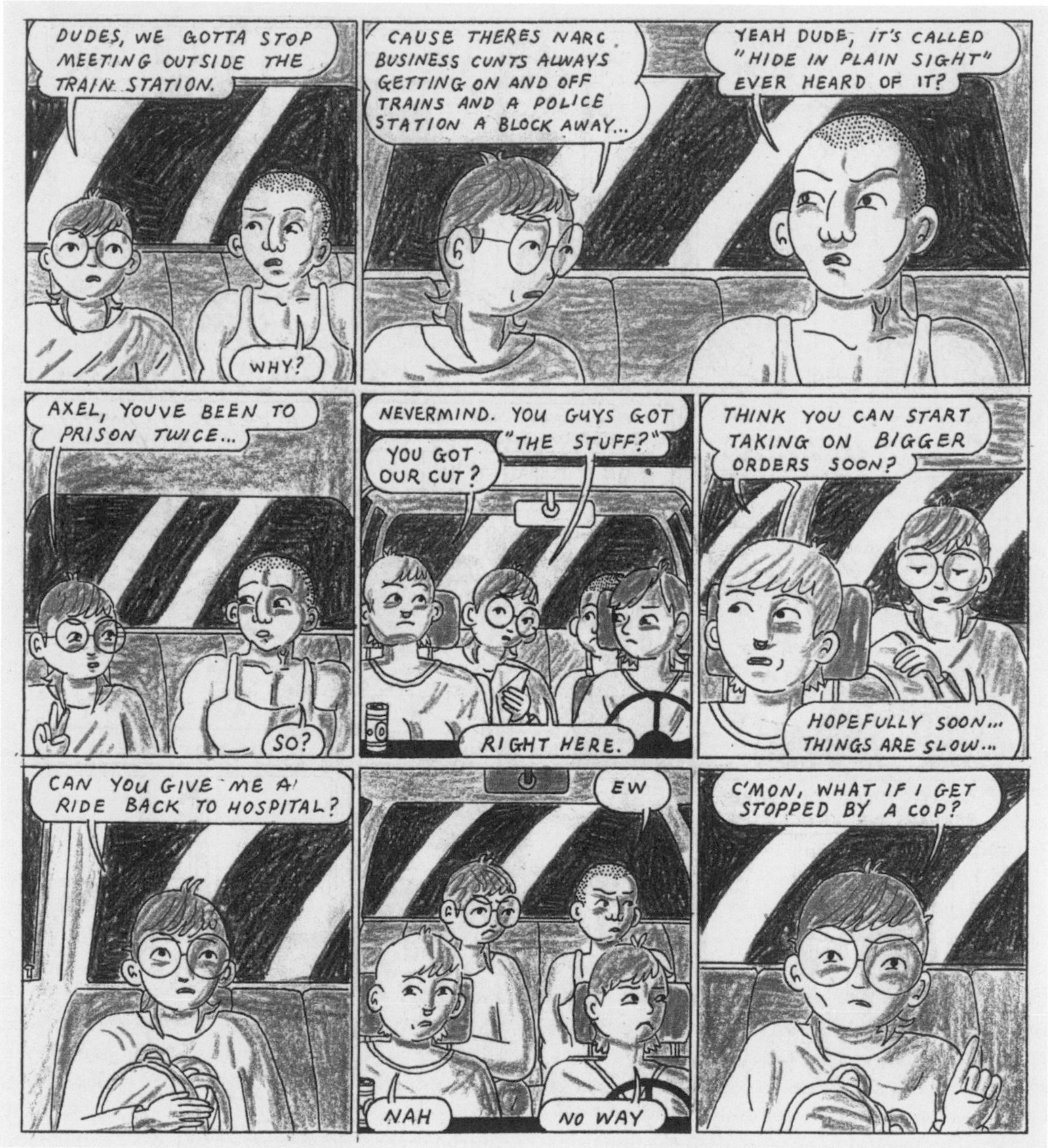

DUDES, WE GOTTA STOP MEETING OUTSIDE THE TRAIN STATION.
WHY?
CAUSE THERES NARC BUSINESS CUNTS ALWAYS GETTING ON AND OFF TRAINS AND A POLICE STATION A BLOCK AWAY...
YEAH DUDE, IT'S CALLED "HIDE IN PLAIN SIGHT" EVER HEARD OF IT?
AXEL, YOUVE BEEN TO PRISON TWICE...
SO?
NEVERMIND. YOU GUYS GOT "THE STUFF?"
YOU GOT OUR CUT?
RIGHT HERE.
THINK YOU CAN START TAKING ON BIGGER ORDERS SOON?
HOPEFULLY SOON... THINGS ARE SLOW...
CAN YOU GIVE ME A RIDE BACK TO HOSPITAL?
EW
NAH
NO WAY
C'MON, WHAT IF I GET STOPPED BY A COP?

HTML FLOWERS: I basically agree with what Kirby is saying. It just is funny shit. Even when I was in school, I was the "funny one," or whatever. I mean, obviously, I was the "hot one," too. [*Laughter.*] I was a chubby, little fuckwit and the way I got by was by telling jokes. I could befriend anyone if I was funny enough. It's how I would stop myself from getting beaten up or disliked. Just tell jokes. When I met Simon, I really started to think that I was a comedy person. "Maybe I should just write comedy now." We started making these comedy comics and I was like, "This is the best shit. I love this so much. It's so much fun." How degrading and absurd your circumstances are when you're sick, that's just genuinely funny.

I'm so tired of stories like *Breaking Bad*. I mean, I love *Breaking Bad*, it's one of my favorite TV shows. It's so well made, but that story is insane. I think everyone who's had cancer has thought, "Maybe I should sell these drugs," you know? How insane that story got! Suddenly, he's blowing up houses and having people assassinated all because he got cancer and never felt important in his life. [*Laughs.*] At the time I was watching that, I was dealing drugs.

KIRBY: Yeah! [*Laughs.*]

HTML FLOWERS: I was already dealing drugs. I was like, "It's really not like this. I'm not better at dealing drugs because I'm sick." If anything, I was much weaker and needed to make friends with competitors so they wouldn't beat me up and take my shit. [*Laughter.*] Maybe if I was a genius chemist! The things I want to write about are the things you never get to see. I hate that it doesn't exist. Like the disabled or sick person who does drugs and doesn't care about their life. The person heading towards death and not really doing anything about it. The person secretly feeling very conflicted because they would never tell this to that fucking narc social worker. I want to write about a useless disabled. You never get to see a useless disabled.

KIRBY: Exactly!

OPPOSITE: Panels from *No Visitors* #4 by HTML Flowers, 2018.

HTML FLOWERS: There's always some special mission they're on. Most of the people I know are useless disableds. They have drug habits because life sucks and they can't actually do any of the shit they want to do and they'll probably kill themselves at some point. [*Laughs.*] I think there's a huge push at the moment in the sick and disabled community to be more positive about living, which is cool, but it doesn't suit me. They're like, "It's not a death sentence."

KIRBY: But it fucking is! I hate this idea.

HTML FLOWERS: It annoys me. Can we just have some stories about how shitty it is first? From the people who experience it, rather than from the point of view from the family members or something. "Aww, Julia has cancer." "It must be so hard for you. How's the business going?" Then you put on a different show.

KIRBY: *Barefoot Contessa*.

HTML FLOWERS: Yeah, *Barefoot Contessa*. [*Laughter.*]

Grant, you once wrote that you like to remind people of death. Is that along the same lines?

HTML FLOWERS: I'm just passing on the favor because I'm constantly reminded of it. If you are ill or disabled, you are like a walking avatar for death. The people around you, many of them never really acknowledge it. I can tell when someone's uncomfortable when I'm talking about health or illness or something. I want to shove it down the world's throat.

Speaking of being slightly uncomfortable here, there's a panel that stuck out when I was reading Rebecca's work —

KIRBY: Oooh, me.

And this has been weighing on me a bit. You wrote, "Am I causing harm by selling my comics about medical and emotional trauma? Am I contributing to the capitalist exploitation of sick people?" And after reading that and preparing for this interview, I was like, "Am I contributing to this exploitation by making this magazine and interviewing both of you?"

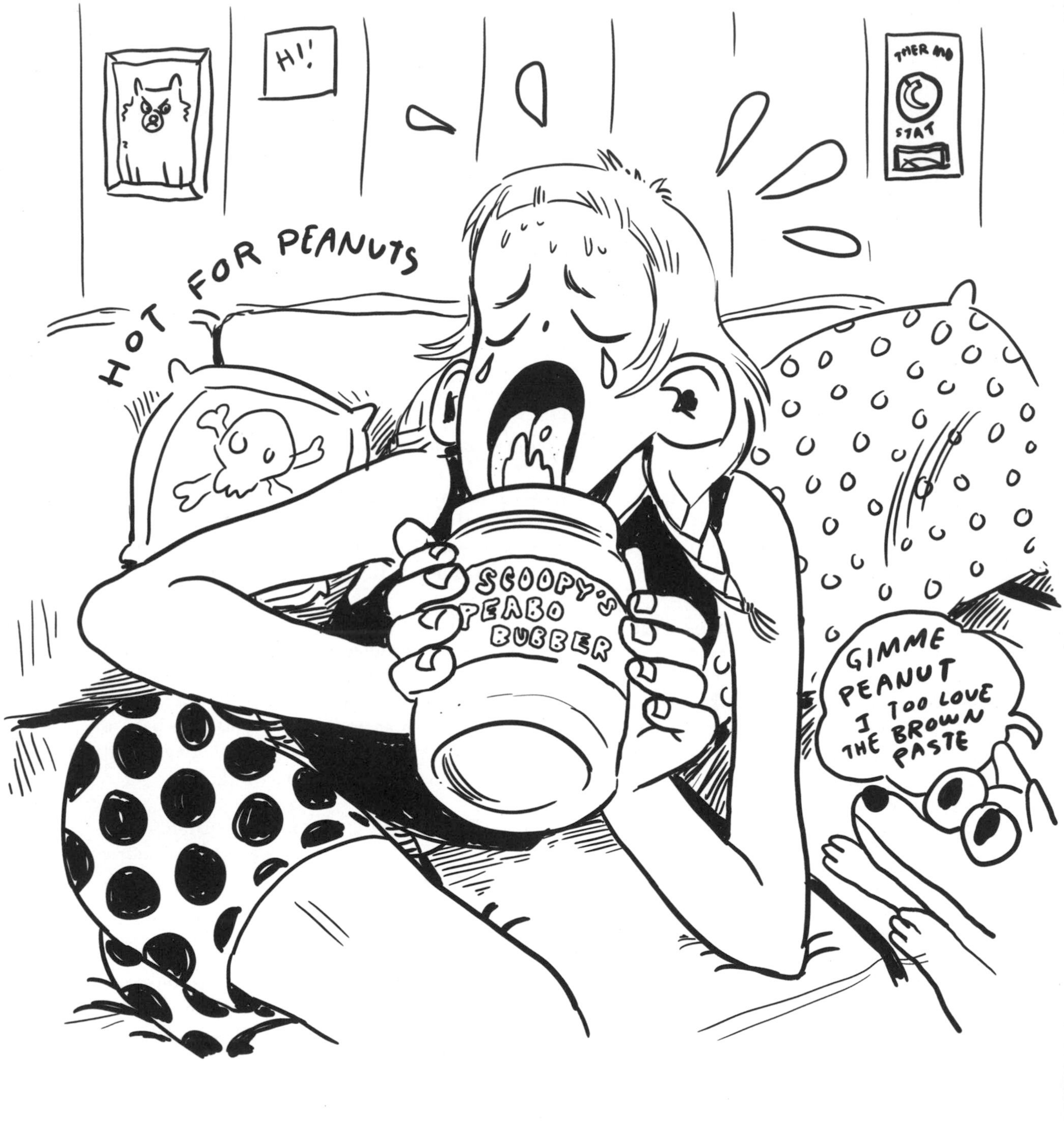
HI!
THER MO
STAT
HOT FOR PEANUTS
SCOOPY'S PEABO BUBBER
GIMME PEANUT
I TOO LOVE THE BROWN PASTE

Kirby expresses her love for peanut butter, 2019.

HTML FLOWERS: You work for Big Pharma, RJ? I fucking knew it! [*Laughter.*]

KIRBY: It is something that I think about. Obviously, the root of this, if I'm getting real deep, is capitalism and commodified health care. I do try to make as much of my chronic illness comics available for free. Also, I make no money because I'm fucking sick constantly. I had to leave a normal job two years ago and my only source of income is this. I worked retail forever and that was the only option, until I couldn't even do that anymore. It's a really weird line to toe and a weird thing to think about philosophically, but …

First of all, no. You're doing good. Thank you. No one ever wants to hear about my vomit and all of that good stuff. Finally, people will hear about all my vomits. I get concerned about how it could be potentially damaging to me. In making confessional comics, I'm also essentially commodifying what could be really private parts of my life. I don't feel bad about doing that, but it feels weird to … The whole practice of what I do —

HTML FLOWERS: That weed's hitting you hard, bro. [*Laughter.*] Kirby accidentally smoked some strong weed before the interview.

KIRBY: I thought maybe I'd need a little bit.

HTML FLOWERS: She was like, "I usually buy bad stuff off of a 12-year-old in a parking lot, but this is really good shit." [*Laughter.*] But I know what you mean.

KIRBY: Obviously, I'm not going to blame myself for being a sickly person and I'm not going to blame myself for being someone who talks about it or makes work about it. None of that is anything I take issue with. I take issue with the fact that the people who want to buy my stuff are probably also fucking disabled and in America. They don't have any money and can't have jobs, because they're like me. That's the problem. It's this weird relationship I have with making this work and then relying on it to be able to go back to the doctor. It's definitely a relationship that I question a lot, but also, I don't have a whole lot of choices at the moment. I'm just going to fucking do it.

HTML FLOWERS: I don't question it. It's so low on the list of my priorities or shit I get worried about.

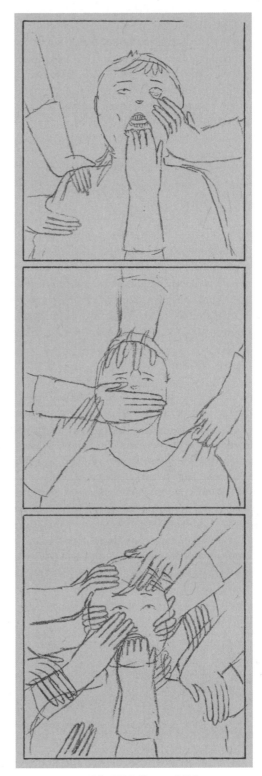

From *No Visitors* #2 by HTML Flowers, 2016.

I absolutely know that I can identify with the concept that Kirby's talking about, but I don't know. I was born sick and I've grown up in hospitals my whole life. Any part of my sense of privacy, any kind of thing that is intimate — my shitting habits, how much blood I'm coughing up, whether or not I'm growing right, if my dick size is normal — has always been a talking point for at least 10 people, plus my mom.

Privacy has never been your concern because you've had no choice.

HTML FLOWERS: I never had it. I don't give a shit about that aspect of my comics. I learned that something people really enjoyed about my work was how intimate I was willing to get. The commodification thing — I just don't give a fuck. If anyone ever tries to criticize me for trying to make rent, they just vanish before my eyes. They become a non-person to me.

KIRBY: Oh, my God.

HTML FLOWERS: I have "no-bullshit vision." They just disappear. Have you tried to live in the world lately? "You work at Safeway? Oh, I guess you're happy with all their farming practices that they engage in." There's no ethical consumption, my guy. What am I going to do? I have to make money, fuckers.

I set up a Patreon where I charge $3 a month for subscription. I hope that most of my fans that are on the poorer side can afford that. I put excerpts from my art and published comics up there for free too, just so my more unwell fans can read them and have access to them. That's about the best I can do. I can't be going around mailing out free comics and shit. Postage is a bitch. I do my part to try to make my work accessible to the sick and poor parts of my audience. That's the best I can do. Otherwise, I feel no conflict whatsoever about selling my work. I expect there's a good deal of people who read my work because they're "inspiration porn" fans.

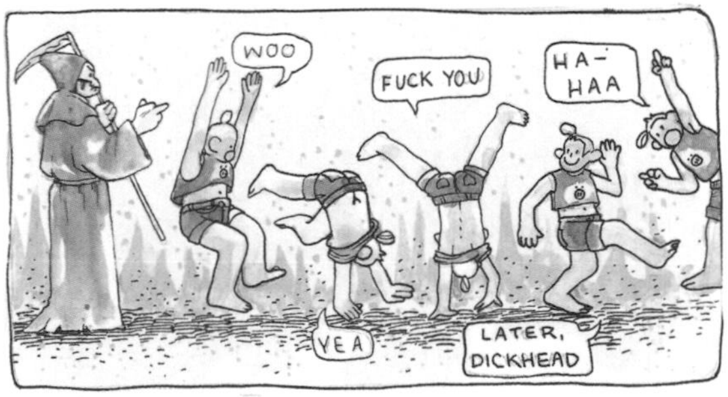
WOO
FUCK YOU
HA-HAA
YEA
LATER, DICKHEAD

A panel from Kirby's *Biopsy*, 2018.

OTHERIZING

What do you consider "inspiration porn?"

HTML FLOWERS: It's like, "Whoa! This guy's got an illness and he's going to die and *he's just writing about it.*"

KIRBY: "We love that he's going to die."

HTML FLOWERS: "It's fucking crazy that this guy gets out of bed every day and he doesn't kill himself. Can you believe it?" I'm sure there's a huge part of my audience that is able-bodied, healthy people obsessed with the story of someone dying. I don't give a shit. Suck my dick. Give me money. You're going to get tokenized one way or another, so you may as well get paid so that you can buy something nice.

KIRBY: For me, it's an impulse. I'm not trying to make this some kind of grand purpose I feel I have because I don't really. The people that consume stories that are "inspirational" or "tragic" about sick people are also the kind of people that are massively afraid of the sick. They are massively afraid of facing that circumstance themselves. In an effort to distance themselves from it, they are drawn in to stories that are outlandish or make-believe, and that keeps people who might otherwise be a burden or disgusting or frightening at arm's length. For people who actually experience this stuff and aren't "inspirational" people or aren't particularly strong, which is the majority of all people, it's different. A lot of time is spent thinking about impending death. That's something nobody really wants to think about facing immediately.

It would be interesting to see the people especially searching for those "inspirational" stories to actually interact with sick people in real life, rather than on the pages.

KIRBY: They think they can identify. When you see someone in Rite-Aid behind somebody in a wheelchair, they're always like, "I really like your sweater. You're doing such a *good job*." [*HTML Flowers laughs.*] "You're so beautiful considering how disgusting you are."

HTML FLOWERS: "That's crazy, you're wearing clothes just like me."

KIRBY: That's the whole thing.

HTML FLOWERS: "I have that jumper. Isn't that nuts?"

KIRBY: It's such a surprise to people who I'm sharing a waiting room with or if I'm in a Lyft or whatever. "Where you going?" "I'm going to fucking hospital." It's a big surprise because I'm not made out of metal or actively bandaged. It's probably really scary for them and that's why they prefer that type of safe story. The fact that they could potentially be facing the same circumstance I am, or that any other sick person is, is so unbelievably terrifying and also gross. This is why media like our comics don't usually exist. And why I think media like our comics is important.

HTML FLOWERS: Mmmm.

KIRBY: I don't think that me making a comic book about that time I fell down the stairs because I was under anesthesia and fought that nurse is going to change societal practices that hand down this type of otherizing. But I do think that having this type of story or information available in a format that's funny and looks good is necessary.

Also for other sick people to see, not just for the people who think we're all really gross. I didn't even know it was OK to talk about this shit, informed by my experience as a girl and as someone who's been in harmful relationships. I didn't even know it was fine to tell my doctors how I was actually doing. There are probably a lot of people who are really sickly and don't have anybody to talk to. They don't feel seen or feel like they're a freak. I want to be like, "Here's a little comic and it's essentially a picture of you." I didn't get to see that until I read Grant's shit. I want to do that for people.

Is your goal to instruct the general public or teach them things? Does that even cross your mind when you're drawing them?

KIRBY: Yeah. I actively have thought that way before.

HTML FLOWERS: Kirby does that.

KIRBY: It's not something I want to do as a practice, but it's something I've had to deal with in terms of handling my other sick loved ones and myself. In America — I don't know how it is in Australia — the process of seeking care is so fucking impossible. Even with the absolute top-tier resources. I made a comic about how to perform patient advocacy. How to record your symptoms and bring them to the doctor so that they'll take you seriously. I did that instructional shit because every single fucking sick person I know has the exact same scenarios play out. Whether you have insurance or not, you're fucking boned. It's so much self-advocacy and nobody knows how to operate within the system, so nobody gets any fucking help either. "OK, this is boring and soulless to make, but here's how you go to the doctor."

It's taken me 10 years and I still don't have a solid diagnosis. I'm 30 years deep into being ill and nobody has listened to me this entire time. On May 1, I'll find out if I have discoid lupus. All anyone had to

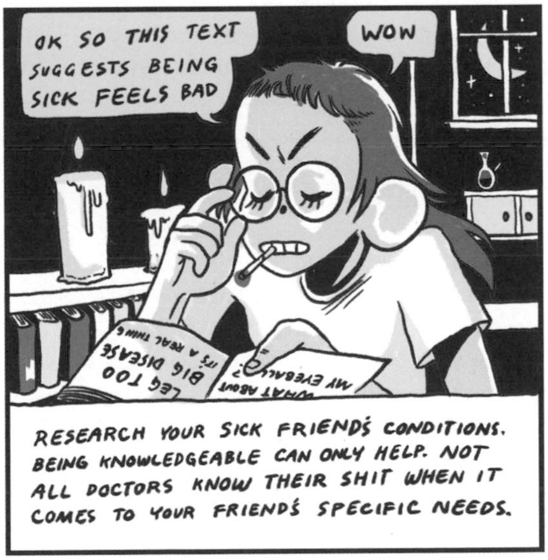

OK SO THIS TEXT SUGGESTS BEING SICK FEELS BAD
WOW
LEG TOO BIG DISEASE
IT'S A REAL THING
WHAT ABOUT MY EYEBALL
RESEARCH YOUR SICK FRIENDS CONDITIONS. BEING KNOWLEDGEABLE CAN ONLY HELP. NOT ALL DOCTORS KNOW THEIR SHIT WHEN IT COMES TO YOUR FRIENDS SPECIFIC NEEDS.

From Kirby's *Sick Day* comic about patient advocacy, 2019.

> **❝ *I just hate the word [self-care] now because of the way it's become this fucking buzzword. For most people, it means putting on Netflix and buying a bath bomb.* ❞**

do this entire time was just to have taken my blood and done an ANA test, but nobody fucking did it. I had to sit there and research and tell them, "I need this test and this test," and bring it in to the doctor. It's crazy that nobody has a step-by-step guide for how to go to the doctor and have someone give a fuck about you. That doesn't exist. There's no accessible resources. How the fuck do you get any help, ever? If that means going to the doctor's office and physically refusing to leave until somebody helps you, then do that. Start screaming. Anything to get someone to ever care about you. It's such a struggle and I think it's ridiculous. I've never seen it anywhere and this isn't in any media that centers on sick people. It's wild. That one was an active decision. That one wasn't an impulse. It's really upsetting. I can only speak to my own experiences. It's not like I'm extremely well-researched in this. But it is something I do feel obligated to discuss.

Grant, do you feel that same obligation?

HTML FLOWERS: Not really. People write me questions a lot, letters, emails. They'll ask questions about what Kirby's talking about. I'm happy to give them answers. But the instructional nature of almost all the literature I've ever seen about being sick has come to bother me so much that I don't have any fucking room to make it myself.

What bothers you about it?

HTML FLOWERS: Growing up, the only literature you're introduced to about illness is like, "What does

it mean to have cystic fibrosis?" Paid for by Verizon or some company. [*Laughter.*] That Ronald McDonald House I used to go to when I was younger, they would have these dumbshit attitudes. "The only disability is a bad attitude."

KIRBY: Oh, my God.

HTML FLOWERS: That stuff started to really bum me out.

Ronald is always creeping around your comics.

HTML FLOWERS: Exactly. I became obsessed with the idea how massive companies parasite off young, sick kids.

KIRBY: Johnson & Johnson can eat my ass, man!

HTML FLOWERS: I don't know what they did, but fuck Johnson & Johnson. [*Casey laughs.*] I think what Kirby does is super important and it's what I've done for heaps of my friends who have become sick. My partner you met just before she was leaving for work, I've been to all her doctor's appointments. I was right there in the ER. I've gotten more than a couple of nurses annoyed with me. I've been like, "She needs some painkillers," and they're like, "I'll get her some Panadol." I'm like, "No, she needs Panadeine. She has a broken thumb." I'm in there doing what I do. I know how to advocate for myself. It's way easier to advocate for someone else.

KIRBY: Yeah.

ADVOCACY

HTML FLOWERS: I'm very much in everyone's face when I advocate for myself, but I go 10 times as hard for someone I care about. That's easy for me. That's just what I do. It's what I learned to do. It's amazing that Kirby has the patience to make those comics and help people out. It's a beautiful thing to do for the community of young, sick kids who follow her work.

KIRBY: Awwww.

HTML FLOWERS: I just don't have the taste for that. I like to show rather than tell most of the time and I'm a selfish artist. [*Laughs.*]

KIRBY: We love a selfish artist.

HTML FLOWERS: Kirby's really out here trying to make moves for the people and I'm just trying to sell my wares. [*Kirby laughs.*]

I don't know much about Australian health care. Do you know the differences between American and Australian health care in layman's terms?

HTML FLOWERS: It's the difference between being shot in the head and asphyxiating. [*Laughs.*] One is a little bit slower and probably a little bit more humane. In Australia's health care system, there is a lot of opportunity to get the care you need but you have to be on your game. It's a full-time job. A lot of people do that thing where they criticize poor people for buying things that they need and everyone's mad about people who are in welfare.

KIRBY: Yeah.

"How dare they go see a movie!"

HTML FLOWERS: Yeah.

KIRBY: "Disgusting!"

HTML FLOWERS: It's harder to be poor and sick in Australia than it is to not be. That's the same for every country in the world, no matter how good the health care is. But the organizational structure of Australia's health care is a fucking mess. It makes it really hard for people living with chronic, severe illnesses like me and people who are worse off. I often think about having an intellectual disability and having to navigate this shit. At least I'm really good one-on-one. I can always talk my way into and out of things. I can advocate for myself. I'm lucid and aware of what's going on. I generally don't forget ... I actually forget heaps of shit. Even I, someone who's pretty switched on, forget a lot of stuff that I need and I still don't know

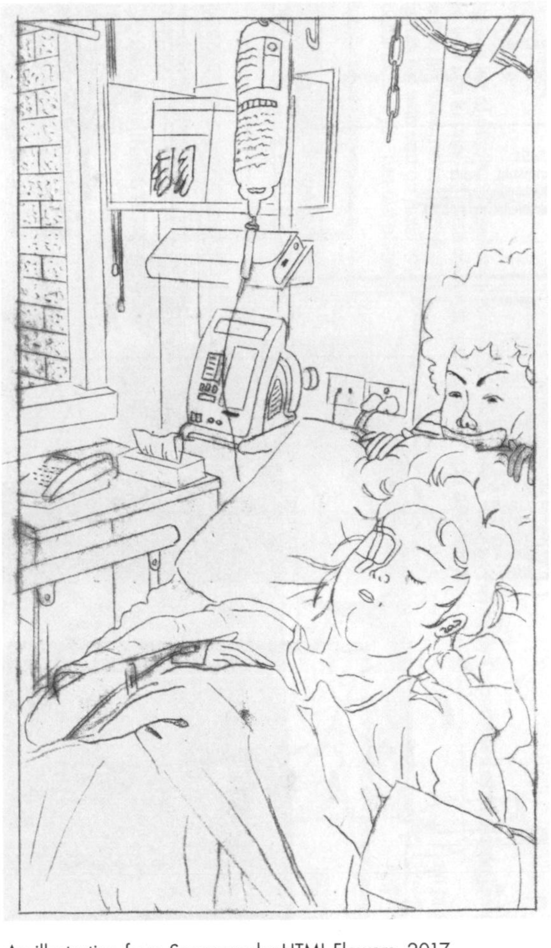

An illustration from *Sonogram* by HTML Flowers, 2017.

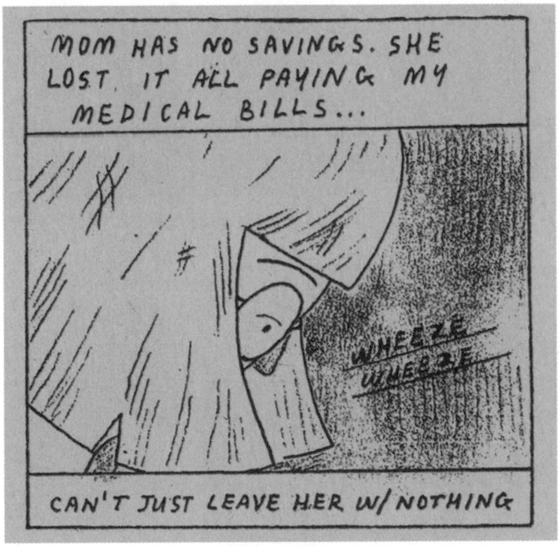
MOM HAS NO SAVINGS. SHE LOST IT ALL PAYING MY MEDICAL BILLS...
WHEEZE
WHEEZE
CAN'T JUST LEAVE HER W/ NOTHING

A panel from HTML Flowers' *No Visitors* #1, 2015.

BIOPSY

REBECCA WELLS KIRBY, 0428638, 1/5   EGD GERD: 530-81-K21-9

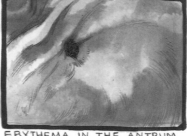

ERYTHEMA IN THE ANTRUM
COMPATIBLE WITH GASTRITIS

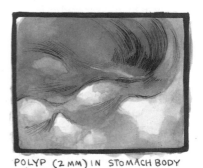

STOMACH BODY

POLYP (2 MM) IN STOMACH BODY

GASTRO-ESOPHAGEAL JUNCTION

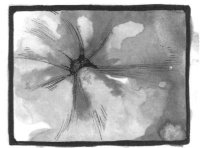

MIDDLE THIRD OF ESOPHAGUS

MUCOSA SUGGESTIVE OF
BARRETT'S ESOPHAGUS

about a lot of stuff that I could have. That's a huge problem.

A lot of people think, "You're in a country where you get subsidized health care." Yeah, but I don't even know half of it that I can get. I do have to take care of every ounce of it myself. It is subsidized, which means I do still pay a bit, and when you take as much medicine as me, that's still a good $100 a month out the window. Wouldn't it be brilliant if I got everything I needed for free? That's the only humane way to approach medicine.

KIRBY: Yeah.

HTML FLOWERS: Another person I follow lives in Canada. A lot of people have this impression that Canada has impeccable health care and being disabled there isn't a big deal. But she's always blowing the lid off. She's always posting bills she has and is like, "That's Canadian health care you're looking at." And it's a big fucking bill for some pills. I think when I first moved here, I was so fucking grateful. One part of my medicine was about the amount of rent that you would have paid in the '80s in the American town that I lived in. That's this bottle here, Creon 4. I need to take one bottle of these a week. I run through them. That would be rent in a week, you know? And that's in the '80s.

Even now, these are like $350 per bottle unless they're subsidized. I was so grateful moving here to not have to pay that much for a bottle, so it wasn't until I was in my mid-20s that I really started to think, "Hang on, this is still hard. Why in the world should this be hard?" How are we, as civilized human beings, not doing everything we possibly can to make the life of someone dealing with an illness much easier? The advocacy around me should be stronger. I'm a great advocate for myself, but there are a lot of people who can't be.

KIRBY: Yup!

HTML FLOWERS: I shouldn't have to be. I should just be making comics, you know? I shouldn't have to spend most of my time organizing an IV that I can take home. Or trying to haggle with the welfare

---

OPPOSITE: Cover for the collected, self-published *Biopsy*, 2018.

department because they found another reason to cut $100 off my monthly payments. "Come on, bitch. You want to go through this again? You tried this last year and I shut it down." [*Laughter.*] That stuff happens all the time. There are social workers, but you get one social worker per department. That department has like 60 people who go to it. That social worker is in charge of all 60 of those peoples' garbage and bullshit. That's not enough. We need personal assistants and people that are going to remind us. There needs to be more advocacy for people in my situation. In my opinion, we should have PAs who help you manage your illness. Like personal illness management assistants.

KIRBY: Yeah.

HTML FLOWERS: PIMAs, we'll call them. [*Laughter.*] We should have that. You know, I missed a really important appointment for a lung transplant consultation the other week. I literally forgot it was happening. No one called me from the hospital to remind me and it was a really important meeting. Consequently, the lung transplant team hasn't gotten back to me. I'm fairly certain that means that they're disappointed in my lack of commitment. If I had someone else in my corner, maybe that wouldn't be a big deal. I could ask my mom, but why should she have to do it? Why should it have to be someone close in my life taking on the second job of looking after me? Subsidize this shit! Pay somebody. Open up a job market for this. People need jobs!

KIRBY: There are titles of professional patient advocates in the U.S. It isn't an actual job title, it's just people who take it on.

They're volunteering?

KIRBY: No, because they can charge whatever the fuck they want for whatever service. Essentially their job is whatever you can afford to pay them. Sometimes it's going to the doctor with you, but they don't always know what the right questions are. Most of them haven't been trained in medicine.

At best, they've helped somebody else and learned through that.

That seems like it could become a scam pretty easily.

KIRBY: Yeah.

HTML FLOWERS: Super easily.

KIRBY: I know one good patient advocate, but I can't afford them. A friend of mine could and they were very helpful. Arguing with your insurance company constantly over the phone adds up to hours a week just to make sure you can go get your endoscopy. That's also going to cost $500. The hours you spend doing that shit are hours you can't spend taking care of yourself or doing anything else.

HTML FLOWERS: Or having love in your life.

KIRBY: Oh, yeah! Or doing things that actually add to your quality of life that you're *still* living. Anything else. But if you are one of these people, it costs as much as your monthly premium, or often more, especially if you have a chronic illness that has no set time limit that it's over. Who the fuck is going to use a patient advocate if you have to pay for it? You could, theoretically, just do all that work yourself and waste hours of your week, but you're not paying someone $500 to come sit next to you at the doctor's. It's definitely a role that should be filled and paid for by not me.

HEALTH CARE PROFESSIONALS

Speaking of health care professionals, both of you have featured in your comics nurses and doctors that haven't been great at their jobs. In Rebecca's *Biopsy* comic —

KIRBY: That nurse can ... Mmmm. Mmmm.

[*Laughs.*] Do you know if any of those types of people have seen your comics?

KIRBY: My phlebotomist has seen my comics.

HTML FLOWERS: Phlebotomist is such a good name.

KIRBY: They think it's funny because they have to deal with everyone else's bullshit, too. I would say that nurses are the unsung heroes of the medical system.

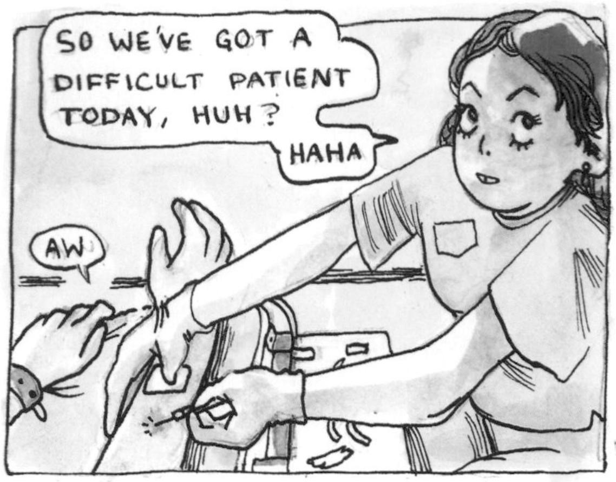
SO WE'VE GOT A DIFFICULT PATIENT TODAY, HUH?
HAHA
AW

From Rebecca Kirby's *Biopsy*, 2018.

HTML FLOWERS: Could be.

KIRBY: I think that a lot of doctors are cops and they're bad. Health professionals are trying to do what they thought was a very important service within a structure that doesn't allow them to actually do that. I had a doctor apologize to me. She was afraid she was going to get in trouble for acknowledging the fact that a lot of doctors outside a specialist's office wouldn't treat me well because I am female. She was afraid to acknowledge this fact to a patient. She could get in trouble. Whatever personal will they had to care for people as individuals is going to be crushed immediately by the system they have to operate within. I am sympathetic to that for medical professionals, except for doctors, because they get paid too much for me to feel sorry for them.

Has anyone read your comics in the hospital, Grant?

HTML FLOWERS: I have to hide them because of the drug content. And the fact that I openly answer questions in the letters section. One of my doctors recently — I don't know what the fuck was up with him, I think he was just having a good morning or something. Bebopping and scatting down the halls. I've never seen him in a good mood before that. He

OPPOSITE: From *No Visitors* #3 by HTML Flowers, 2018.

was whistling and said, "You got any stuff online?" [*Makes whistling noise.*] I was like, "Uhhh, yeah." He was like, "Maybe I could check it out. I'd love to get to know you a little bit better."

KIRBY: Nope!

HTML FLOWERS: I was like, "Ugh." And he was like, "What if I just Google your name?" "Nooo, don't do that." I have been talking about my drug use and the limitations of my drug use by the lung transplant for years in interviews now. [*Laughs.*] I gave some comics to a social worker in 2017 because I trusted her. She'd been my social worker for years and I know for a fact that she would never show anyone. I don't know if comics are covered under the client/patient privilege thing.

[*Laughs.*] I don't know.

HTML FLOWERS: But I trust her. She's an amazing social worker that did a lot of good for me. I told her a lot of things in confidence. I did pass on some work to her. And also, a physio that I knew wouldn't narc on me. She was like, "Don't worry, I'm not going to show anyone." [*Laughter.*]

Did you get any feedback?

HTML FLOWERS: They were both going away or ending their time with me, so no. The comics were like a thanks for everything they'd done, you know? I never got any feedback. Sometimes nurses look at my work while I'm making it in the hospital room. They're like, "*Interesting.*"

KIRBY: Love that. My doctors would be pissed, I think.

HTML FLOWERS: "I've never done a drug." I can't let my doctors look at my work.

KIRBY: For you, there's an actual solid punishment that would come of that. For me, it's a lot more

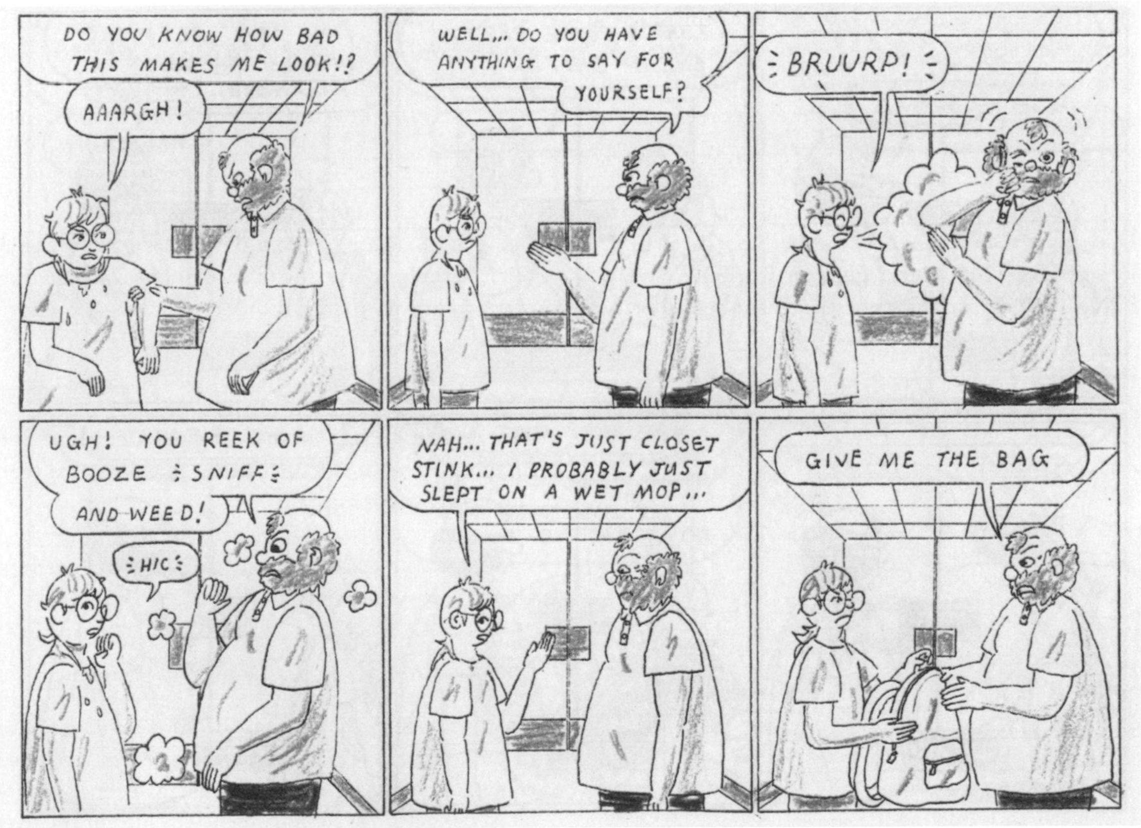
DO YOU KNOW HOW BAD THIS MAKES ME LOOK!?
AAARGH!
WELL... DO YOU HAVE ANYTHING TO SAY FOR YOURSELF?
BRUURP!
UGH! YOU REEK OF BOOZE SNIFF AND WEED!
HIC
NAH... THAT'S JUST CLOSET STINK... I PROBABLY JUST SLEPT ON A WET MOP...
GIVE ME THE BAG

abstract. I don't get taken seriously anyway. I draw my doctors as what they look like. If they're going to be a piece of shit, then I'm going to be a piece of shit. They don't like to be called out, even in the appointment. If they're behaving in a way that's fucked and I say, "Hey, you're wrong," they just end the appointment and I spend $250 to go home with nothing. That's the biggest punishment I'll face. "No medicine for you."

HTML FLOWERS: "You're being mean to me and I'm a doctor! You can't be mean to me."

KIRBY: I saw a new dermatologist for the discoids that I get. I get big, distinct discs. I went to a new dermatologist and was like, "Hello, here's my entire file that I bought. Here's photos of all my symptoms. Here's a timeline. I would like you to run these blood tests." I'm sure they don't like to be told by some stinky asshole what to do, but also, if they did their jobs in the first ... Whatever. We went through all my symptoms and I brought a list. She left the room for a minute, then came back and was looking at my skin. She was asking me questions about my other symptoms and I answered one of them, I think it was about the body pain. I mentioned the hernia, the enterocele, and she was like, "Oh, well, that one's real." Without even taking a breath. "That's a real one."

I was like, "You're fucking joking, right? You know I have paid so much money to sit here and listen to you be a piece of shit to me, right now, while I'm covered in bleeding discs." Our appointment ended after that and she wrote me a prescription for fungus cream, which I did not need. Then I went home after paying a lot of money, but then they claimed that I needed to pay more, so now I owe more to the hospital. Good. They can fucking look at my comics. I'll see someone else, I have an HMO.

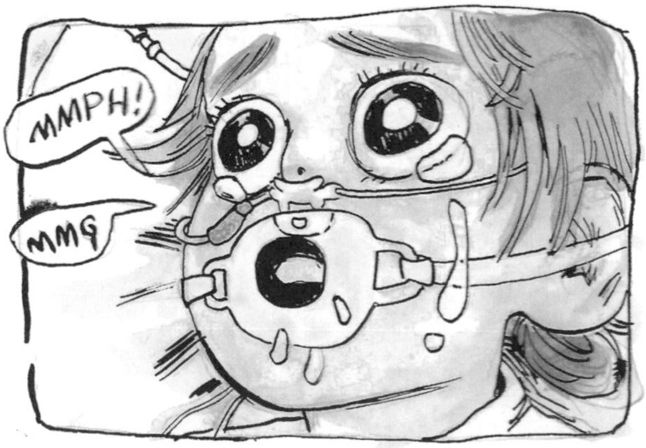
MMPH!
MMG

Kirby is about to undergo medical testing in *Biopsy*, 2018.

What's your relationship with the pharmaceutical industry?

HTML FLOWERS: Uhhhhhhh, I hate it. [*Kirby laughs.*] I spend a lot of my time trying to highlight why it's a nightmare. I mean, I'm taking this medication right now that almost no one else has access to in the U.K. and in America and it's a life-saving drug for people with CF. It's a gene medication, so it alters my genetic makeup as I take it. That company, Vertex, they won't make a proper deal with the government in either America or the U.K. to have it even a little subsidized. They just want more money for it. Kill 'em all. World is a fuck. Every pharmaceutical corporation is run by cops.

KIRBY: Yup.

HTML FLOWERS: What are you going to do? I hate those cunts.

KIRBY: It's the most disgusting job you can work. I hate it. I hate anybody who works a job that's complicit in robbing sick and dying people of any chance of managing their condition.

POLITICS

Are you following the health care debate as it's heating up with the upcoming presidential election and everything?

HTML FLOWERS: Absolutely. I read some garbage about it every fucking day.

KIRBY: Yup.

HTML FLOWERS: There's a lot of shit being done here in Australia as well. We have a government that has reinvigorated its popularity with its latest budget. Its latest budget saves something like $7 billion and part

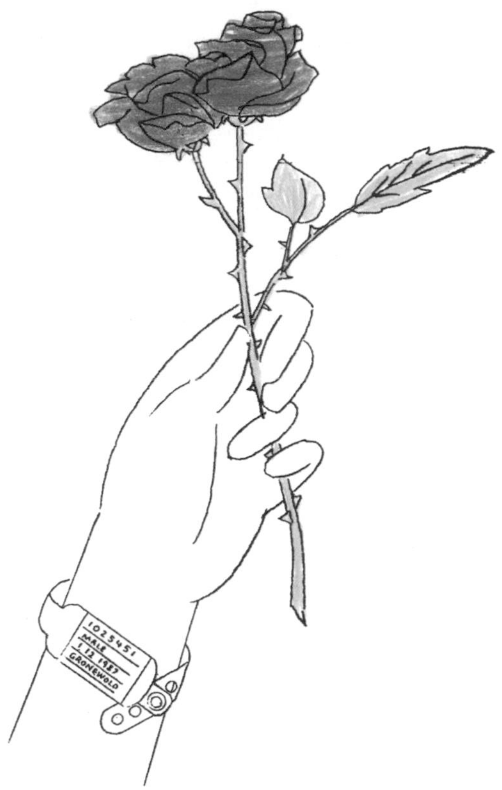

From the cover to HTML Flowers' *Incision*, 2017.

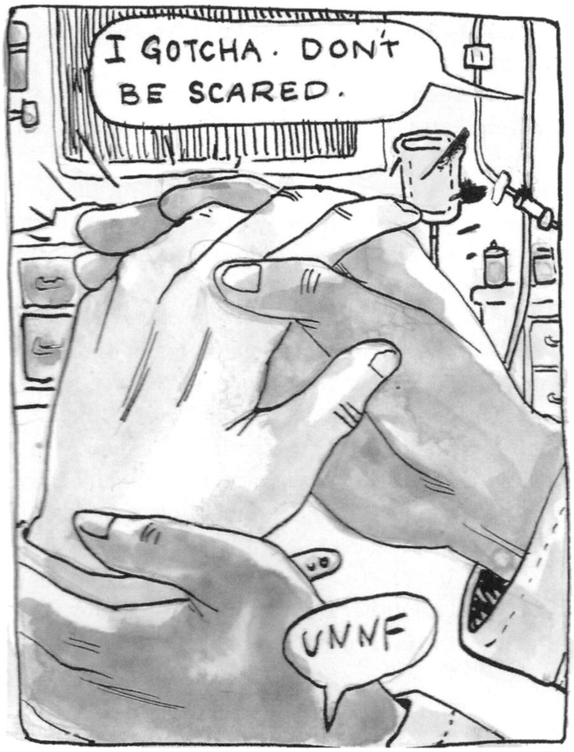
I GOTCHA. DON'T BE SCARED.
UNNF

From Kirby's *Biopsy*, 2018.

of that is from cutbacks on a program called NDIS. That's the National Disability Insurance Scheme.

KIRBY: Oh, my God.

HTML FLOWERS: That was an initiative that was started about seven years ago and has never been funded the way it was promised to be funded in the first place. It's an initiative that buys people wheelchairs who can't afford them, it helps anyone who has severe limitations doing day-to-day things. They pay for nurses to help their families deal with their illnesses. They cut the funding on that by $7 billion. In a show of lip-service to seem like they still give a shit, they decided to open a royal commission into the abuse of helpless, disabled people. And that commission is going to cost $600,000. Maybe they'll just employ their friends who work in various government branches to ask the most docile patients if they've ever been abused, you know? That's what they do. They cut back where it's really needed then do some garbage shit that will make the front page. Scott Morrison, who's our Prime Minister, "He really cares about the disabled." Of course, I'm still obsessed with American health care because it ruined my life. I'm always wondering how close those crazy ol' Yanks are getting to having subsidized health care. [*Laughs.*]

That affects your politics too, Rebecca, I'm assuming.

KIRBY: Without a shadow of a doubt. I obviously try to inform myself in part out of obligation, but knowing full well that in the near future there's absolutely nothing that's going to be done that will actively impact my quality of care. It's just not a possibility now, apparently. Everybody knows they need to talk about it and it needs to be discussed, but I don't see universal health care becoming a thing. I don't think anyone's going to swoop in and control insurance providers to make them less of a nightmare. I know that

I should be involving myself and educating myself as much as humanly possible, but I can only take so much of being faced with the reality of having to continue operating this way. There's only so much I can actually absorb and force myself to care about. No one else does, either. It's not going to get me the care I need, or the care that my family needs or anybody else that needs help. There's only so much investment I can muster. Presently, anyway.

I have been trying my best with this boring-ass shit [*holds up book*] to read about the history of American health care and how we got here. How it is presently selective on who it treats and everything. It's really frightening how little has … I don't know. We're just so far from where we need to be to make anything even a little bit more humane for people who are sickly and disabled.

Are you at all hopeful for 2020? With the election and a potential regime change.

HTML FLOWERS: [*In old man voice*:] Hopeful? Hopeful? I haven't heard that name in a long time. [*Laughter.*] Who's this whippersnapper asking us about hope, Kirby? Who is this young man with his big dreams?

KIRBY: In a sense that there is a potential that something might be different than it has been for the past couple of years, but not in any big way. Yes, I'm a little hopeful, but no … [*Laughs.*] Nope.

#SELFCARE

I want to shift gears back towards your art. Thinking about online culture and a lot of little webcomics that go viral, they deal a lot in #selfcare.

KIRBY: Ahhhhh. Grant, your favorite!

HTML FLOWERS: You dirty old bitch! I see what you're doing!

For some reason, I figured both of you might have opinions on this.

HTML FLOWERS: I'm about to get us canceled, Kirby. [*Laughter.*]

KIRBY: You're really digging in, RJ.

Do you have opinions on that trend in art and that general way of thinking?

HTML FLOWERS: I'll say my piece real quick. It's just bullshit. [*Casey laughs.*] It's very much a great way to sell things to people now.

KIRBY: Yes!

HTML FLOWERS: I read an article about how real self-care isn't actually easy. Real self-care is about doing work that supports the people around you and yourself. It makes you feel fulfilled. That's always been my conception of self-care. I just hate the word now because of the way it's become this fucking buzzword. For most people, it means putting on Netflix and buying a bath bomb.

Real self-care is donating whatever small amount of money you have to a friend who's too sick to get any dinner tonight. That's self-care. It takes something away from you, but also satisfies you, you know? For me, self-care is hard work. It's knowing that I was able to get my mom a fair amount of money towards a house last year. That was 10 years of selling drugs and art and working side-jobs and saving that money. The fulfillment I have from that, that's a lot of fucking self-care right there. That's some grueling-ass self-care. The way it's applied and the way it's sort of constantly bandied about at disabled people like it's going to benefit us at all, as if it's not just the latest bullshit to come out of the "wellness warrior" society. I'm sick of it. I hate it. It's facile garbage that just serves to de-tooth what should be rabid, angry disableds. We *need* rabid, angry disabled people. We don't need people who are like, "I couldn't get the medicine I need this week, but I was actually able to afford some lavender to drop into my bath, so …" [*Casey laughs.*] "Check out this self-care."

KIRBY: It's a fucking disgusting concept. I remember Grant talking about some company being, "How do we be more inclusive to our disabled audience?" that they're trying to market to. I think that was the

---

OPPOSITE: A meeting from HTML Flowers's *No Visitors* #4, 2018.

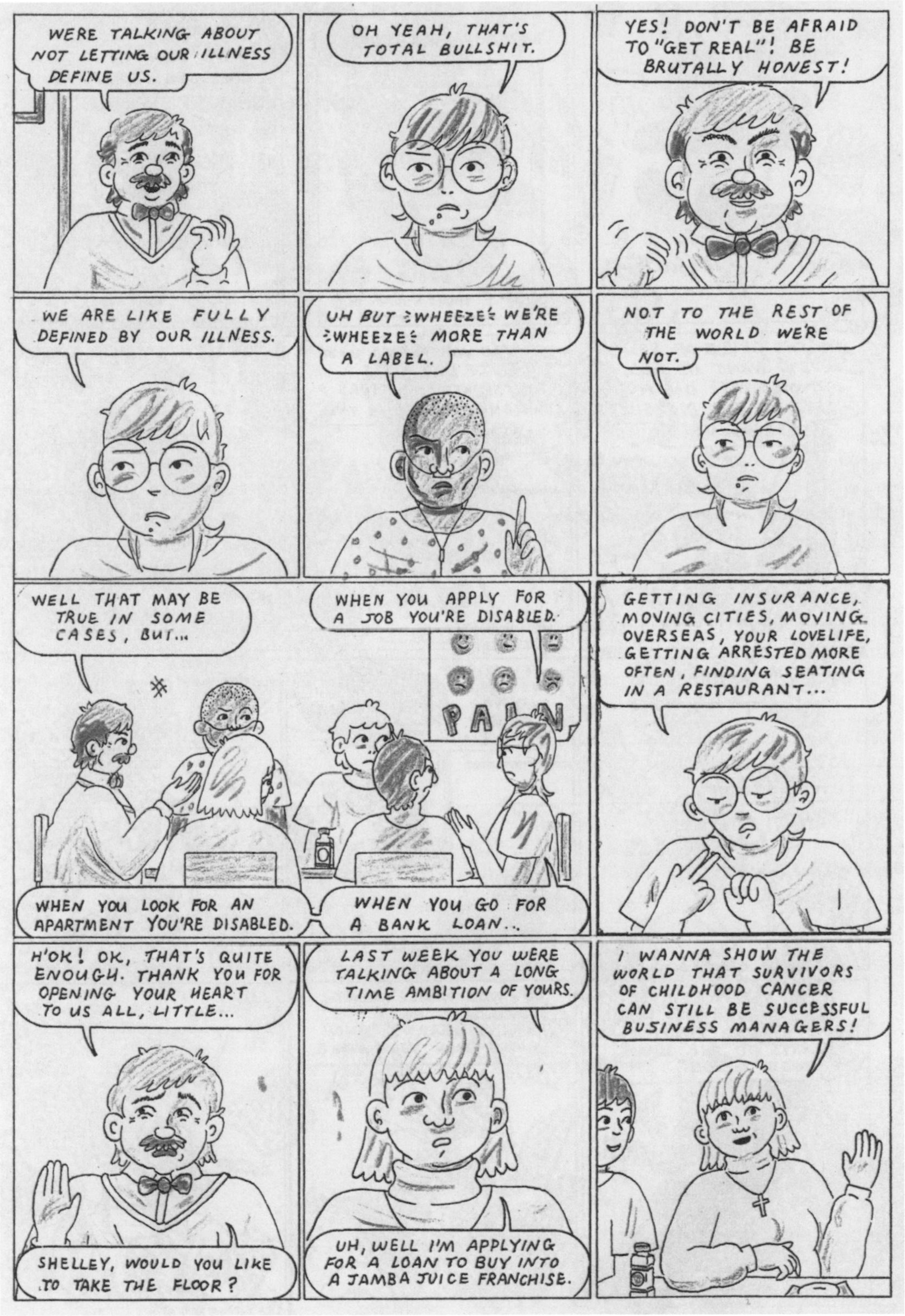
WERE TALKING ABOUT NOT LETTING OUR ILLNESS DEFINE US.
OH YEAH, THAT'S TOTAL BULLSHIT.
YES! DON'T BE AFRAID TO "GET REAL"! BE BRUTALLY HONEST!
WE ARE LIKE FULLY DEFINED BY OUR ILLNESS.
UH BUT *WHEEZE* WE'RE *WHEEZE* MORE THAN A LABEL.
NOT TO THE REST OF THE WORLD WE'RE NOT.
WELL THAT MAY BE TRUE IN SOME CASES, BUT...
WHEN YOU APPLY FOR A JOB YOU'RE DISABLED.
PAIN
WHEN YOU LOOK FOR AN APARTMENT YOU'RE DISABLED.
WHEN YOU GO FOR A BANK LOAN...
GETTING INSURANCE, MOVING CITIES, MOVING OVERSEAS, YOUR LOVELIFE, GETTING ARRESTED MORE OFTEN, FINDING SEATING IN A RESTAURANT...
H'OK! OK, THAT'S QUITE ENOUGH. THANK YOU FOR OPENING YOUR HEART TO US ALL, LITTLE...
SHELLEY, WOULD YOU LIKE TO TAKE THE FLOOR?
LAST WEEK YOU WERE TALKING ABOUT A LONG TIME AMBITION OF YOURS.
UH, WELL I'M APPLYING FOR A LOAN TO BUY INTO A JAMBA JUICE FRANCHISE.
I WANNA SHOW THE WORLD THAT SURVIVORS OF CHILDHOOD CANCER CAN STILL BE SUCCESSFUL BUSINESS MANAGERS!

> *“I’m 30 years deep into being ill and nobody has listened to me this entire time.”*

first thing I ever heard you dig into and rant about. [*Laughter.*]

HTML FLOWERS: I get mad about it.

For both of you, your comics output is nearly the definition of actual self-care. You’re taking care of yourself, put simply. But if anyone explored social media #selfcare, your comics might be the last thing people want to see.

KIRBY: Yeah! It’s not easy. Nobody wants to consume media that’s a realistic depiction of what it means to be a disabled person or what it means to be chronically ill. It’s a little too difficult to swallow for most people. In the same way, the practice of examining of who you are as a person and what steps would be beneficial to take not only to make you a better person, but to make your life more manageable. Those are too difficult. So, buy a fucking face mask with slime on it and tell yourself you’re doing good tonight. That’s the least challenging avenue. But it’s easy to sell. It’s taking what could be a spiritual and beneficial concept and boiling it down to sell something like a candle with fucking oatmeal on it. These are the things that people can sell...

HTML FLOWERS: [*Laughs.*] Oatmeal candles!

KIRBY: I saw it yesterday! I went to fucking Whole Foods—

HTML FLOWERS: I’m not laughing at you, I’m laughing at oatmeal candles.

KIRBY: So, I went to Whole Foods. I needed broccoli, right? I know I’m a horrible person for going to fucking Whole Foods, but whatever. [*Casey laughs.*]

HTML FLOWERS: That’s an American thing, I don’t get it.

KIRBY: It’s owned by Amazon. There you go. I went and I was like, “I’m going to buy myself a candle because my house stinks like shit. It’s going to be great.” It had fucking oatmeal on top and costs $19.99 for that hunk of shit.

In any case, it’s a very common practice in the beautiful capitalist society that we live in to take a definition or a concept from the community of people that desperately need it and then make it the absolute easiest to spread and use it to sell shit. Who uses self-care to sell stuff? Cosmetic companies, companies that produce soap—

Well, some artists. People making prints on Etsy.

HTML Flowers panels from *No Visitors* #4, 2018.

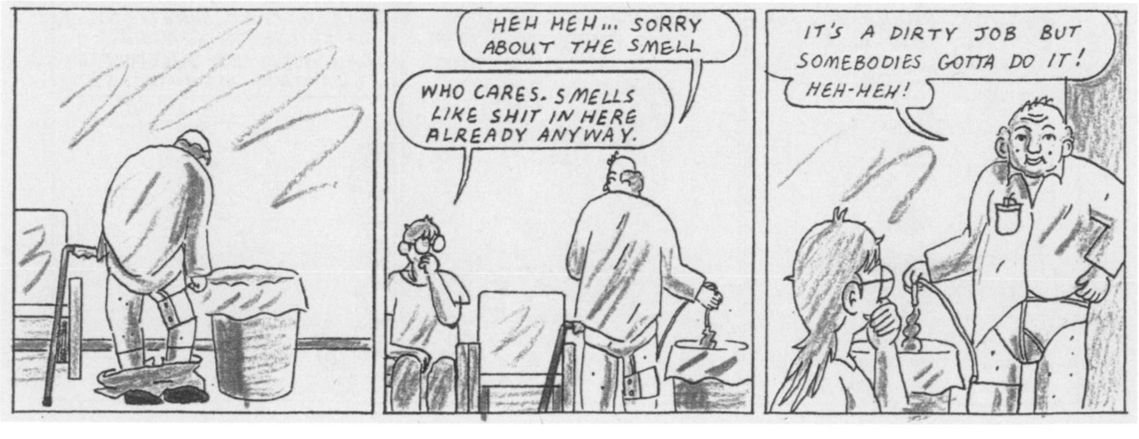
HEH HEH... SORRY ABOUT THE SMELL
WHO CARES. SMELLS LIKE SHIT IN HERE ALREADY ANYWAY.
IT'S A DIRTY JOB BUT SOMEBODIES GOTTA DO IT! HEH-HEH!

A *Sonogram* illustration, HTML Flowers, 2017.

KIRBY: "It's self-care. It's just so good." It's remark-able. Maybe our concept that was intended to sell to people that needed to heal something isn't available and non-inclusive to people who are sick and need actual care. But also, I'm sure they're like, "How do we sell it to them next?" That's their self-righteous mission that falls so short of what it's claiming to do. That's everyone selling shit at a massive profit at the expense of somebody else. It's so fucking insulting, and it's the exact same thing as people making movies that star some character with a health issue —

HTML FLOWERS: Cole Sprouse.

"I WANT TO BE A BURDEN"

What's that movie called that's out?

HTML FLOWERS: *Five Feet Apart.* The inspirational story of two people with cystic fibrosis who want to fuck.

Have you seen it?

HTML FLOWERS: No, I haven't. But I did write a diss track about Cole Sprouse though. [*Laughter.*] It's really dumb, but I've been filming a video for it. I mostly just get drunk and naked. My girlfriend is filming it. [*Casey laughs.*] We filmed a scene where I was naked on the toilet and you know when you're on the toilet, I just accidentally did a bit of a shit while we were filming. [*Laughter.*] I couldn't help myself. I was sitting naked on the toilet. I was like six double-strength ciders in, so I was deep. "It feels good to sit down. Uppp…"

KIRBY: [*Laughs.*] It was inevitable, man.

HTML FLOWERS: Kate was like, "Did you shit?" And I was like, "Yeah, just give me a second." [*Laughter.*] She's got all that on camera.

KIRBY: Beautiful.

This is definitely the most times anybody's talked about shit in a *Comics Journal* interview, probably. [*Laughter.*]

KIRBY: We love to talk about shit.

HTML FLOWERS: Shit Gang, baby. But, with *Five Feet Apart*, I honestly only watched an interview with Cole Sprouse and Haley Richardson, and don't tell anyone I said this, but it seems like they went about it the right way. [*Laughs.*] I'm still mad. I don't care. I don't want any more inspirational dumb-ass John Green-type *Fault in Our Balls* movies about somebody with cancer who "just wants to love."

KIRBY: "They're just like us." Those movies can actu-ally eat my ass. I'm so sick of it. First of all, no. Every single narrative made about sickly people is always just like, "What do we think they're like without

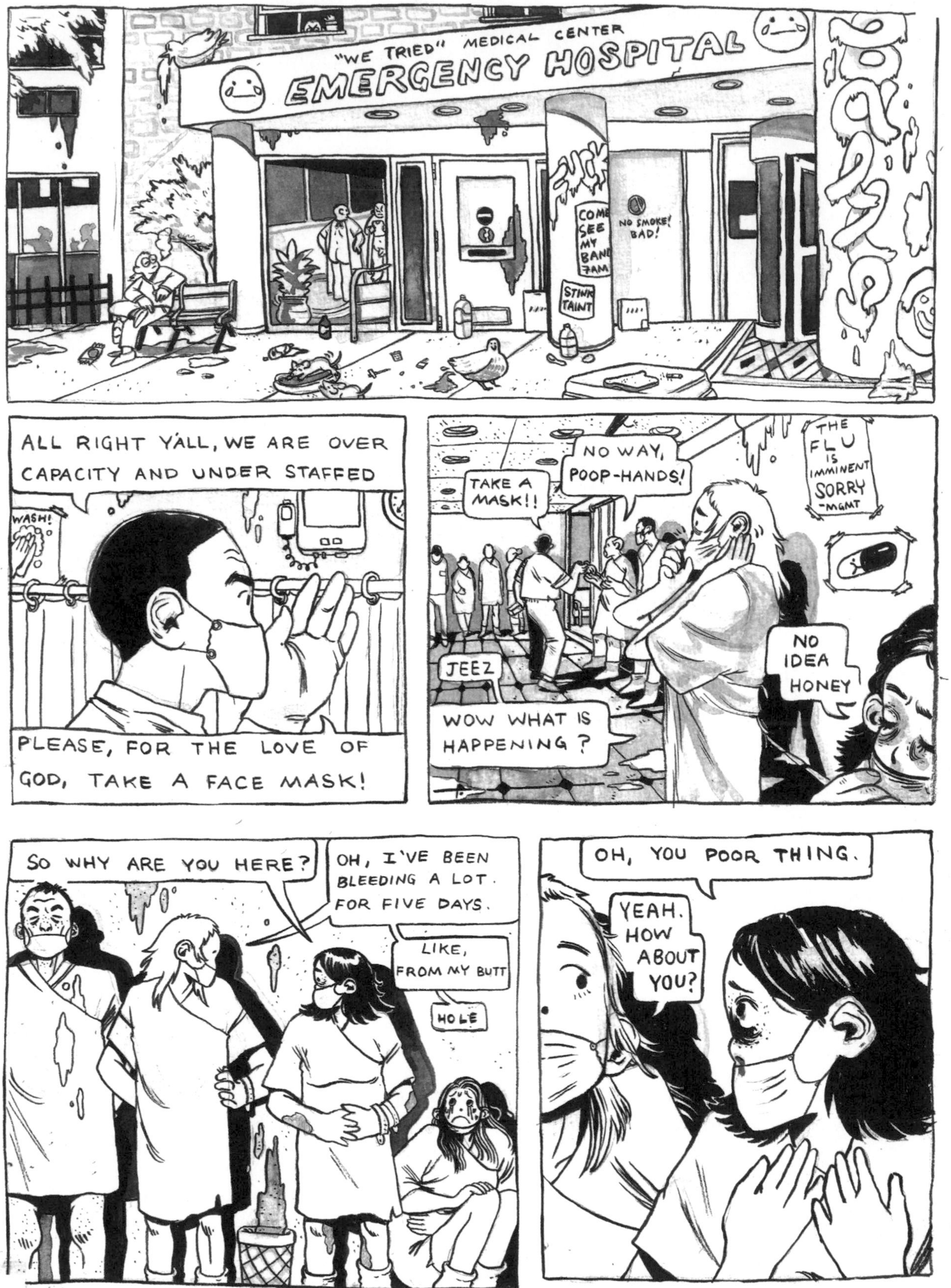
"WE TRIED" MEDICAL CENTER
EMERGENCY HOSPITAL
COME SEE MY BAND 7AM
NO SMOKE! BAD!
STINK TAINT
ALL RIGHT Y'ALL, WE ARE OVER CAPACITY AND UNDER STAFFED
WASH!
PLEASE, FOR THE LOVE OF GOD, TAKE A FACE MASK!
THE FLU IS IMMINENT SORRY -MGMT
TAKE A MASK!!
NO WAY, POOP-HANDS!
JEEZ
WOW WHAT IS HAPPENING?
NO IDEA HONEY
SO WHY ARE YOU HERE?
OH, I'VE BEEN BLEEDING A LOT. FOR FIVE DAYS.
LIKE, FROM MY BUTT
HOLE
OH, YOU POOR THING.
YEAH. HOW ABOUT YOU?

having to talk to them? What do you think they may love doing? Do they love fucking? Let's make a movie about it!"

HTML FLOWERS: "They're trying to be just like us, so they probably want to fuck. Write that down! Somebody write down the fucking aspect." [*Casey laughs.*]

KIRBY: It's so wild. It's always avoiding the point that there's a complete resigning of normalcy and a redefinition of normalcy. Nobody wants that. Or they do, because we both make comics and sell them on the internet. But we didn't know anyone would want them. It's like able-bodied people making movies that really want to sell a trope to sickly consumers. "Heeey, you're not a burden." But yes, I fucking am! I am absolutely a burden. Anyone trying to comfort an audience by saying like, "They're just the same as everybody else," is also insulting. It's fucking dumb as shit.

HTML FLOWERS: It's like the same "You're not like other girls" line.

KIRBY: Yeah! Yeah!

HTML FLOWERS: Those guys who are like, "You're not like other girls." Well, what's wrong with other girls? [*Laughs.*] "You're not a burden, you can be anything you want to be." Well, I am absolutely a burden.

KIRBY: I want to be a burden.

HTML FLOWERS: I very much can't do half the things I want to do or be. Part of the reason I'm a burden is because of how the world is run. Why don't they make movies about that? Maybe they're complicit. Don't think about how much you can actually do for us, they just have a story they can sell.

KIRBY: A well-meaning person I talk to, I was like, "Wow, I always thought I would have a baby and a family." She was like, "You can still do that!" No, I can't. I can't and that's very sad. I don't want to be told the only avenue to hope and fulfillment is to maintain

OPPOSITE: A page from *Sicky*, an upcoming collaboration between HTML Flowers and Rebecca Kirby.

> *"'Heeey, you're not a burden.' But yes, I fucking am! I am absolutely a burden."*

a standard of life that is as similar to a healthy and financially stable person's life as I can get. There are many other avenues to fulfillment. Or not. You can also be fucking miserable and unfortunate forever. People are like, "Death is the worst thing that can happen to you," but it's a perfect normal thing.

HTML FLOWERS: Death seems chill.

KIRBY: It's always the same.

What you just explained, for both of you, does this give you a bigger sense of urgency to create more art and get more art out in the world?

KIRBY: Yes.

HTML FLOWERS: A lot of the time it makes me feel a little defeatist. It's definitely good fodder, though. Me and my friend Elliott, who also has a couple of different illnesses, we have a completely unspoken mutual interest in any inspirational movie about disabilities. Elliott is constantly screencapping shit she's found. It's like the Jake Gyllenhaal Boston Marathon bombers movie. He loses his legs and it's about his inspirational journey to walk again. I'm like, "Yes, let's do it." It's garbage. Half the time it's really wrecked, but every now and then you get one where you get mad. "Goddammit, they actually kind of got some of the emotions right." [*Laughter.*] It's like I'm crying against my will. But I'm a sucker for Jake, so what're you going to do. [*Casey laughs.*] I just want to make a story about a useless, dumbshit disabled person. That's all I want. That's all I've ever wanted to see. That's who I am. I just want to see it one time before I die, that's it.

KIRBY: Yep.

HTML FLOWERS: I want to see a book filled with stories about the dumbest disabled person you've ever seen. [*Laughter.*] Making no effort to improve his life. That's all I want. It's a small thing to dream of.

COLLABORATION

I heard you may be working together on something right now?

HTML FLOWERS: We're doing a little mini together.

KIRBY: Yeah.

HTML FLOWERS: We've got to steal each other's fans. [*Laughs.*]

KIRBY: We've got to exchange which babies love me and which babies love you. It's going to be great.

HTML FLOWERS: Yeah. It's a pretty fair exchange. My 15k to Kirby's 45k. [*Laughs.*]

KIRBY: If only followers were currency, baby. [*Laughter.*] We'll make a fun mini. Then I want to do a big one and I don't know what's going to happen with the big one. I don't have anything else to possibly talk about for a while.

HTML FLOWERS: Yeah. All my minis, I'm saving them up and coloring them. That's what I'm doing. I thought it was going to be this year, but I keep getting so fucking sick. I just lost three weeks because Kate couldn't do anything alone and was one-handed. I was cutting up her food for her, helping her put on socks in the morning, stuff like that. I don't know. I just want to see that book before I die.

KIRBY: You're going to get it.

HTML FLOWERS: *No Visitors: The Useless Disabled* series. What a way to ruin a fucking book before you open it. [*Laughs.*]

"THE MOON ONLY SHINES FOR THE DYING AND SICKLY."

Let me bring up one last thing. Grant, you've written a few times in you comics, "The moon only shines for the dying and sickly." Can you explain that?

HTML FLOWERS: Yes. That's a flex on healthy people. I like the idea of taking the moon away from them. [*Laughter.*] I think that staying up late is a disabled freedom.

KIRBY: It is.

HTML FLOWERS: I think when healthy people do it, they're appropriating. Just a little bit. [*Casey laughs.*] The moon is not down with healthy people walking around at all hours of the night. What do they have to think about? "My favorite Panera up the street has closed down. I've got to go for a long walk at night." [*Laughter.*] I love the moon and I have a lot of formidable memories of the way the moon looked through hospital windows. They are always double-paned and the moon always looks particularly beautiful and strange out of them. I remember as a kid, I'd put my head on the window and roll my head back and forth. With the double pane, the moon always looks really interesting. Just growing up in hospitals and staying up late, the moon has become a big thing in my life and has been since I was so little. I've decided the moon is mine. And it's Kirby's.

KIRBY: Thank you for sharing the moon with me.

HTML FLOWERS: I'm taking it away from healthy people. The moon belongs to us now.

KIRBY: We get one thing. ✿

OPPOSITE: From HTML Flowers's *No Visitors* #4, 2018.

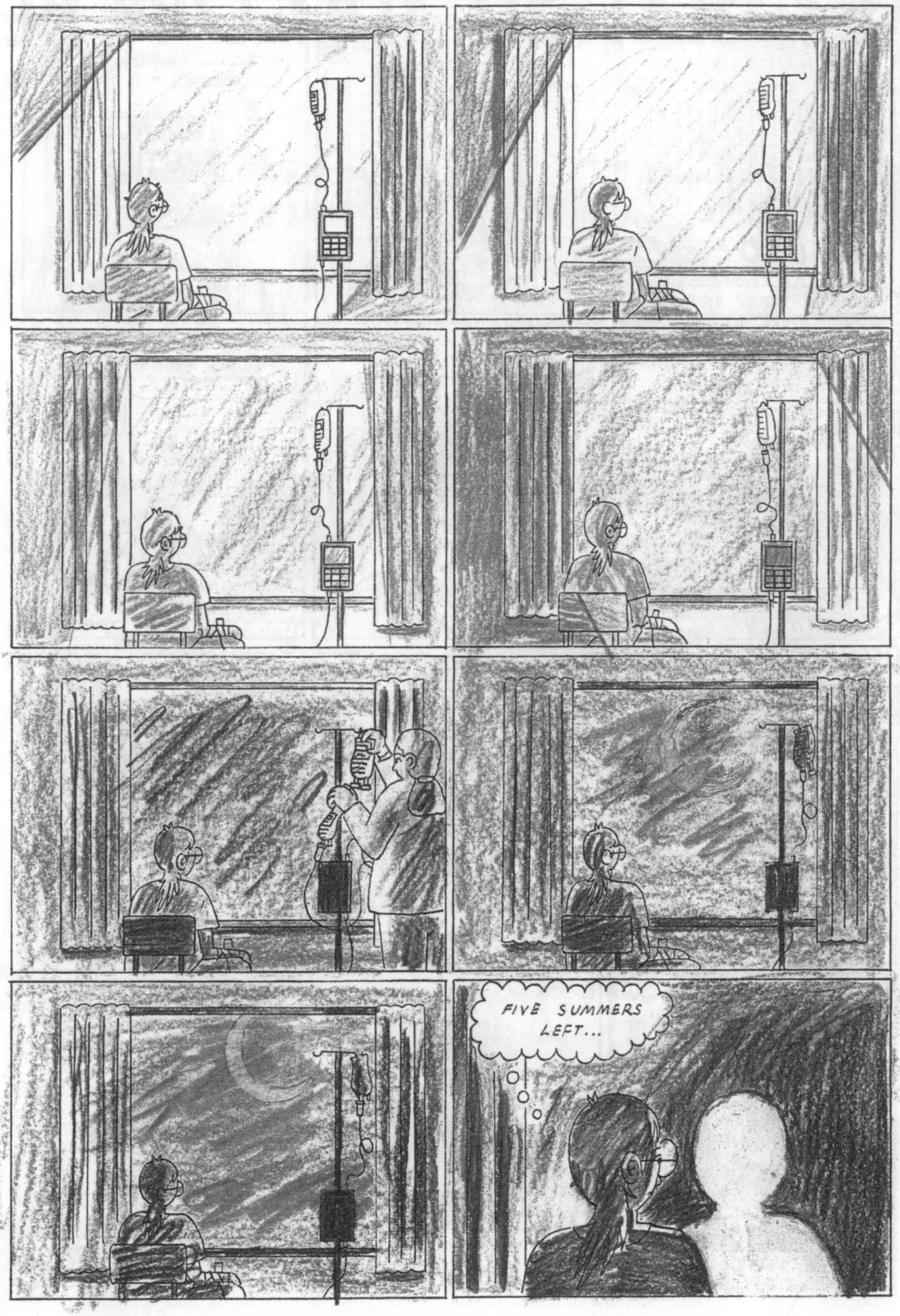
FIVE SUMMERS LEFT...

FEATURE

Vision Mapping Health Care for 2030

By Alece Birnbach

WHEN THE Association of Rheumatology Health Professionals (ARHP) asked me to create a vision map for their conference — in real time — about what health care might look like in 2030, I didn't know anything about rheumatology's place in the medical field or why its future might be in jeopardy. As a graphic facilitator, I do three things: listen, synthesize and draw. Learning about a topic I don't know anything about that I'm asked to create a vision for is almost as fun as drawing it. Often, I'm listening live to a keynote speaker or panel discussion, and rapidly translating a 60-90-minute session into a visual story. But for this vision map, the process was a little different. I wanted to include ideas from as many attendees as possible, and I had two days to do it.

Before I arrived at the conference in Chicago, I spent several hours prepping. I read through the ARHP website, followed links to learn more about rheumatology and searched YouTube for any videos on the subject. This research gave me an overview of the subject matter, enough information so that I could have a conversation with the actual experts — the conference attendees. I knew that making a personal connection with these health care professionals — and hearing the passion in their voices as they shared their challenges, concerns and hopes for the future — would give me the data I would need to craft their collaborative vision.

And that's important to note: I was tasked with creating their vision, not my own. Which meant I needed a way to invite them to share their ideas. My 4-by-16-foot foam board was strategically placed in a very high-traffic area, so attendees would walk past me on their way to and from sessions. I placed a second, smaller board next to mine, and wrote this question on it: "Where do you see health care in 2030?" I left markers next to the board with instructions for people to write or draw their thoughts and ideas on it. I then left the board and markers for a few hours while I attended a couple of morning sessions. There, I gathered important data points. Such as, "By 2030, demand for rheumatology doctors will exceed supply by 4,000 doctors worldwide, and it's worse in pediatrics." When I heard that statement, I knew I had my opening anchor image that would be the beginning of the visual story. By stating the biggest challenge first, I knew I could focus the rest of the story on ways to solve it.

I have a background in fine art. Like most artists, I use my pencil to block in the shapes and define each area, much like a quick gesture drawing. Once the big chunks are penciled in, I write the big anchor words. The drawing surface for this vision map is made up of two 4-foot-by-8½-foot-thick, white foam core boards taped together to create one 16-foot-long surface. I used my favorite Neuland markers, which are

Penny Fox Internship Fellowship. *Brittle Joints*, a collection of comics about her life with Bruck Syndrome (a rare congenital condition with symptoms that include bone fragility, thin blood vessels and muscle weakness) came out in 2018 with funding from a Massachusetts Independent Comics Expo Mini-Grant. On a sepia background, with greens and blues bathed in golden light, Sweeney uses traditional art mediums, such as watercolor and light hatching. Through charting her own path, literally and figuratively, Sweeney advocates for legal medical marijuana and accessibility.

In June 2019, Sweeney, Webber and I spoke over the phone (Webber said, at this point, she's able to talk on the phone, as long as there's a time limit) about graphic medicine, urban environments and their mutual dislike of "inspiration porn."

COMPLETENESS OF EXPERIENCE

KRISTY VALENTI: I was moderating a panel, and we had a medical librarian ask for suggestions. She said she wanted to find graphic works to help create empathy in doctors. Are you trying to create empathy, and, if so, what visual and storytelling techniques would you be using to do that?

MARIA SWEENEY: One focus of *Brittle Joints* is making that connection to facilitators of health, including doctors. One of the stories that I wrote includes my doctor, who I've been with for over a decade, and the goal is to make him see that he, too, is part of the disabled experience. His words or his actions for good — or maybe not so good — have an impact on that experience. And, while I'm not seeking the ultimate goal of getting empathy from everyone in it, I think that is very much a subliminal goal of writing autobio comics from a disability experience.

Georgia, I know you had discussions about doctors as well in your comic. I imagine that's part of the focus for you, enlightening people of that relationship?

GEORGIA WEBBER: My approach to the whole work of communicating my experience is to fill it out from the one-dimensional narratives that have existed in our more broad pop culture world about disability, and about health in general. There's so many details of life that you don't consider to be a part of health until you have a compromise, and then suddenly everything is a challenge. I'm similarly not thinking when I'm creating anything, "I wanna create empathy in anyone for this particular experience." I want to convey the completeness of this experience. I think the search, for me, is just for understanding and expression and communication, so surely empathy is a part of that.

SWEENEY: I agree.

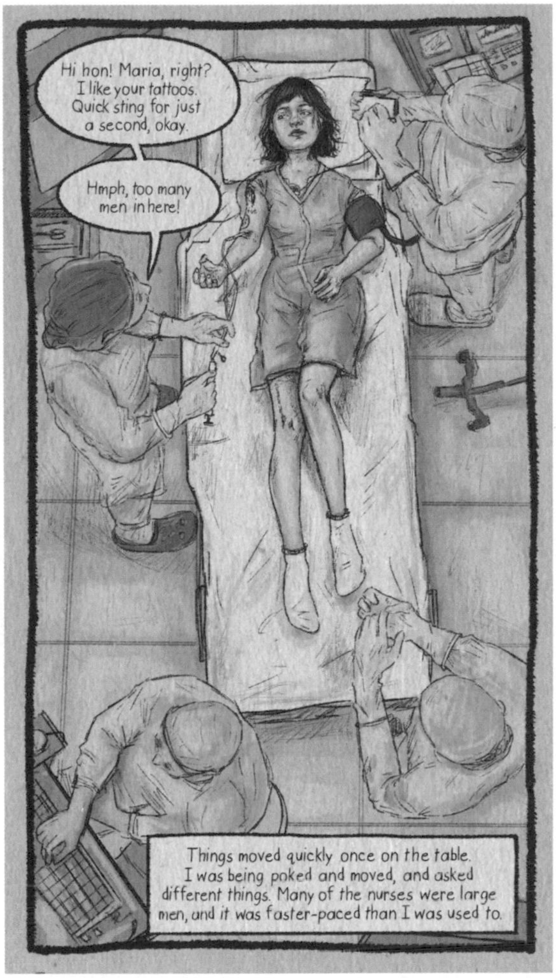

Hi hon! Maria, right? I like your tattoos. Quick sting for just a second, okay.
Hmph, too many men in here!
Things moved quickly once on the table. I was being poked and moved, and asked different things. Many of the nurses were large men, and it was faster-paced than I was used to.

From "Nerves" in Maria Sweeney's 2018 comic, *Brittle Joints*.

OPPOSITE: From the prologue to Georgia Webber's 2018 graphic memoir, *Dumb: Living Without a Voice*.

From Sweeney's "Nerves," *Brittle Joints*, 2018.

In "Nerves," Maria, you take the reader through the very common doctor's office experience, where you get your blood pressure, and all that.

I thought that was a really good tool — we've all been there — and then you individualize your experience after that.

SWEENEY: I think a big part is that disabled experiences seem, if not off-limits, certainly a level of taboo. It was definitely the case for me growing up. Words like "accessibility," "inclusivity" — even the word "disabled" — was not something that was considered OK as a child. It was in our early adulthood that I've seen very much the inclusiveness, as we've had marginalized groups speak out. And that includes the disabled groups.

I think that doctors are seeing that they're part of that, and I wanted to capture that as well. People do go to doctor appointments and they do have to take care of their health, and I think that's hard for people who maybe aren't disabled young — they're faced with this: "Oh my gosh, I have to facilitate these things

and the health care system is not inviting and is not inclusive." And that can be a struggle, no matter at what point you become disabled.

SERIALIZING

You both serialize in minicomics.

SWEENEY: Yeah.

Could you talk about how that shapes your narrative? How does feedback work with a minicomic and the next minicomic, and how does that work into the collection, etcetera?

WEBBER: I serialized [*Dumb*] for the purpose of staying sane through the process. Because I envisioned that I wanted to create something longer — to make sure that I could communicate all the elements of my experience that I thought were worth communicating. It just seemed like the best way to encourage myself to keep going would be to have smaller deadlines and more manageable story pieces, so that I could work with them without getting overwhelmed by the whole process.

And that ended up working into the narrative just because, for me, the form of the comic is so important to the content, because they're constantly feeding one another, and the reader's experience is the first of everything. So, when I decided to draw shorter stories, I also decided that I would treat the story as a collection of shorter pieces; and then I could make those pieces feel very complete on their own, and then when they came together, that was just gonna be the feeling of the book. It had things to say in small pieces, and then the through line was the continuity, time-wise, of one person's experience. But it's bitten into these smaller bites because it needs to be digestible. [*Laughs.*]

SWEENEY: I would say that my experience is paralleled with that as well, that having the stories broken down and having a deadline separating each is good for organization purposes for me. Another part of writing about a disabled experience is that not every day is filled with, quote-unquote, a "disabled experience." And sometimes you have days where you're just doing regular things, and it's a blessing that something is not obstructing your access. I think that collecting stories of the minute moments and the more aggressive times of being disabled is powerful, and mirrors days that people have. People have off days, and people have really great days, and Georgia, I certainly think you capture when days are going really well and accessible for you but, of course, days that are not. Not every day is going to be one after another and consecutive, and allowing the comics to be broken into different experiences allows for a more natural readership between people, and also mirrors the everyday life of someone who's not disabled.

WEBBER: Yeah, we share many things, like, it's not that you cease to be human once you're disabled, which is a thing I think it's really important to remember. That's why those fluctuations of experience are important, in any story. Also, so that the reader doesn't feel just blocked out and overwhelmed, like they need to be invited to connect to things that they're familiar with as well as connect to things that they're not. And I also have to say that the serialization gives me a chance to build in breaks, so if I was not feeling good, and not feeling capable of drawing, I could do that. I ended up just stopping drawing for about a year and a half, two years, because of another chronic pain issue that

> ❝ *You question your worthiness to live if no one thinks that it's worth helping you … to execute whatever task is on your list for the day. It's not just uncomfortable, it's fundamentally, existentially disturbing.* ❞

arose from actually trying to push myself too hard. So, I learned a lot from that process, too.

SWEENEY: Yeah, that comes from a hustler mentality and we are very much conditioned to work, work, work. It doesn't really account for: If we draw all day, can we cook a meal in the evening? Can we use our hands to rely on furniture to walk? And these things seem very small, but they indicate what kind of day you have, what food you ate, did you go outside or not. So, comics have to weave your way into all those other decisions that maybe aren't part of everyone's everyday choices.

Georgia, I have a question about how you structured your minicomics to culminate in the party. I was curious how you came to that, with the layered, overlapping panels.

WEBBER: The New Year's scene in the middle of the final book — it was closer to the end of the minicomic series. I briefly mentioned earlier that the reader's experience is at the forefront for me of what I'm trying to craft. There's a climax for me in the story — just in

OVERLEAF, LEFT: From Webber's "Paperwork," *Dumb*, 2018.

OVERLEAF, RIGHT: From Sweeney's "Cannabis," *Brittle Joints*, 2018.

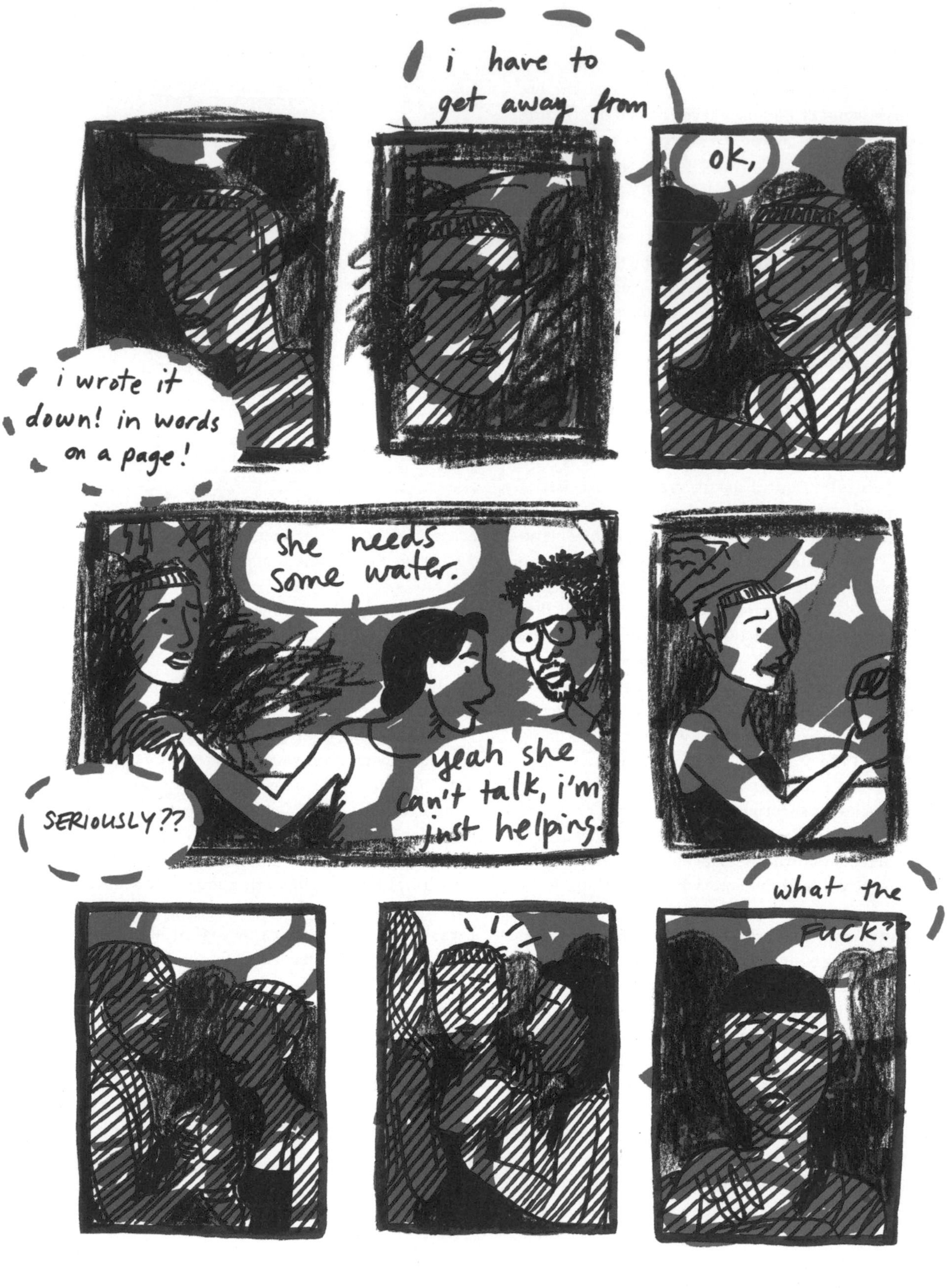
i have to get away from
ok,
i wrote it down! in words on a page!
she needs some water.
yeah she can't talk, i'm just helping.
SERIOUSLY??
what the FUCK??

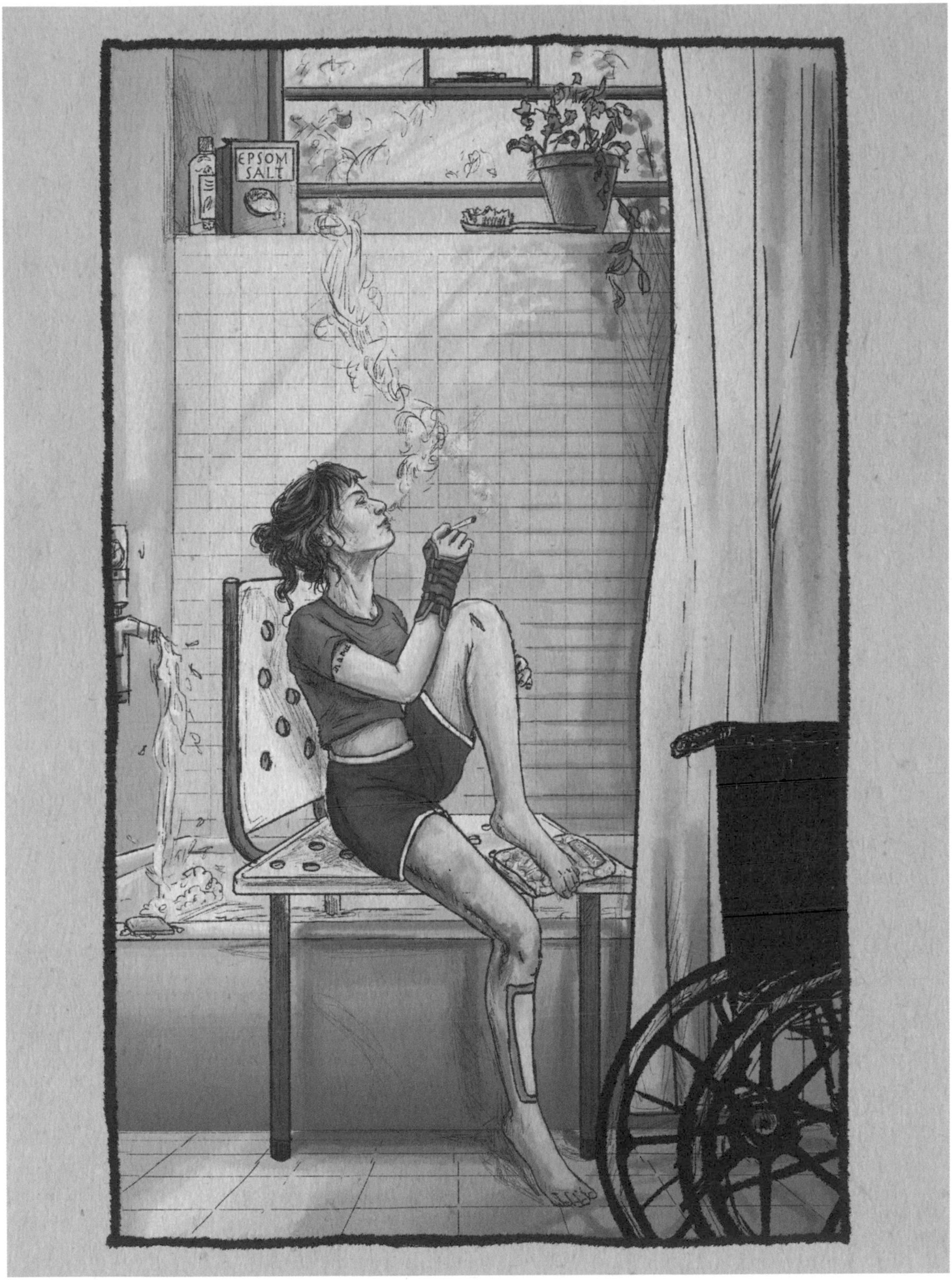
EPSOM SALT

> **❝** *This question of access, and this push away from thinking you need it, is foolish. … We're all gonna be equal, develop all kinds of issues in the future.* **❞**

the passage of time and the realization of how deeply I felt my identity was linked to my voice. Both the sound and the way that I choose to use it, and always have, and all of these memories that were overlapping my present experience of moments when someone complimented me, or my aspirations to sing when I was younger. It went from an immediate, acute situation that I was in that I thought would end soon (and so I was very open to it and willing to go through it) to something that felt like it was the new normal, the new permanent situation of my life. Then I was suddenly having to confront — and maybe let go of — all the things that I had felt were so strongly a part of my identity for so long.

It was a build, and it was really painful for me, and it happened around the same time as something that I didn't really communicate very well in the book, that party that I convey, where things are overlapping and falling apart. There's a moment that's acknowledging New Year's — that was actually something that I organized without my voice over several months to have a group of seven or eight of my cartoonist friends who live all over North America to join me in Montreal for a New Year's week of just hanging out. Because we liked each other and didn't see each other very often. I made a New Year's party that was a drink-and-draw blanket-fort party, just for them to have a good time, and I just did all of it without my voice at all. So, it was also a moment of really striving to accomplish something that I would've done anyway, and also experiencing my sense of identity falling apart around me. I needed to include that kind of duality, even though the details of that are not clear in the book — I thought that was just too

much information to give everybody, because there's a lot going on.

But, for me, that was a subversion of the "inspiration porn" narrative of the disabled person experiencing health adversity who just triumphs so far beyond what they're supposed to be capable of, what people expect of them, and then maybe even what someone who is able-bodied and healthy would do. I just hate those stories so much. I don't think they do anyone a service of understanding. It's just very thin and doesn't convey the fullness of that experience, and how complicated it can be. Life is not easing up on you because you have a harder time navigating some situations.

RESOURCES

Cartoonists are resourceful in that they're always figuring out everything they can do to get that comic into print. Maria, you received a grant. How does the resourcefulness you need as a cartoonist mirror the resourcefulness you need when dealing with systems surrounding illness? For example, you both have those paperwork sections.

SWEENEY: Resourcefulness is definitely in the artist realm, and it's definitely part of the disabled experience, no matter at what point. People are really resilient, and people do comment on my experience from a disability standpoint. "Oh, you come up with this to alleviate things," whether it's using tools to get a sock on, or bringing a cushion pillow to work, these really small things are thought of as very clever. And while I'm not removing credit from that, I do think a lot of people don't realize that they too would have to be forced to be really resourceful and look for things for themselves, from either furthering their art in a very competitive field, or allowing them some comfortability in the workplace. Having the knowledge of being resourceful from either a young age, with a disability experience, or through art and having the struggles of self-publishing and everything. That is why we stand with strength. That is why work gets completed. Even if it means you need to take a year off because of your health. Somehow that is more powerful to me because you have acknowledged, perhaps not a limitation, but a change in schedule to allow for greater things to come forward. That to me is the best part of being resourceful. It gives longevity to your goals.

WEBBER: I totally agree, Maria. The basic fact of resourcefulness becomes incredibly important for survival as well as continuing passion in things that matter. In a world that is not prepared to make everything accessible to all people with different needs, you don't have a choice. Just the simple stuff like you had in your comic with deciding to take your wheelchair or not take it, and what that is going to mean for you, and the sort of calculation that you have to do based on where you're trying to go and whether or not that accessibility is going to be available. Then knowing that when it is not available, what's that going to mean for your body and how you're feeling later in the day because you needed to go to this place, and that place was not ready to accommodate you. So now you're accommodating it, and it is just happening whether or not you identify as resourceful. It's happening whether or not it's about art, or about groceries.

One of my issues with the inspiration-porn style of disability narrative is that it really casts the disabled person as so different from other people because that resourcefulness is present in their life. It means that people who don't have a disability or don't identify that way are immediately thinking of themselves as people who wouldn't think that, wouldn't do that, wouldn't have that kind of creativity.

SWEENEY: And it's odd.

WEBBER: Absolutely. I firmly believe that every person has the capacity for that kind of creativity, and that they would do what they had to do in that situation. But also, the ideas that we espouse in our maybe more unconscious or subtle culture. I don't think anyone out there is explicitly saying that disability is a horror, but it's the communication that is taking place in culture all the time, anyway. When people who are completely able-bodied, or believe themselves to be because that line has been drawn with such a harsh division, see that resourcefulness, it is immediately saying that people who aren't disabled aren't resourceful. You're just living in a world where everything is made for you so you never have to think about it. Which actually means that you think you can't do challenging things because you're not

being challenged in the same way. It's weird because we could all connect over that if we want to.

People who choose to have artistic careers, not just cartoonists but all kinds of art, are facing those systemic challenges as well, just to make money to survive and contribute what we fully have to contribute to the world. So, there's a good crossover of disabled artists who have resourcefulness totally in spades because they have to. Anytime you perceive something uncomfortable for you in your life, you're going to be resourceful about it. It's just a weird box that we put ourselves in, this idea of being able-bodied and therefore not resourceful because everything is easy for you or disabled and having to be resourceful because everything is hard for you. Nothing is that cut-and-dry.

SWEENEY: No, not at all.

BENEFITS AND FINANCIAL TRANSPARENCY

SWEENEY: It reminded me I have two parallels. The paperwork, and seeking out benefits that, I'd like to point out, we are actually entitled to when we become disabled. But it doesn't feel like you are entitled to them.

WEBBER: That imposter syndrome. It's so hard. [*Laughter.*]

SWEENEY: You are in Montreal and, I'm sorry, but I was disappointed to see that your paperwork, bureaucracy struggles, very much parallel the American experience. There's all this jargon and talk and misuse of "free health care" in Canada, which we know, in a general standpoint, sure, but that's not all that's entailed. It's far more complicated than that. We got to see a glimpse of that. I think that resonated with a lot of folks who are always struggling to get on disability, or recently — no matter at what point they needed it. It's a really big narrative here in the United States that a lot of people just get disabled benefits, and that it's very easy to get and straightforward. It's a hundred

OVERLEAF: From Webber's "Paperwork," *Dumb*, 2018.

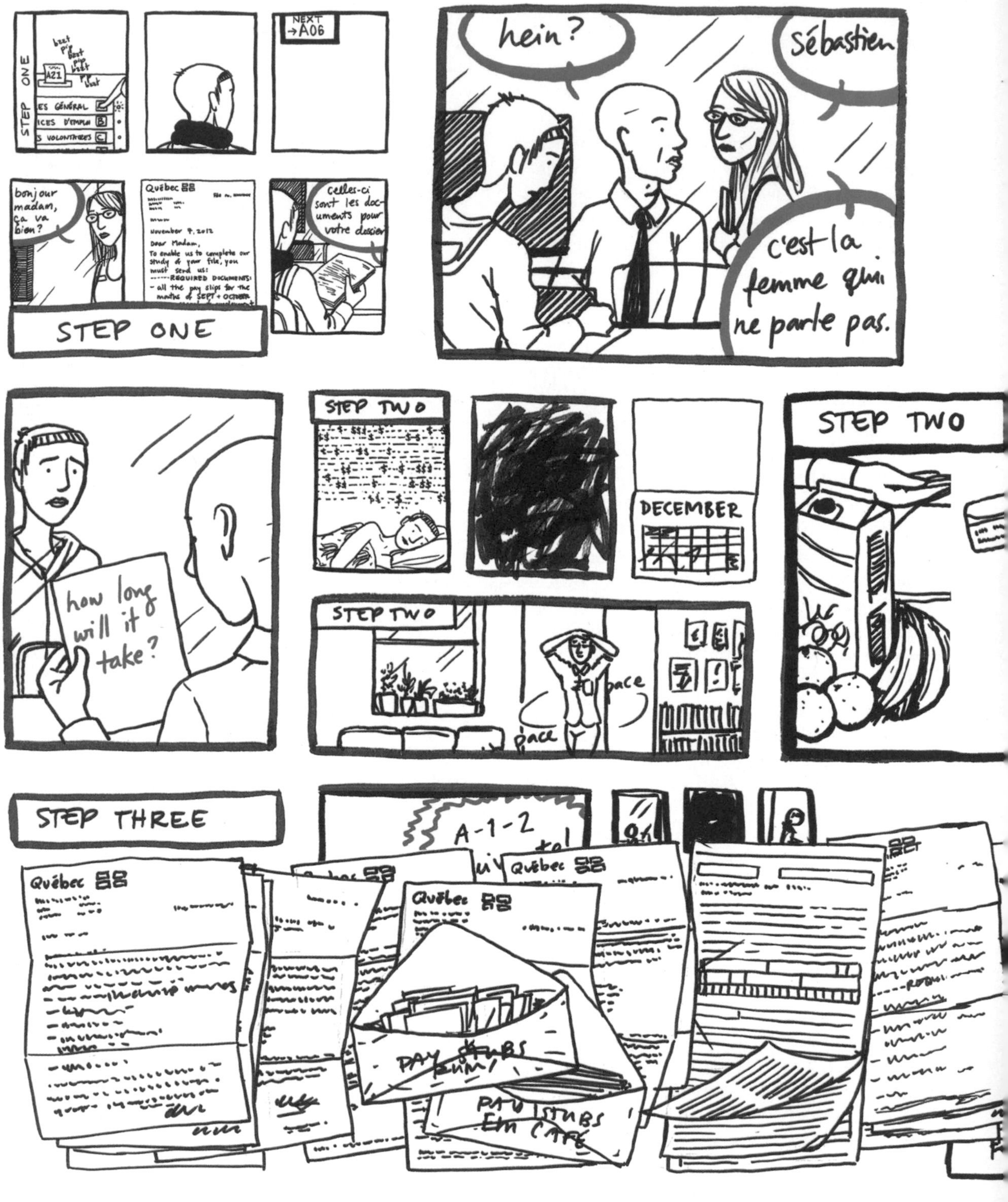

STEP ONE
A21
NEXT →A06
bonjour madam, ça va bien?
Québec
November 9, 2012
Dear Madam,
To enable us to complete our study of your file, you must send us:
REQUIRED DOCUMENTS:
- all the pay slips for the months of SEPT + OCTOBER
celles-ci sont les documents pour votre dossie
STEP ONE
hein?
Sébastien
c'est la femme qui ne parle pas.
how long will it take?
STEP TWO
DECEMBER
STEP TWO
STEP TWO
pace
pace
STEP THREE
A-1-2
Québec
Québec
Québec
PAY STUBS
PAY STUBS
Em CAFÉ

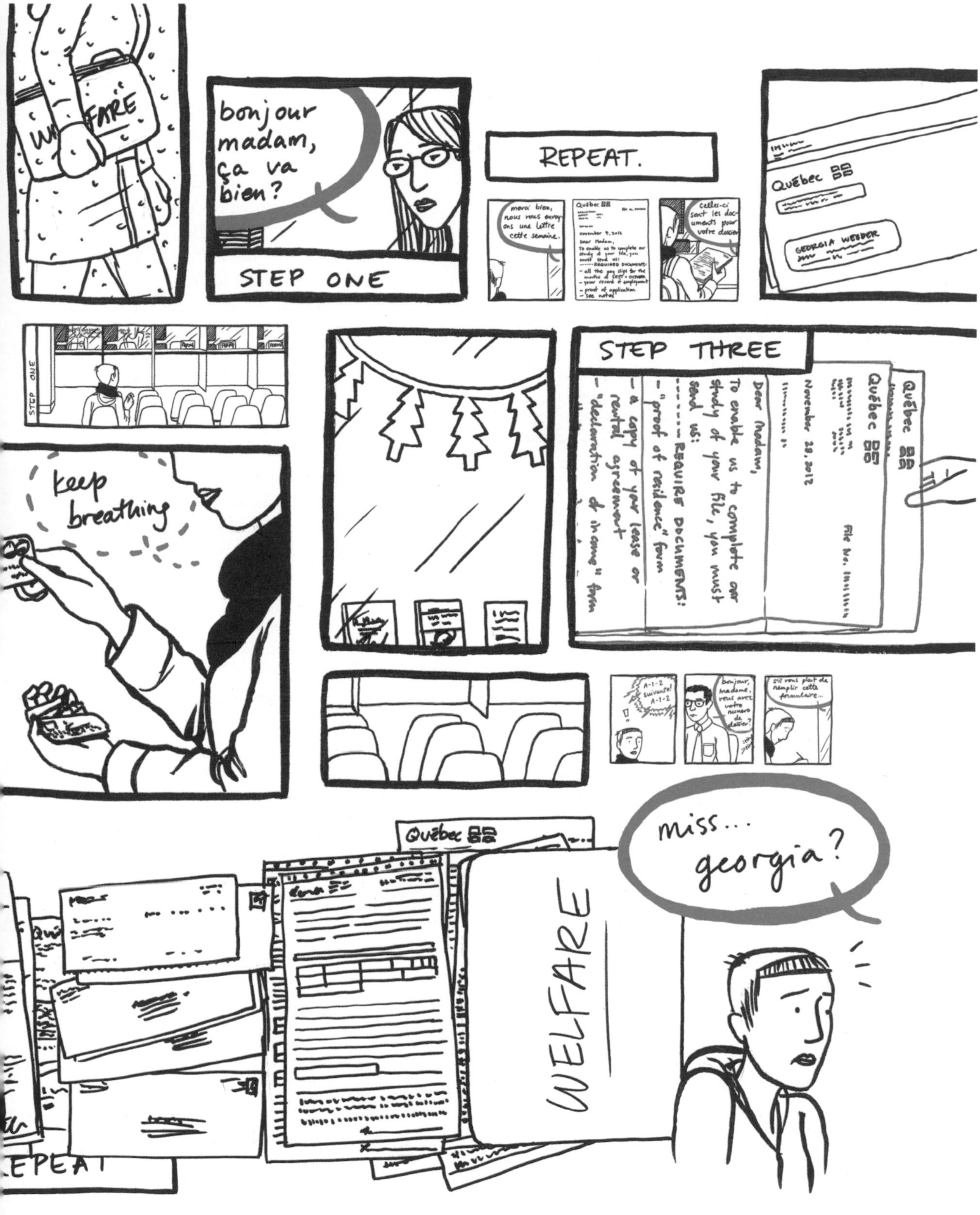
WELFARE
bonjour madam, ça va bien?
STEP ONE
REPEAT.
merci bien, nous vous envoyons une lettre cette semaine.
Québec
November 9, 2012
Dear Madam,
To enable us to complete our study of your file, you must send us:
REQUIRED DOCUMENTS:
- all the pay slips for the months of SEPT + OCTOBER
- your record of employment
- proof of application
- see notes
celles-ci sont les documents pour votre dossier
Québec
GEORGIA WEBBER
STEP ONE
keep breathing
STEP THREE
Québec
Québec
November 28, 2012
Dear Madam,
To enable us to complete our study of your file, you must send us:
REQUIRED DOCUMENTS:
- "proof of residence" form
- a copy of your lease or rental agreement
- "declaration of income" form
File No.
A-1-2 suivante! A-1-2
!
bonjour, madame, vous avez votre numero de dossier?
s'il vous plait de remplir cette formulaire...
Québec
WELFARE
miss... georgia?
REPEAT

Sweeney's "A Good Day," *Brittle Joints*, 2018.

percent not and most people are denied. People with genetic disorders, such as me, were denied several times. Basically, it's a ploy to get you to pay attorneys so that they would help you with that case. It's a long-winded thing.

Is it just that you were like, "Yup, this is part of the story. This needs to be included," or did you also sense the way, that sharing that information — because myself, it was a very structured and important segment, when I'm talking about getting on the medical marijuana program in the "Cannabis" story, and the process of very restrictive paperwork. This is just a small example of a lifetime of paperwork for being disabled and seeking benefits. So, did you know, like, "Hey, this needs to have a light shined on it." Or, not that you were cavalier about it [*Webber laughs*], but did you also think, "Yes, this is part of the story."

WEBBER: I think so. I personally feel as an artist for my whole life that the financial aspect of things — like when you talk to other artists about it, we're all just like, "Yeah, it's a struggle, we know how hard it is." But we don't actually discuss the very specific details of our finances with each other. Like, "Yeah, how much did it cost you to get these things printed?" and then, "How much do you spend on all

of your shipping supplies?" and, "How much were you donated from that campaign? So, if you subtract all your expenses from that — Oh, you *lost* money on this!" We kind of know that, and that's a hard element of life, and has been a hard element of my life for a long time.

But then, when I introduced a health struggle into it — frankly, I'd been struggling with depression and anxiety for years before that point, but I did not consider those things to be legitimate, and so I didn't seek help for them and I didn't include that. Then when it came to me having a physical issue that, honestly — even though it was so painful for me to speak that I wouldn't do it — I was still questioning all the time how real it could be because I've just absorbed a lot of skepticism for people taking care of themselves, and taboo feelings of the inability to touch anything to do with the link between finances and health. For me, like I said, the story I was telling was just meant to be complete, it was just meant to not leave out any ugly detail or any uncomfortable detail, because for me the whole story is much more interesting than just the slices of it that tell a very one-dimensional, emotional narrative or arc.

So, the financial aspect was actually, for me, probably one of the biggest ones because it was the hardest decision to leave my job, and it was the hardest decision to walk into that office and ask for assistance. Then, my process of receiving assistance took so long because they have an "hours" requirement for how many hours you've worked in the past two years to qualify for even welfare. I wasn't even going on disability, because you had to get welfare and then apply for disability as the next step. So, I was applying for welfare, and they were asking for all my paystubs, and asking me for all this proof of the money I had made. I was working part-time because Montreal is so cheap — or it was so cheap, I think that's changed a lot now — but it was so cheap that I only had to work three days a week to live my life and feel comfortable. So, when I came in with all my paperwork and they were like, "You haven't worked enough hours in a year."

I was like, "Well, so what? I haven't worked enough hours? That doesn't mean I can work more now because I haven't worked enough hours. I'm still in trouble and I still need this help." So, it was a really long process because they just couldn't make that work in the system, and I was really lucky in the end to have a worker just come in and sit down with me and I tried to share with her what was going on. But obviously, without being able to speak, it was extremely hard. She just was like, "OK, I have to find a way to make an exception here, because I don't know how to fix this for you, but it isn't right." And so, she did. It was amazing, but I'm really sad that other people don't have that. Or I could have had a worker who was not sympathetic to me at all and that I don't know where I'd be today, like I have no idea what would have happened.

SWEENEY: It makes me anxious hearing about it.

WEBBER: I was trying to make people feel that. I was trying to take the financial aspect of it because it's so uncomfortable, and it did include a lot of luck for me, and it did include a lot of red tape that didn't make sense in my situation. Letting people know that when they saw me on a day-to-day basis, and they're wondering how I was doing, that yes, it was emotionally complicated to have the social structures of life totally shift. It felt very uncomfortable to be in pain and that made me very sad, and that was very hard to deal with on a mental and emotional level by itself. But that over all of this stuff, was also the pressure of financially surviving when I was just trying to get through the process of receiving any help, and having to make every single decision of mine a decision of, "How much faith am I going to put into this system helping me?" How much can I put on credit before I start losing my mind? What's going to happen if I can't pay this back?" Even paying rent, all of that being so difficult made the disability experience of pain and of the social changes in my life so much harder, that if I'd had financial support then it would have been still hard, but way less so.

SWEENEY: Yeah, very much.

WEBBER: Years later, I still have passion and anger about it because it was so ridiculous. But anyway, you are obviously dealing with a lifetime of it. I don't have to explain it to you. I feel strongly that everyone having the voice that they want to share their story just means that all of our stories have room. If no one

Busted city sidewalks
DELI MARKET
Stairs to get into stores, restaurants, offices
OPEN
Public transit without wheelchair ramps or lower steps
SEPTA
113
SEPTA

Sweeney's "A Good Day," *Brittle Joints*, 2018.

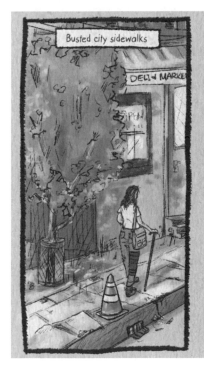

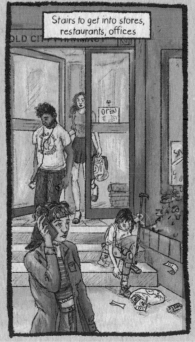

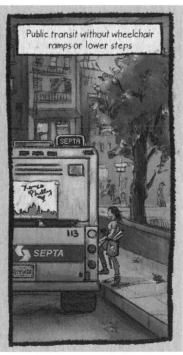

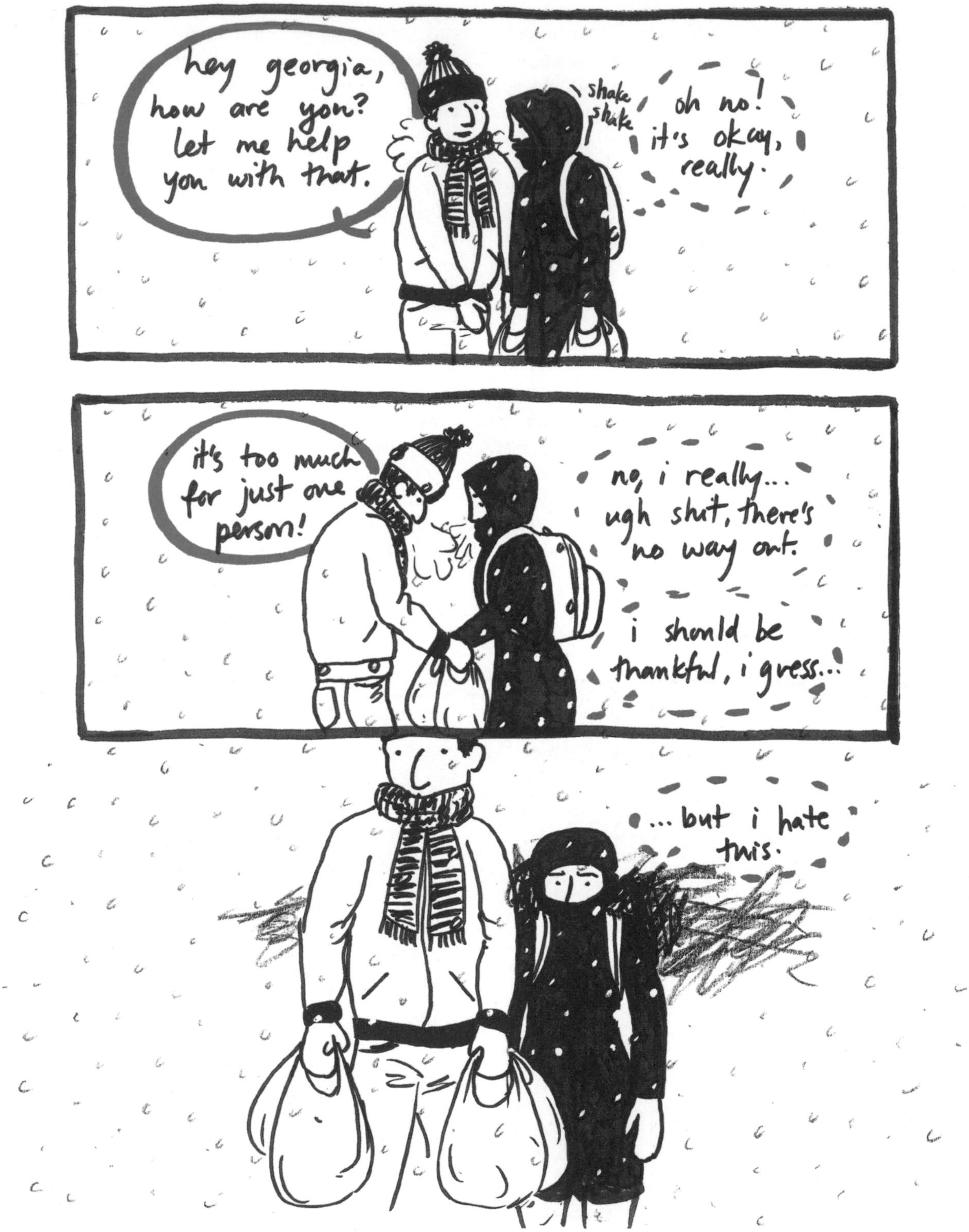
hey georgia, how are you? let me help you with that.
shake shake
oh no! it's okay, really.
it's too much for just one person!
no, i really... ugh shit, there's no way out.
i should be thankful, i guess...
... but i hate this.

is talking about something, then we all take the cue. Instead of letting that roll endlessly, I wanted to tell how hard it was for me to be like, "This is a part of my life, I'm sure it's a part of yours," and that's OK, we can talk about how hard this is.

Or we can talk about debt, or we can talk about how being an artist feels so undervalued that you question your worthiness to live if no one is going to pay you for the work that you're making. You question your worthiness to live if no one thinks that it's worth helping you get into the building you need to, to execute whatever task is on your list for the day. It's not just uncomfortable, it's fundamentally, existentially disturbing. And everyone deals with some element of that, whether it's totally life-changing or just a sidebar to whatever else is going on. It still affects you, and it's still there and it's still real, and I don't want anyone to feel like me talking about my story means they can't talk about their story.

SWEENEY: Same.

WORLD-BUILDING

A memoir has just as much world-building as anything else. It's very important in your memoirs, specifically, to build a world and then navigate it. Both of you had a more urban setting for your comics. Could you talk about the thought process?

SWEENEY: A lot of *Brittle Joints* focuses on some of my college times, so that was more in Center City, Philadelphia, New York City, and as you said, these are urban places. I think Georgia and I can both relate — accessibility in urban cities is not good, to say the least, in lot of realms.

A big part of being disabled and trying to navigate in a city is finance. The only way for wheelchair users to safely navigate in Philadelphia is really using rideshare apps, or cabs, and a lot of times there's minute issues that aren't minute for the disabled person in terms of getting from point A to B. Where people have not picked me up because I said I use a wheelchair, and they don't want it to damage their car or something

like that. That means I can't go somewhere. Or they will come and sort of take a long route so I will cancel their ride and then when I have to do the ride again, I usually get the same person, because they're in the same area. And now I eventually — if they do accept the ride — I know I'm sitting with somebody that originally didn't want me in the car. That happens, honestly, as long as I use a wheelchair, in perpetuity. It's always a constant fear, as soon as I get out the door. It's a matter of whether I feel like I can go anywhere, or not. That happens in Philly, that happens in New York.

A big part of me navigating the city was trying to find pain management tools to allow me to walk short distances to complete errands, because I couldn't get a wheelchair down my dorm stairs. I can't actually wheel myself in my wheelchair; it's a transport wheelchair, it is not one that people live in. And that has to do with Medicare and bureaucracy, as we talked about, but that is actually what a lot of disabled people deal with. People kind of assume I have a ramp up into my home. I've never lived in an accessible home. Ever. And that seems really harsh, but also, it's just the reality, so even with fractures and concurrent bone issues, if I got to go upstairs, that has to be accomplished somehow, whether that wheelchair goes up there or not. But not everybody can do it, of course, not everybody has to push themselves in this way.

When people hear that, their first thought is, "Wow." Again, like you talked about, Georgia, this inspiration porn kind of thing. And really, it's very tiresome because all I'm trying to do is get to the second floor of wherever I live. And again, it's never been a place where I can easily access. So, if my home is not accessible, I'm already armored for the world that is not accessible to me either. People are very nice but they can also extend help where it isn't needed to the point where I become injured. That's a whole discussion. It's just a very layered experience to get to a café.

I wonder, Georgia, if you've struggled a lot with not being able to speak to people to either get directions, or if there's a change in schedule? How is it being in such a loud environment? And even if you can walk and get on a bus, does that mean you know it's the right bus? If that makes sense?

WEBBER: Yeah, for sure. The amount of mental energy going into all those interactions for me is

---

OPPOSITE: From Webber's "Paperwork," *Dumb*, 2018.

what I end up focusing a lot on when I was building the world of the comic. It's definitely less important to me, the physical space that I'm in, because I'm not someone dealing with physical disability, so I didn't have to do really detailed or lush examinations of the environment, which I really appreciated in your story that you just mentioned about going to a coffee shop. The slow pace of walking down the sidewalk and encountering cracks on the sidewalk, and how that could be a part of your experience that I would never have thought about. I wouldn't have imagined it at all.

My difficulties are mostly communicating with people and, in doing so, it made a lot of my world-building stuff about making clear the physical language we are communicating, with or the lack of language, or someone's lack of understanding in a moment when I'm trying really hard. And having similar experiences like you just mentioned, about someone trying to help and just being really harmful. There's only a couple of examples that I give in *Dumb*, of small moments where someone's really got the best of intentions, and it's so humiliating. If I wanted help, I would be happy to ask you for it, and if you asked me, I would be happy to give you an answer, but this assumption that they know what's best definitely caused me a lot of distress. I mean, maybe that's sort of my ego just wanting to be independent, but it's also a matter of respecting me as a person. I'm pretty sure you would ask anybody if they wanted the help, or you would be expecting them to give you an answer, yes or no. But with me and my lack of voice, you're not even gonna wait, you're just gonna do it.

I actually had a turning point in drawing *Dumb* where I was super focused on the bodies, and where each person and each character was in a panel in relation to me, and in what they were saying, and if there was space for the way that I would communicate. But then I had a friend say something about my style being really stripped down, just all white backgrounds. And I was like, "Oh! Backgrounds. Uh, right. This happens in a room, I am in a world. I have to remember that and continue to include that."

So, I ended up building a world outside of me a little bit more, which makes a lot of sense even in the flow of introducing someone to a whole bunch of information, to give very simplified and direct information and then add to that some space and understanding for it, and maybe make it more complex with more detail later. That ended up working in my favor without it being intended.

SWEENEY: Gotcha. But in terms of background and world-building, you including the context, at least of the party, to other people who have been to parties, perhaps, the next time they're at one, and there is somebody who does not have the ability to speak, perhaps that will be a little bit more of a learning experience.

WEBBER: I hope so.

SWEENEY: People connect with things that have happened to them. It's a little — not pessimistic, but people only care what they care about. That applies to the disabled experience. A lot of people are beginning to care when they see their friends struggle, and they're like, "Oh, I didn't think of that. I didn't think of how difficult it is to not have to use my voice. I didn't think of how it is to walk down the street." You, me, our comics and the graphic-art community, they're smart, and they're willing to care. But a big group outside of that, I think, they're not going to know what it's like to be disabled until it happens to them, and then they're gonna care.

WEBBER: Yeah, it's true.

SWEENEY: But I think we changed that.

WEBBER: Yeah, I hope so. The thing that I really focus on, too, and I continue to make graphic medicine — is that my work is always gonna be health-focused in some way, or another — but also bridging the gap between our understanding of health and health conditions, and disability conditions, which are, to me, conditions of health. They don't have a separation in my view of it. The thing is, everyone has health, and everyone has health issues, and so if we can understand disability as a matter of health — which is not to say that people who are disabled are *unhealthy* — but when we look at them in the spectrum of health conditions, as ways in which we can differ in our health, and all of those things being valid for care. Because we all deserve health, and we all deserve comfort in our health. I think that's one of the ways people are afraid of disability and afraid of the accommodations they would have to make, is just the idea that their body would be any less healthy. Again, I don't wanna imply that disabled people are unhealthy, because that's super not true.

SWEENEY: No, they're not.

WEBBER: They can run a spectrum between losing a limb to having a genetic condition that is very much a continuing health condition that needs care all the time, to mental health … It's really a huge spectrum of possibility that fits into that umbrella of disability. For me, I've come to understand that people are so uncomfortable with the idea of disability because they're terrified of their health condition being different, their body being different. Obviously, the sense that they might lose something, lose the ability to do things, is terrifying. Ultimately, the only ability that would be lost would be to navigate the world that they presently do with their bodies. But it's the world that doesn't have space for them to have another body, and they don't know what that's like.

And ultimately, looking at someone who's struggling with having access to somewhere can be as simple as, "Well, OK, if I think about myself as a person who's healthy, and something happens to me and I'm sick, and someone offers to help me when I'm sick, how would I feel about that? Probably, I would feel grateful that they were offering, and then I could make the choice whether or not I wanted to accept it." Instead of having the immediate sense when someone is disabled, and may be struggling with something that I think I could help with, me thinking, "Well, disability is different, and that means that I should not engage with this part of this person's experience because that's rude, or overstepping some boundary or something."

I don't think that we have a unified concept of all of us as having bodies, and all of those bodies having various levels of health, and all of us needing various levels of help at different times. There's a blanket of fear around, "Oh, I don't know about that, so I shouldn't ask about that," or, "I don't know about that, so I'm not sure why it matters." It's making everything relatable. If you're alive, then you're having an experience of a body, and this other person is also alive and they're having an experience of a body. That's a

pretty basic thing to connect over. Then navigating that specific situation doesn't have to be terrifying.

SWEENEY: There's a lot of commonality.

DRAWING BODIES

You both have to draw yourselves and you have to draw other people in other bodies, interacting. You have to think about how you're going present yourself.

SWEENEY: I had a comment on drawing of the self, and one thing that you have in the comic, Georgia, is the fatigue and routine, being bored, of drawing *you*, again and again. I definitely struggle presently with that. [*Webber laughs.*] I love portraiture — and my aesthetic is very much based in illustration — I struggled a lot having to continually draw myself. It reopens old wounds — that's a double entendre, there! [*Laughter.*] Sometimes, having to draw myself at a doctor appointment, or undergoing surgery — or, currently, I'm drawing the relationships of people out in the city, and the things they've said to me, or the help that

From Webber's "Splitting," *Dumb*, 2018.

they've extended that we talked about, and how that is problematic more often than not. Especially in a boisterous, gritty city like Philadelphia, there's a lot of characters and a lot of assumptions made.

While it's getting done, I currently struggle with sitting down, removing me from the situation so that I can just draw the lines that look like me, that have my nose, that have my face, and then drawing the people that have done me wrong and done things that bother me. It's not this existential, traumatic experience that I have to undergo every time I get the Photoshop open, but it is very much something that I have to divide and conquer and compartmentalize. I wondered if you had any strategies, artist to artist, to alleviate some of that struggle.

WEBBER: I totally took the opposite tack when I was finishing my book, after I had to take a year and a half off because of chronic hand pain. I really wanted to finish it and I did not take into account how emotionally stressful it was gonna be for me to reenter my headspace and my experiences to draw them. I can definitely tell you how *not* to do it. Don't do it all at once on a very short timeline. That's a very bad idea.

SWEENEY: Yeah.

STRATEGIES

WEBBER: Now, I am writing and drawing a book about trauma. And it's not memoir in the same way, but it is coming from my interest in trauma, which is because of my experience with it. It's a similar situation where I'm looking at this subject and thinking I have a lot to say about this that relates very deeply to where I've been, but also where I still am in my life, and I really want to do it carefully.

Resourcing is an ongoing process for me: finding or creating resources for wellness and happiness and relief after something has been stirred. I'm very much in the thick of figuring out what that looks like for me, because there's a lot. I have PTSD, and one of the symptoms and common occurrences in people with PTSD is a hypervigilance and a very low tolerance for calm or pleasure. The hypervigilance comes into play, looking for the danger that is probably about to happen, just having had an experience of it and not

knowing if it will recur, or not having processed a current feeling of safety.

I'm just trying to preface by saying that for me, it's still not easy and it's not always working, but if I know I'm gonna tackle a difficult topic or a page of drawing, just trying to prepare myself for that by doing things that I really like. That can be being a friend and talking about it, or eating a really nice meal that I really enjoy cooking, because that's one of my pleasures, is cooking. It could also mean, "I am definitely going to do yoga this morning," because for me that's another source of wellness. So, if I know I'm gonna have a hard day, choosing to do something really good for myself before it starts, but then also giving myself permission to stop and reach for another one of those things at the moment that I'm starting to feel overwhelmed. Even if it's just like, "I made a plan to see my friend at 3 PM today, I'm going to yoga at 9 AM today, and between those hours, I'm gonna try and tackle some of this stuff." However it is that I'm feeling, hopefully I'll be ready to walk away from it at the time that I need to go meet my friend, and then I know I have the support of that person to help me if I need it.

SWEENEY: Thank you. Friends, connecting and allowing you to give some space to share what you're gonna have to write or tackle has been important for me. It's not something that comes very easily because I'm kind of a solitary worker. I'll work on the comic, and then it's done, and my friends don't really see it until it's done. That makes it a lonely and probably not a healthy process, so for the second issue of *Brittle Bones*, a lot of it has been sharing the story, perhaps not in detail, but, "Oh yeah, this is about this person that did this." In that way, it becomes a little bit more normal, it's been voiced. It brings power to share it with somebody. Then it doesn't feel as taboo when you have to draw it, y'know?

WEBBER: Absolutely. Because sharing it in a comic is sending it out into the widest world possible. Especially if you go online, it ends up just going into the hands of whoever, which really doesn't allow for a lot of grounding in the connection that it's offering. You have solitarily created something and deposited it somewhere, and then you've walked away, and you don't know who's gonna come upon it and be touched

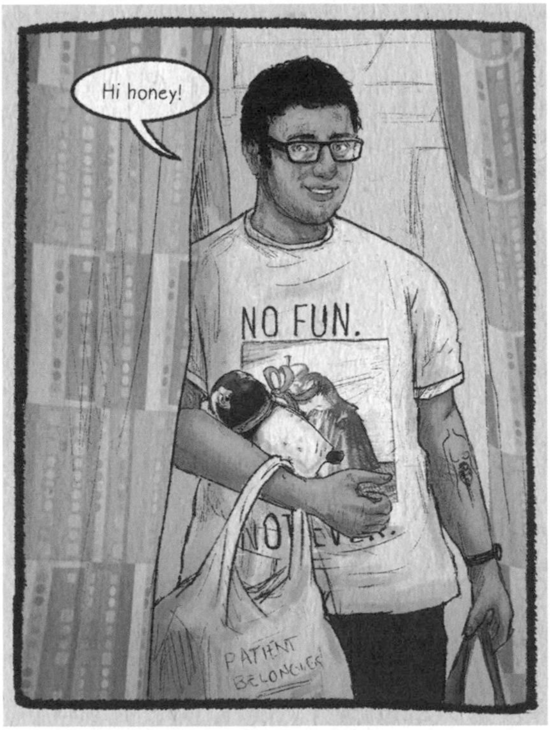
Hi honey!
NO FUN.

From "Nerves," *Brittle Joints*, 2018.

by it. And when they are, who knows if they'll let you know. There's so many parts of that, that we have to put a lot of faith in existing, and of that being the value of the work being out in the world, and also whatever value we take from personally expressing. Having the actual experience of creation still include connecting with other people, even if it's just the activity you do after you spend some time working in solitude.

SWEENEY: Yeah, even if it's just a discussion that isn't about that.

WEBBER: It's just having days that aren't totally locked up in the comics world and the comics creation. Especially if you know you're dealing with challenging stuff, figure out how to be really, really nice to yourself about that. Which I say lightly, but know is an extremely difficult thing for some people, like myself. It's very simple and basic stuff, but building in breaks or having some exercises that you can do to keep yourself feeling good while you're in the process of physically producing, eating, sleeping ... It's very, very basic, but I can't understate how important those things are for me, no matter what I'm working on. But I just happen to choose really challenging, personal topics for myself. [*Laughter.*]

COLLABORATION AND ONGOING PROJECTS

You are both collaborating. You have *Dancing After TEN*, Georgia, and I know you've done *In a Rut Comics*, Maria. Do you want to talk about collaborating and your projects?

SWEENEY: *In a Rut Comics* was sort of my segue into comics in general. It's a collaborative series I work on with my partner, Eros Livieratos. He's the writer, and I'm the illustrator. It was him that pushed me into comics as a whole. He is very well-versed in indie comics and being a writer himself, it was of very deep interest for him, and I had never really dabbled into comics prior to us meeting. That was very cool. It is still very cool.

The first issue, back in 2015, is very much an exploration of that process. We weren't together for some of the creating, so there were always different roadblocks, different things when you're not with the person you're collaborating with. That was definitely a learning curve, but we continued through. We did the second issue for my senior thesis in art school, and then the third issue is our most recent, and it came out last year. This is a stand-alone issue, and Eros made a lot of things relating to being in the punk-noise scene in New Jersey that he works in, an urban kind of neighborhood. It aims to connect people in the slice-of-life genre, adding personal struggles, things that people don't normally think about when transitioning from young adulthood, and that's sort of the process of *In a Rut*.

We also do other projects together, poetry zines, and that helps give me a lot of confidence to pursue *Brittle Joints* on my own. Because up until that time I was pretty comfortable collaborating, and while I was encouraged in college about comics, there were no comic professors at the time, and there were no comic classes. It was like, "You do you, Maria. OK. You do those comics." It was encouraging, and sometimes it wasn't. There was a lot of pressure: "You know, Maria, you can make your own comics." And I did know that, but at the time I was still very comfortable and was happy to collaborate with someone and learn through them, and really take the time to build the art style that I wanted.

I'm very happy it worked out that way, because then in 2017, I really pursued narrating my own work. I had already felt really comfortable with the art I was pursuing, the style and process of working. And that, I think, is a big challenge too. When you go into comics, you've got a blank page. How do you start? Do you start simply as budgeting off the sides of your bleeds? Do you start with just the panels, the thumbnails? It's just a little bit different than when you approach an illustration, that's just a single piece.

So, having those two years of collaborating really allowed me to harness my skills in art so that when I focus on telling my own story, which we talked

---

From *Dancing after TEN,* an introduction to Georgia Webber's collaboration with Vivian Chong.

about can be sort of painful and difficult to bring up, the art — while I always love learning and improving — was a little more secondary. I was able to focus on the narration. That's how *In a Rut Comics* came. It continues to be a place for me to work on, collaborate with. We've worked on anthologies with other artists from either Marvel or the indie scene, and having the *In a Rut* project allows me to take a break from me, and pursue other things. I'm very proud of that.

WEBBER: That's awesome. I would say I've been experiencing a similar relief in collaborating with Vivian [Chong], because that book that you mentioned, the little 20-page intro called *Vivian's Image,* is actually just a teaser for our full graphic memoir we're doing about her life called *Dancing After TEN* [toxic epidermal necrolysis]. So that process is actually a really long and in-depth one. It started in March and we're just a few months in, and I have a deadline of October to get her whole story down on paper.

Just to clarify, this is the project about a woman who went blind when she had a reaction?

This is Vivian's image.

These are lines on a page.

WEBBER: The TEN reaction is really non-specific. Almost any medication can cause it because it's just a very rare combination of physiology and some sort of stimulus, and it even happens somehow just from autoimmune conditions. So, it's really not about the dangers of a particular medication, but the dangers of that medication to Vivian, because she just happened to have that right combination to spur this reaction, and then have a huge life-changing experience from it. So yeah, that's the project.

She's telling her story to you. She has her own materials, and you're adapting that into a graphic memoir?

WEBBER: Yeah, because she wrote and drew about 100 images of a comic that were a memoir of what was happening to her, but she drew that while it was happening, and while she was losing her sight, so she did lose her sight and had to stop. She couldn't finish the story, and I don't even know if she had an end in mind. She was just documenting. So, I have those drawings, and then that was 14 years ago, so the way she tells me the story now includes a lot of perspectives from all the things she's learned and done since then. I'm telling multiple perspectives at once: incorporating what she drew before; incorporating how she feels about it now and what she's gone through since then; and also, incorporating our relationship because the story of the book is her losing her sight. We need to acknowledge that this is a visual medium, and, clearly, she's not the person writing and drawing it. Clearly, there's another perspective interpreting it. I'm in there somewhere, and that's just another layer to the process. It's really her story, so we're trying to make that as much in her voice, as much from her perspective as possible, with her at the center.

The collaboration experience is different than [how] I've ever worked, because I have only ever worked on my own, and have mostly preferred it that way, except for when I was much younger and just out of high school and organized and ran an anthology zine for a little while. So, it's collaborating in a sense, but not really directly on, like, someone making words and me making art, or vice versa. But with Vivian, the process is also a very planning-heavy version of what I might do for myself, because when I'm on my own, I'm throwing things on the page and

making it messy and allowing that mess to be there, and that was also me teaching myself and learning for myself how to make a comic, especially something long form.

But with Vivian, I know what I'm doing. I'm definitely still learning a lot, but I feel like having been through the process before, I at least know I can reasonably expect it's gonna take me this long, and here are the things I'd really like to do with it. The detachment from the contents, because they're not my life and I don't have to build that stuff into my day when I'm working on Vivian's story, because I'm not emotionally pulled through it in the same way that I was pulled through my own work. Collaborating is a bit of a break in the sense that there is hard work to do on the craft of what I'm making, but there isn't the same hard work to do emotionally to keep myself afloat through the process.

Working with her has been very easy. We agree a lot, so it's been very comfortable to choose what happens next in the story, or which things to convey, or what wording to use. We're very connected that way, and that's been great. The only thing that's tough about it for me is, because she's blind, I have to plan everything very intensely so that I can describe down to the panel the aesthetics of what I'm trying to convey and the references I'm trying to make and the words that I'm gonna use. All of that has to be described to her before I actually start because she wants to give input on whether or not she thinks I'm headed in the right direction, and if I've got anything factually wrong, and if there's something that isn't quite her voice, it's not what she would say, or it's not what she would like to share. She needs a chance to look at that.

And by "look at it," I mean have her computer read the document to her, so the shorthand of a sighted person is not super-inclusive to her experience. The back and forth that we do does take a long time, and I have to type everything out and think it out and then it changes as I go, and then once it's finished, I type it out again, and she gets a chance to look at, or to have the reader read that to her, and then there's an access facilitator who actually visually looks at the pieces, and then talks to her about her impressions. So, the two of them have a process. And then they both come back to me with their suggestions about what to change, and then I repeat it with the changes.

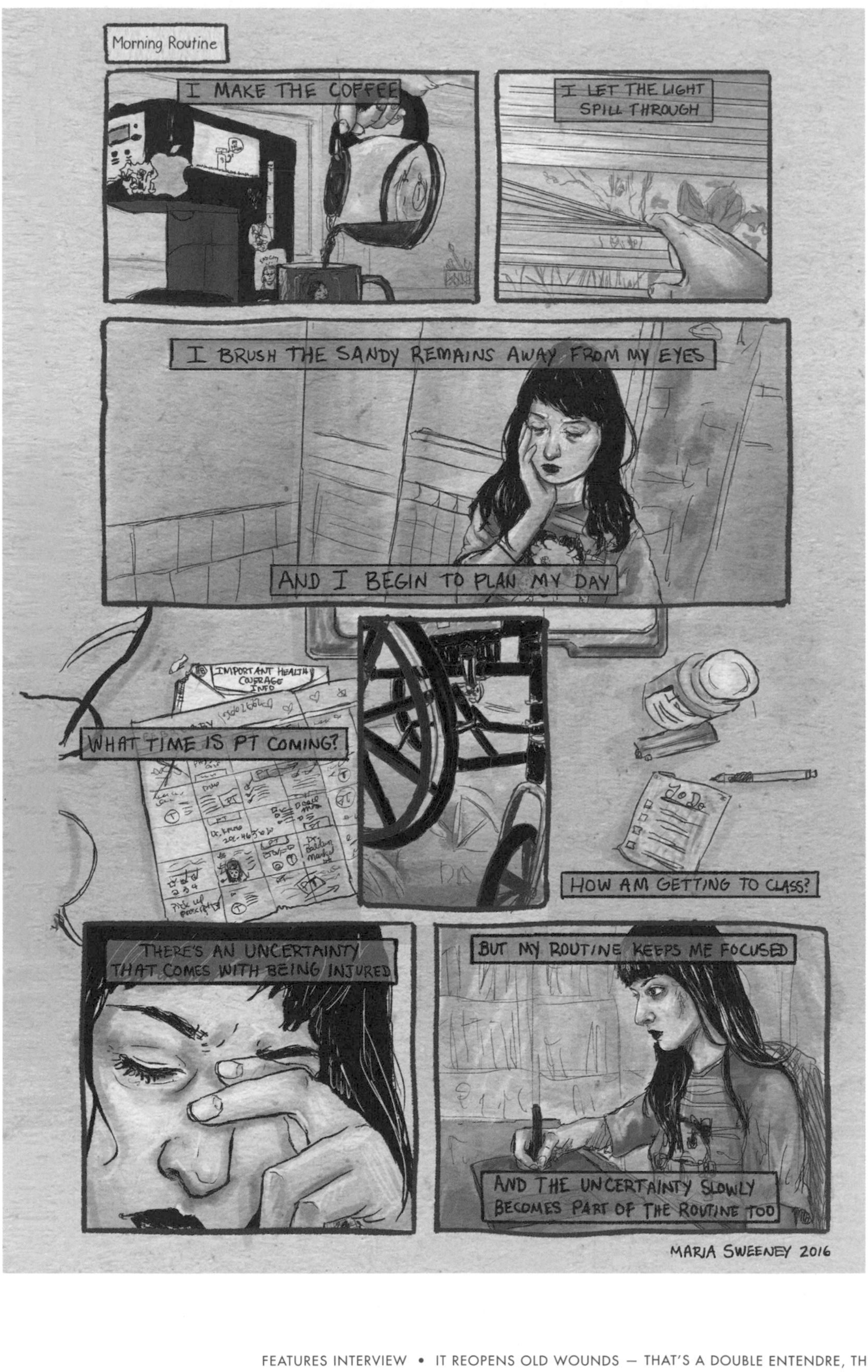
Morning Routine
I MAKE THE COFFEE
I LET THE LIGHT SPILL THROUGH
I BRUSH THE SANDY REMAINS AWAY FROM MY EYES
AND I BEGIN TO PLAN MY DAY
IMPORTANT HEALTH COVERAGE INFO
WHAT TIME IS PT COMING?
To Do
HOW AM GETTING TO CLASS?
THERE'S AN UNCERTAINTY THAT COMES WITH BEING INJURED
BUT MY ROUTINE KEEPS ME FOCUSED
AND THE UNCERTAINTY SLOWLY BECOMES PART OF THE ROUTINE TOO
MARIA SWEENEY 2016

Everything I do has a multi-stage process, and it's been really good for me to learn about planning and how I would approach this from a purely production, efficiency and consideration standpoint. Because when I'm just working with myself, I can be brutal with myself, and I can grind through something that really sucks for me to do. I can write something just because that's the only way I can write it right now, and then walk away later, and I might come back with another opinion, but there's no one who's gonna push me on it, and there's no one who's gonna nitpick.

Which is kind of unfortunate, because I'm also a comics editor, and so I find that process of editing and having another set of eyes and another perspective, another heart looking at it, that's so valuable, but I've not found anyone who can do that for me. So, it just feels more chaotic. It all feels more like I'm just throwing this spaghetti at the wall, and I'll see what sticks and the kind of mess I can make. Which I think is pretty clear in the book itself, but the way that I'm working now, with this collaborator, just forces me to be structured, and it's a cool thing to learn that I can actually do that.

SWEENEY: Awesome.

I'm very interested in your upcoming work with trauma. Especially, again, while it is going to incorporate your own personal experiences, it's going to probably illuminate a lot of where trauma comes from. Which will be very helpful for not just me, but for everyone [*Webber laughs*] with trauma.

I was very excited to see a lot of parallels in our experience. I know that you even said they're very different, but well, they are and they're not, especially when we make the connection of how this is a human issue. I think it's important to note that everybody becomes a level of disabled at some point of their lives, whether it's temporarily or through age, eventually. This question of access, and this push away from thinking you need it, is foolish. We all are gonna need to access buildings when we're older. We're all gonna be equal, develop all kinds of issues in the future. It may be that it will be difficult for older folks *to* speak and use their voice, which I find a lot where I work.

I felt like you brought a lot to the conversation about the disabled experience, and despite ours being different, they're quite the same in a lot of ways.

WEBBER: Yeah, absolutely. I really appreciate every story about health, every story about disability that has the courage to come into the world. Because it does mean that everyone will have the chance, at least to find it when they need it, or see parts of themselves and people they love in those experiences. It's a common humanity thing, which I actually am touched by even though it's a generic phrase at this point.

SWEENEY: No, I agree. It means a lot to me.

WEBBER: And I am very happy to see that things like graphic medicine are growing so quickly right now, so as to just keep including more and more and more stories. Because accessibility is not about everyone having exactly the same access to everything — but just that there's room for every kind of access, and there's openness to those differences. I'm so pleased when there's another story in the world because it creates that space, just by existing. It's so valuable. ✿

OPPOSITE: This one-page comic is called "Morning Routine," from Sweeney's *Brittle Joints*, 2018.

My Life with the Worst-Case Scenario

Patrick Dean

FUNNY STORY: My symptoms began a year before my diagnosis in June of 2018. I had trouble pronouncing certain sounds and my voice became nasally, as if someone were pinching my nose while I talked. This went on for a while and my wife suggested I see a doctor, but I was in my early 40s and it was probably nothing serious. Insisting my problems would iron themselves out, I told her that my voice would come back — and the cough that developed would disappear, too.

Sometime after New Year's, my wife put her foot down after it took me longer to spit out basic sentences. We saw my general practitioner who stated that whatever this was, it wasn't neurological. Blood tests and an MRI later, I was referred to an allergist because the MRI showed I had a severe sinus infection. Spent a few months treating this sinus infection with saline and steroid sprays, but my speech only got worse. The allergist referred us to an ENT. The ENT shoved a camera up my nose and saw that my muscles in the palate weren't working. He said that this issue was neuromuscular. The word was like a punch in the face.

My wife and I threw out some worst-case scenarios, but the ENT reassured us that "neuromuscular" could refer to about 200 different diseases. From there he referred us to a local neurologist, who gave me a quick examination and said, "Yeah, this looks like ALS [amyotrophic lateral sclerosis]." He ran blood work to rule out treatable diseases. The following week, we came back to his office for another MRI and tests that would pinpoint what this was. The first test was being shocked up and down my body, which hurt — but it was a walk in the park compared to the next test. Then, the neurologist came in and stuck electric needles from my feet to my neck that listened to deteriorating

muscles. His conclusion was he didn't want to make the call, so he referred us to the ALS clinics in Augusta and Atlanta. The lab work also came back negative, further eliminating the hope that my issues would be treatable.

Since Augusta had the first opening, my wife and I traveled there for a definite diagnosis. The grumpy sonuvabitch doctor basically redid the tests I had done in Athens, Georgia, but he was more thorough and, for good measure, stuck some needles in my chin and tongue. After leaving the room for what felt like an eternity, the doctor came back in and confirmed I did indeed have bulbar onset ALS.

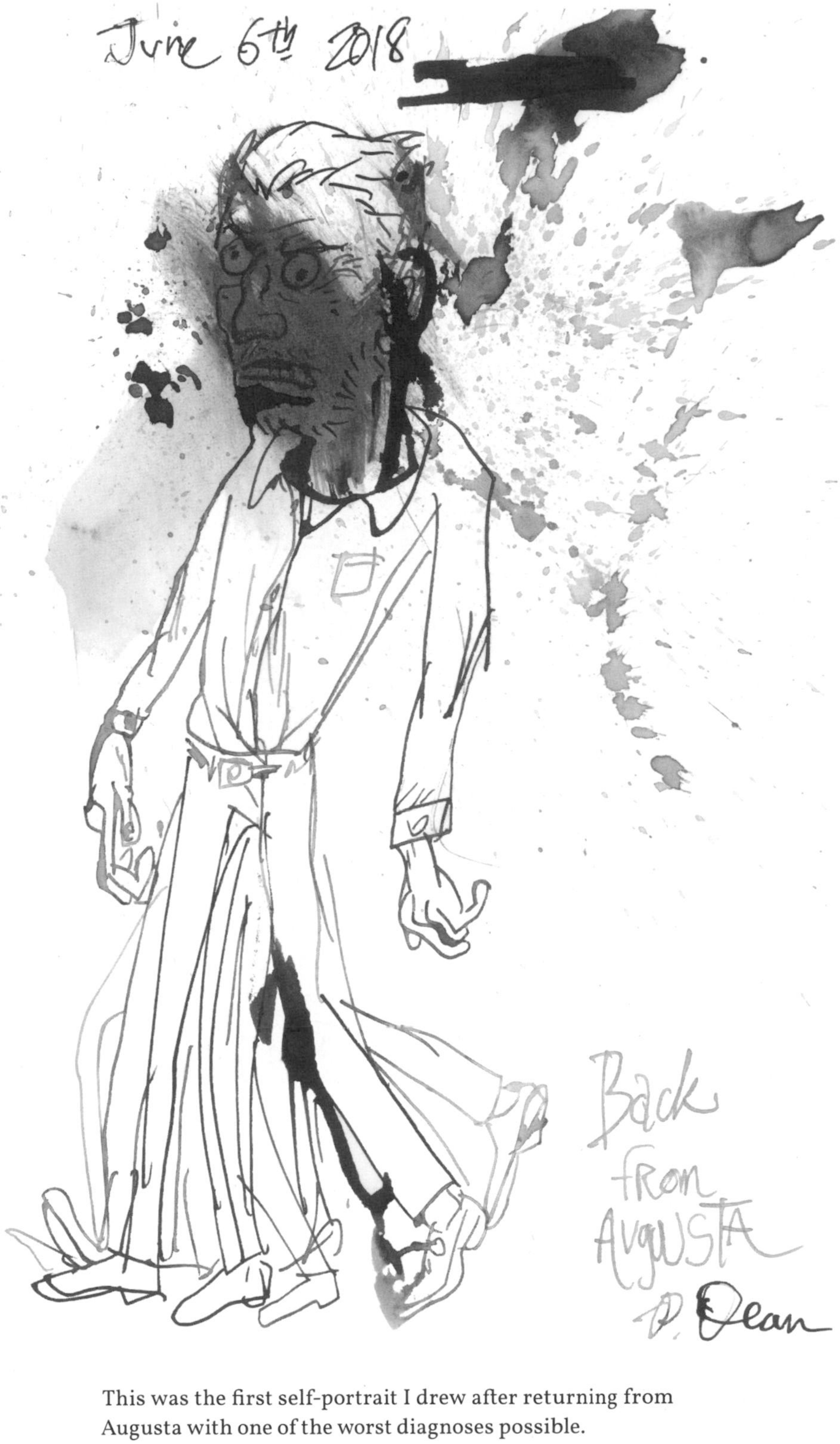
June 6th 2018
Back from AUGUSTA
R Dean

This was the first self-portrait I drew after returning from Augusta with one of the worst diagnoses possible.

I made the announcement public with the following comic...

I HAVE BEEN GIVEN AN ALS DIAGNOSIS
THIS FACT MAKES ME FURIOUS...
...AND VERY HEARTBROKEN.
IT'S MESSED UP MY VOICE FOR MONTHS NOW AND MOVING ONTO MY BREATHING AND SWALLOWING

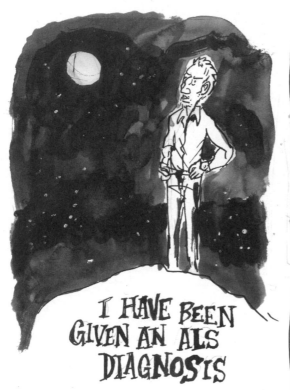

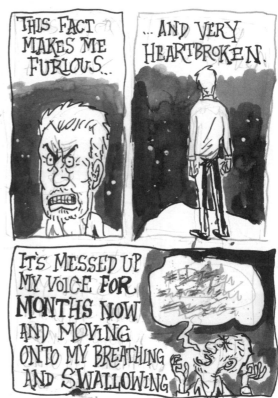

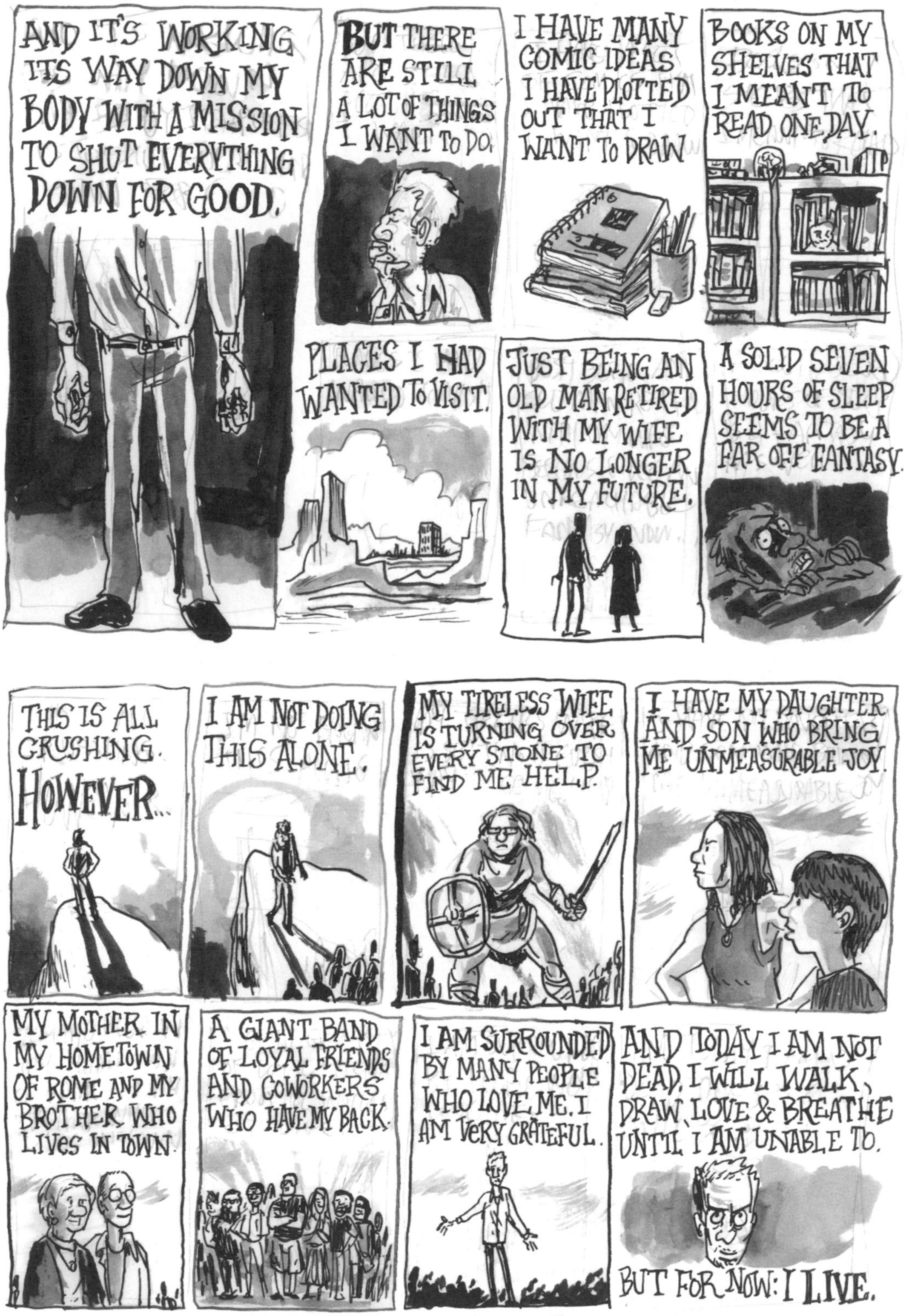
AND IT'S WORKING ITS WAY DOWN MY BODY WITH A MISSION TO SHUT EVERYTHING DOWN FOR GOOD.
BUT THERE ARE STILL A LOT OF THINGS I WANT TO DO.
I HAVE MANY COMIC IDEAS I HAVE PLOTTED OUT THAT I WANT TO DRAW
BOOKS ON MY SHELVES THAT I MEANT TO READ ONE DAY.
PLACES I HAD WANTED TO VISIT.
JUST BEING AN OLD MAN RETIRED WITH MY WIFE IS NO LONGER IN MY FUTURE.
A SOLID SEVEN HOURS OF SLEEP SEEMS TO BE A FAR OFF FANTASY.
THIS IS ALL CRUSHING. HOWEVER...
I AM NOT DOING THIS ALONE.
MY TIRELESS WIFE IS TURNING OVER EVERY STONE TO FIND ME HELP.
I HAVE MY DAUGHTER AND SON WHO BRING ME UNMEASURABLE JOY.
MY MOTHER IN MY HOMETOWN OF ROME AND MY BROTHER WHO LIVES IN TOWN.
A GIANT BAND OF LOYAL FRIENDS AND COWORKERS WHO HAVE MY BACK.
I AM SURROUNDED BY MANY PEOPLE WHO LOVE ME. I AM VERY GRATEFUL.
AND TODAY I AM NOT DEAD. I WILL WALK, DRAW, LOVE & BREATHE UNTIL I AM UNABLE TO.
BUT FOR NOW: I LIVE.

JULY 23d, 2018

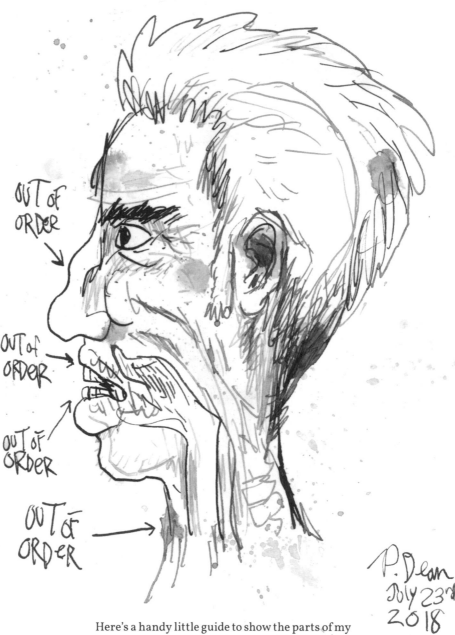

OUT OF ORDER

OUT of ORDER

OUT of ORDER

OUT of ORDER

P. Dean
July 23d
2018

Here's a handy little guide to show the parts of my head that were affected by bulbar onset ALS, in the beginning. Pretty much everything involved with speaking, swallowing and breathing. No big deal.

A GOOD DAY WITH BULBAR ALS...

COUGH

In the beginning, when my symptoms were relatively mild, I drew this to show even the best days kind of suck.

July 21st, 2018 → Saturday

Coughing a lot, some drooling but I've also gained back the weight I lost when I was diagnosed.

This disease comes with a lot of machinery to help me breathe and to keep me from choking. One is like a fancy CPAP machine that pushes air into my lungs, synched with my breathing patterns, and the other has different settings that can pull food and gunk out of my throat. Both have saved my life on a few occasions.

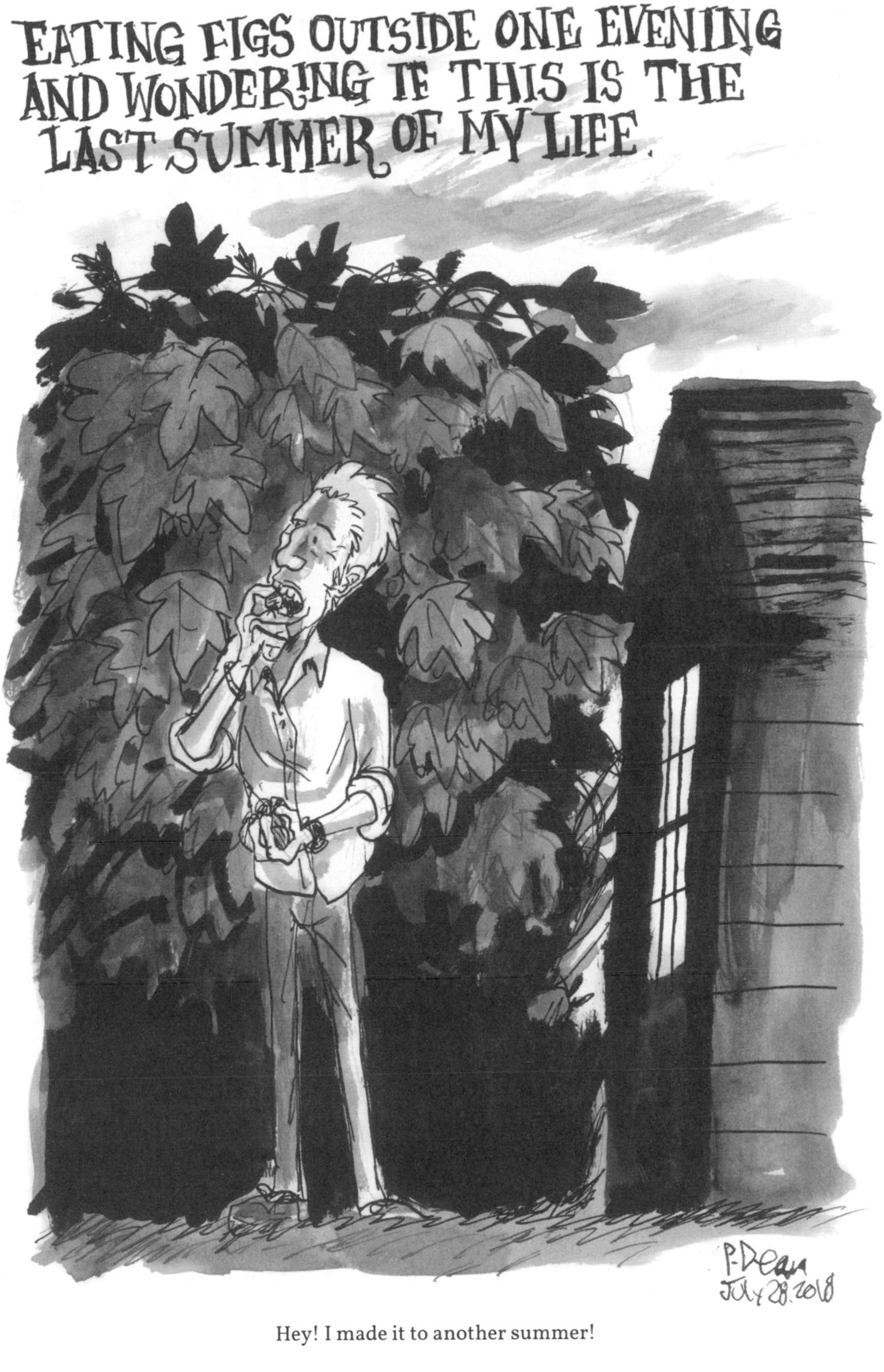
EATING FIGS OUTSIDE ONE EVENING AND WONDERING IF THIS IS THE LAST SUMMER OF MY LIFE.
P-Dean
July 28.2018

Hey! I made it to another summer!

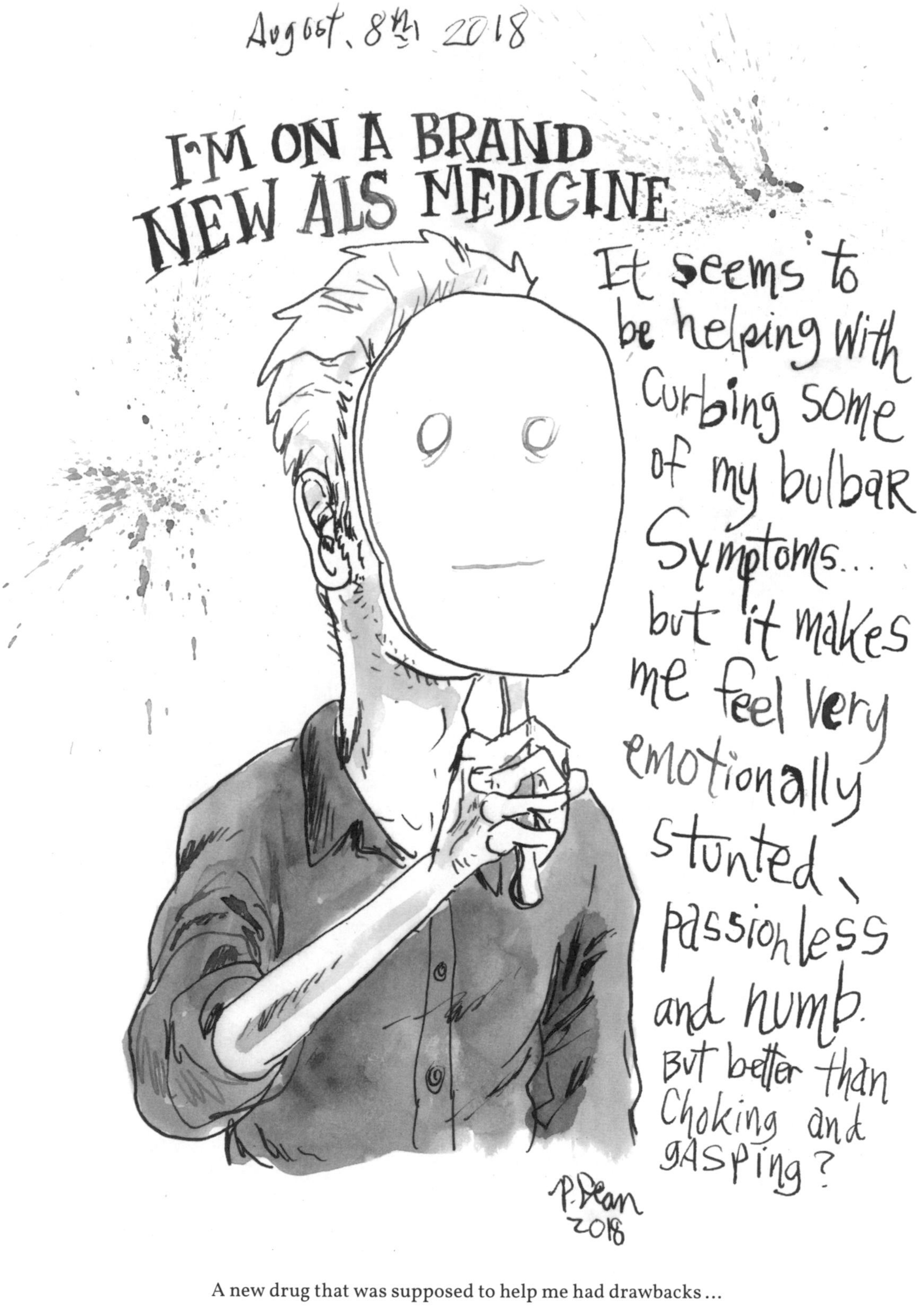
August, 8th, 2018
I'M ON A BRAND NEW ALS MEDICINE
It seems to be helping with curbing some of my bulbar symptoms… but it makes me feel very emotionally stunted, passionless and numb.
But better than choking and gasping?
P. Dean 2018

A new drug that was supposed to help me had drawbacks…

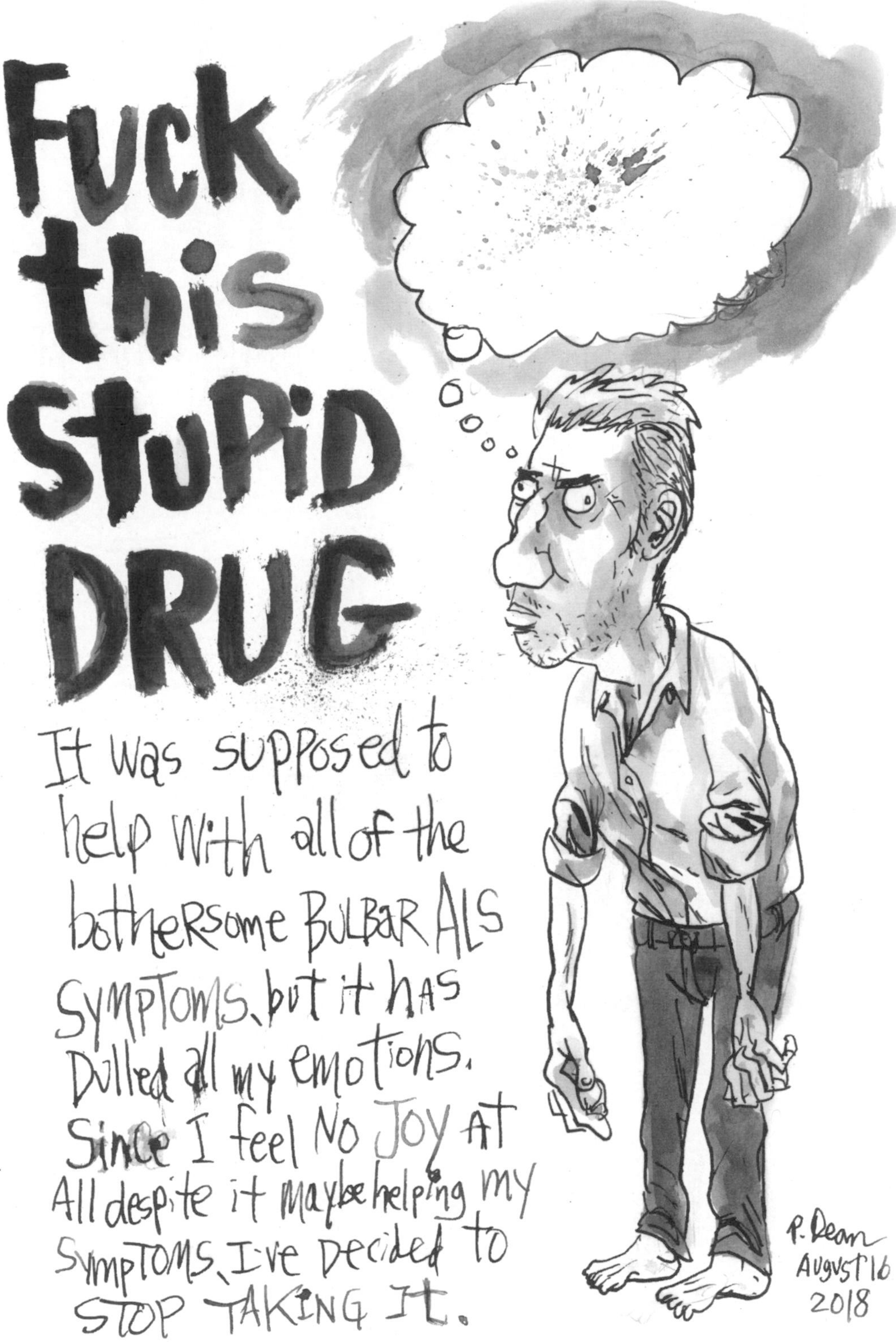
Fuck this Stupid DRUG
It was supposed to help with all of the bothersome BULBAR ALS SYMPTOMS, but it HAS Dulled all my emotions. Since I feel No JOY AT All despite it maybe helping my SYMPTOMS, I've Decided to STOP TAKING IT.
P. Dean August 16 2018

... and I don't regret dropping it. Well, maybe a little bit.

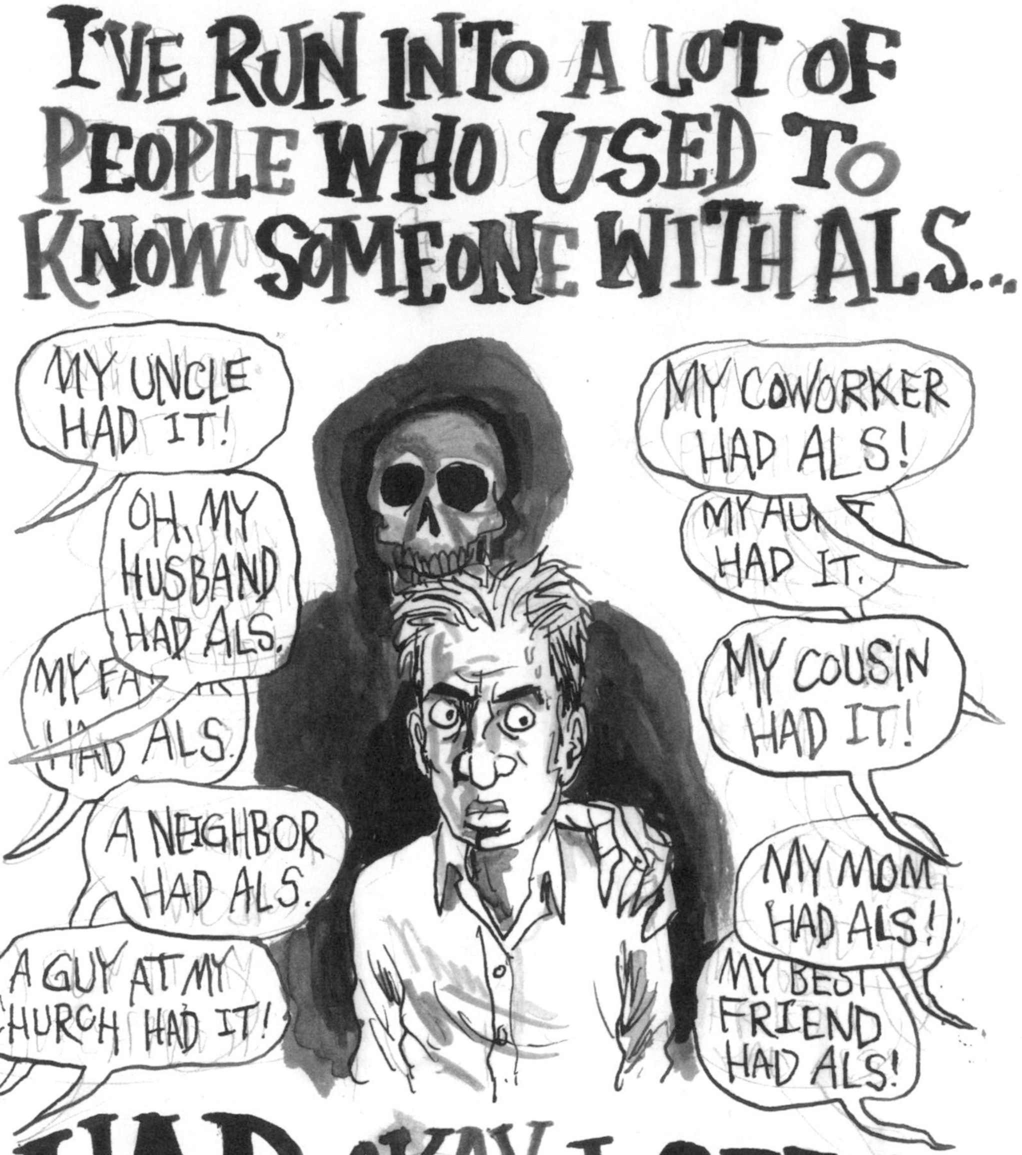
I'VE RUN INTO A LOT OF PEOPLE WHO USED TO KNOW SOMEONE WITH ALS...
MY UNCLE HAD IT!
OH, MY HUSBAND HAD ALS.
HAD ALS.
A NEIGHBOR HAD ALS.
A GUY AT MY CHURCH HAD IT!
MY COWORKER HAD ALS!
HAD IT.
MY COUSIN HAD IT!
MY MOM HAD ALS!
MY BEST FRIEND HAD ALS!
HAD. OKAY, I GET IT. THIS WILL KILL ME.

Pretty much anyone with a "I know someone with ALS" story always talks about that person in the past tense. I've yet to hear anyone tell me, "I know someone with ALS and they're doing great!"

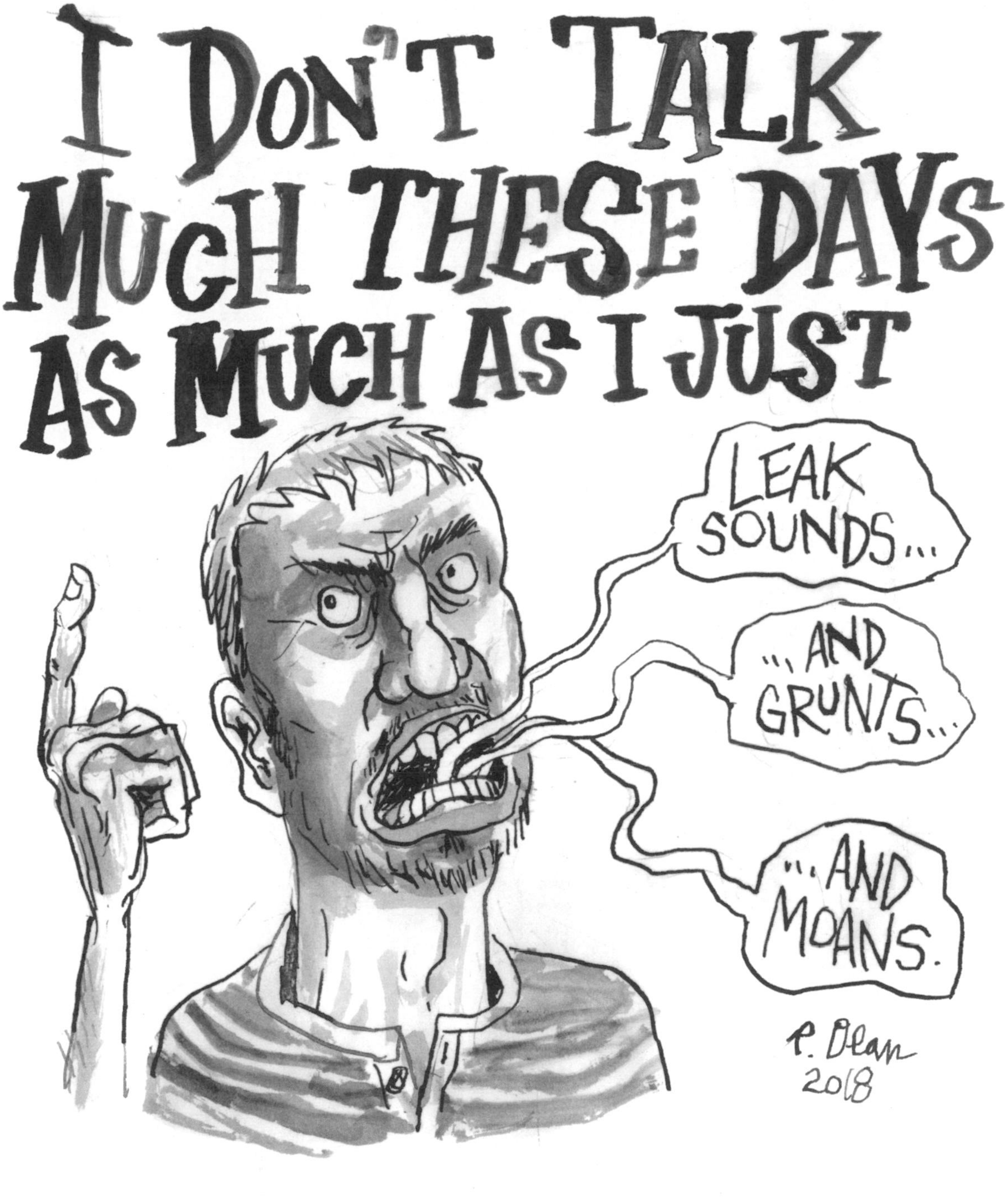
I DON'T TALK MUCH THESE DAYS AS MUCH AS I JUST
LEAK SOUNDS...
...AND GRUNTS...
...AND MOANS.
P. Dean 2018

Speech was the first thing to go. It's been a long time since I've been able to talk my head off. I miss not shutting up and chatting with friends. I miss telling my wife and kids I love them without whispering and gasping. To add insult to injury: Even when I'm trying to keep quiet my chest does something weird, and I blurt out a moan or grunt.

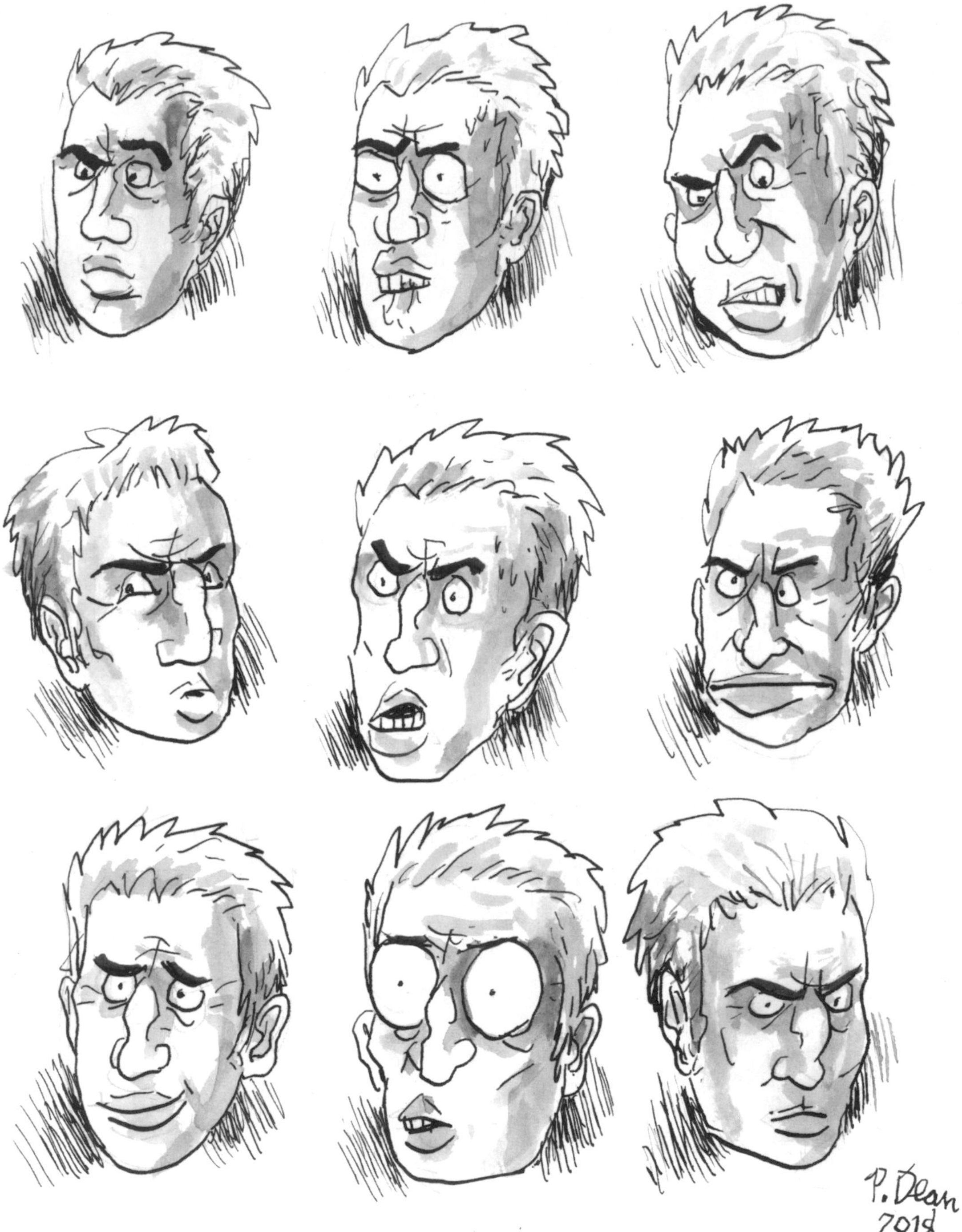
P. Dean
2018

In December of last year, we made the decision to go ahead and have a feeding peg placed in my stomach before I became too weak to have a surgery free of complications. I had never had surgery before, so here's the faces I made while listening to the surgeon describe the procedure to me.

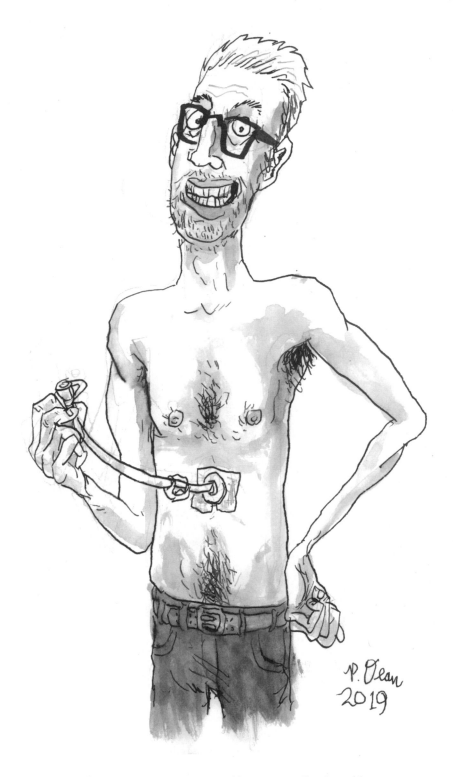

The surgery was a success and it went as well as it could
have gone, but it's still a lot to get used to. It's how I get
all my meals now that my swallowing has declined.

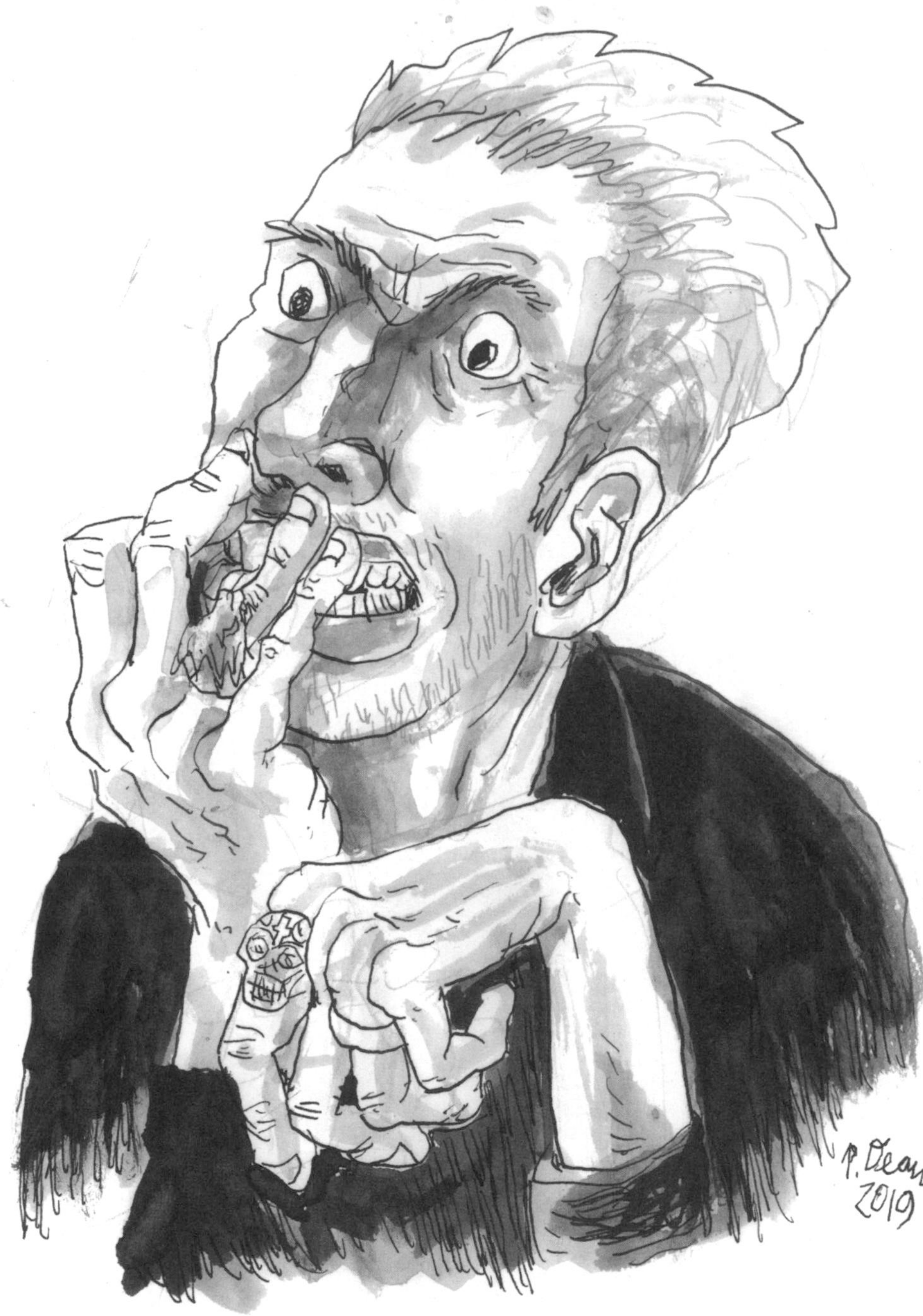
P. Dean
2019

Self-portrait of me trying to get my mouth to work with my hands. It's infuriating that my mouth can't make essential sounds anymore. My wife has had to represent me through phone calls to insurance and medical companies. Even after explaining how I'm unable to talk, they still have to have a verbal confirmation from me that is followed with a series of questions. They're required to do this, but it's humiliating.

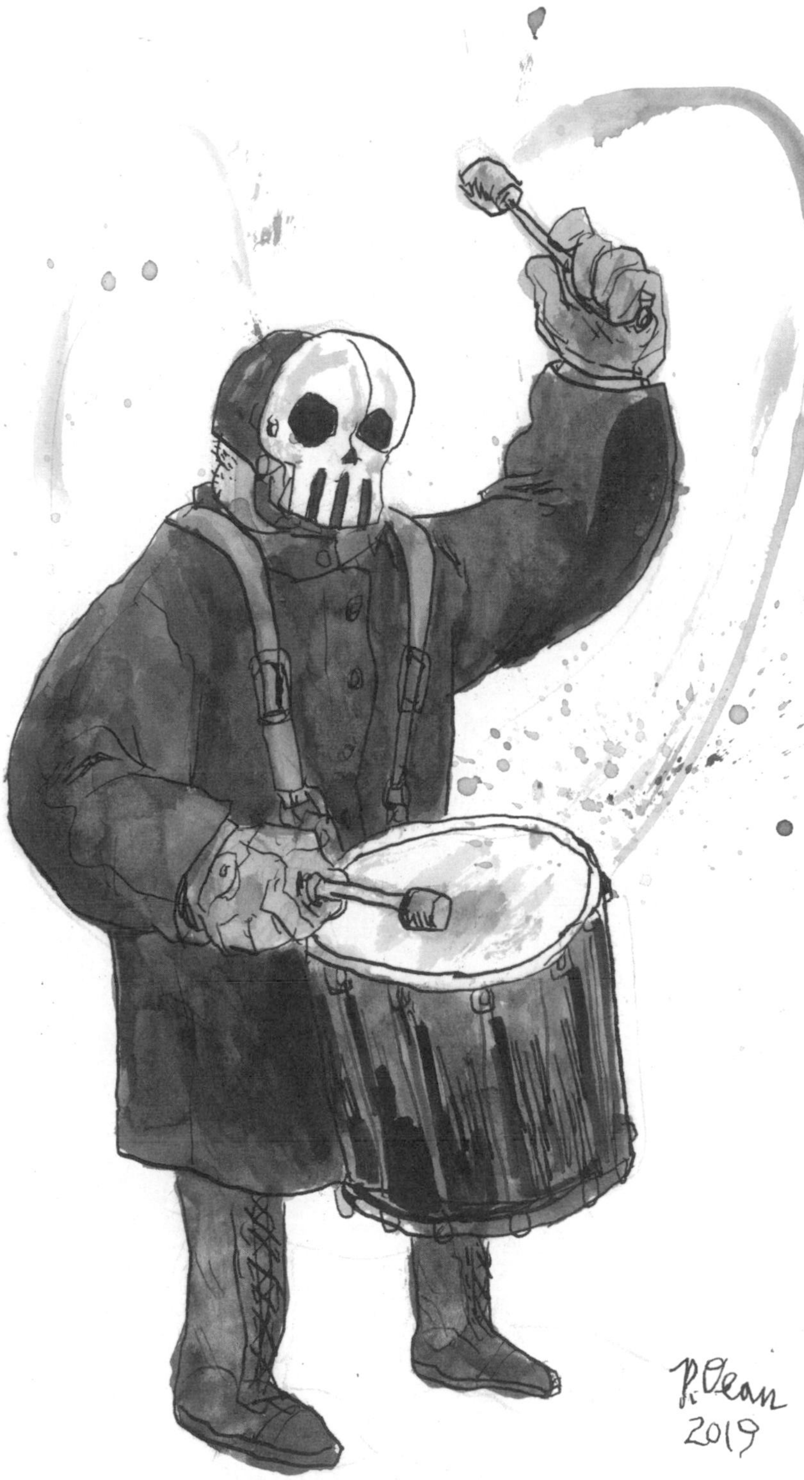
P. Dean
2019

Every time we jump forward and worry about something awful and inevitable in the future, we call that "beating the drum." Sometimes we have to bring these terrible subjects up — but it's wonderful when we don't.

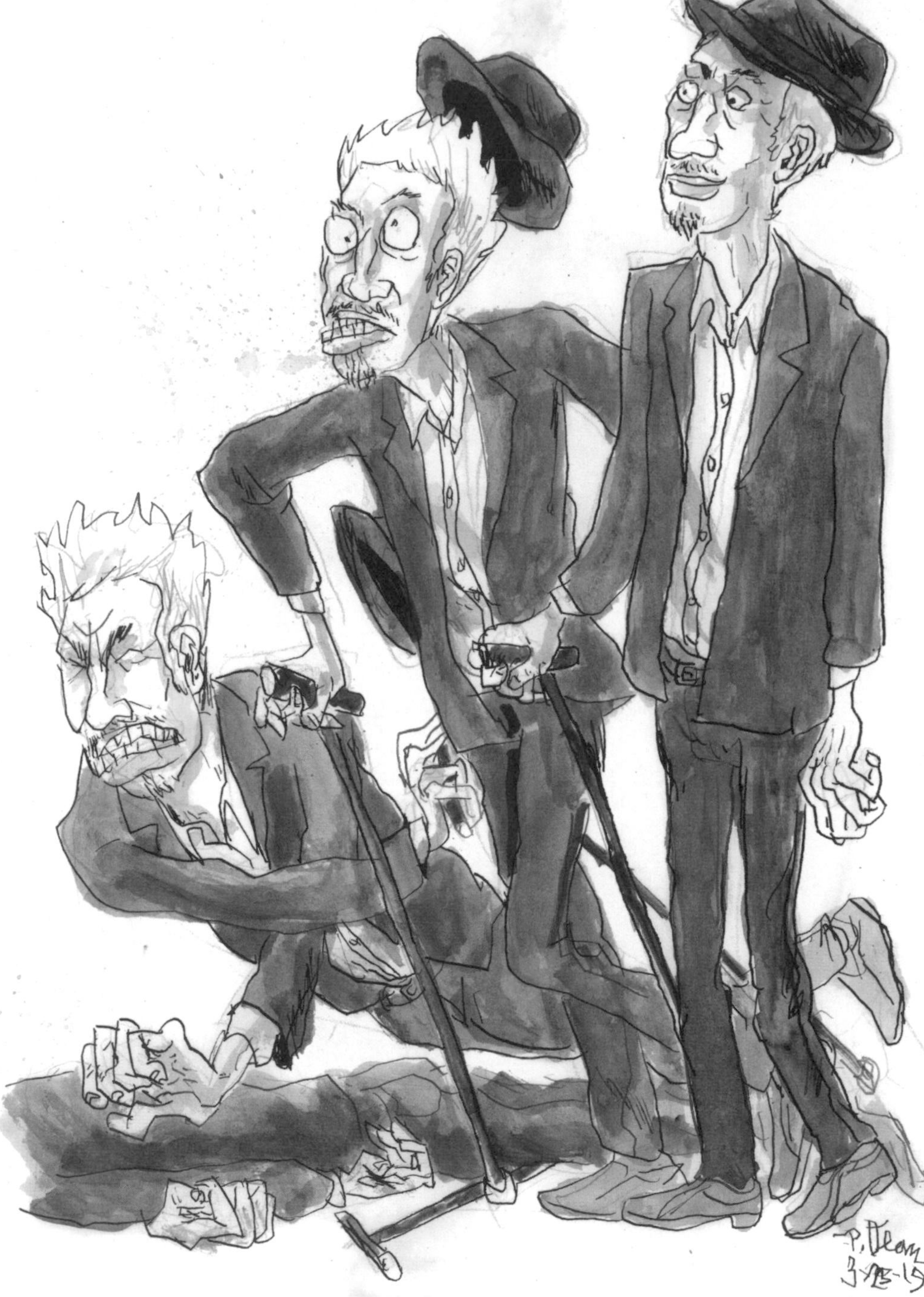

With the disease working its way down my body, my legs have become affected. Weakened muscles mean I'm unsteady when I walk, and I have had some real hard falls lately. It's made me feel less sure of myself and I need a cane at all times.

ONE YEAR AFTER DIAGNOSIS

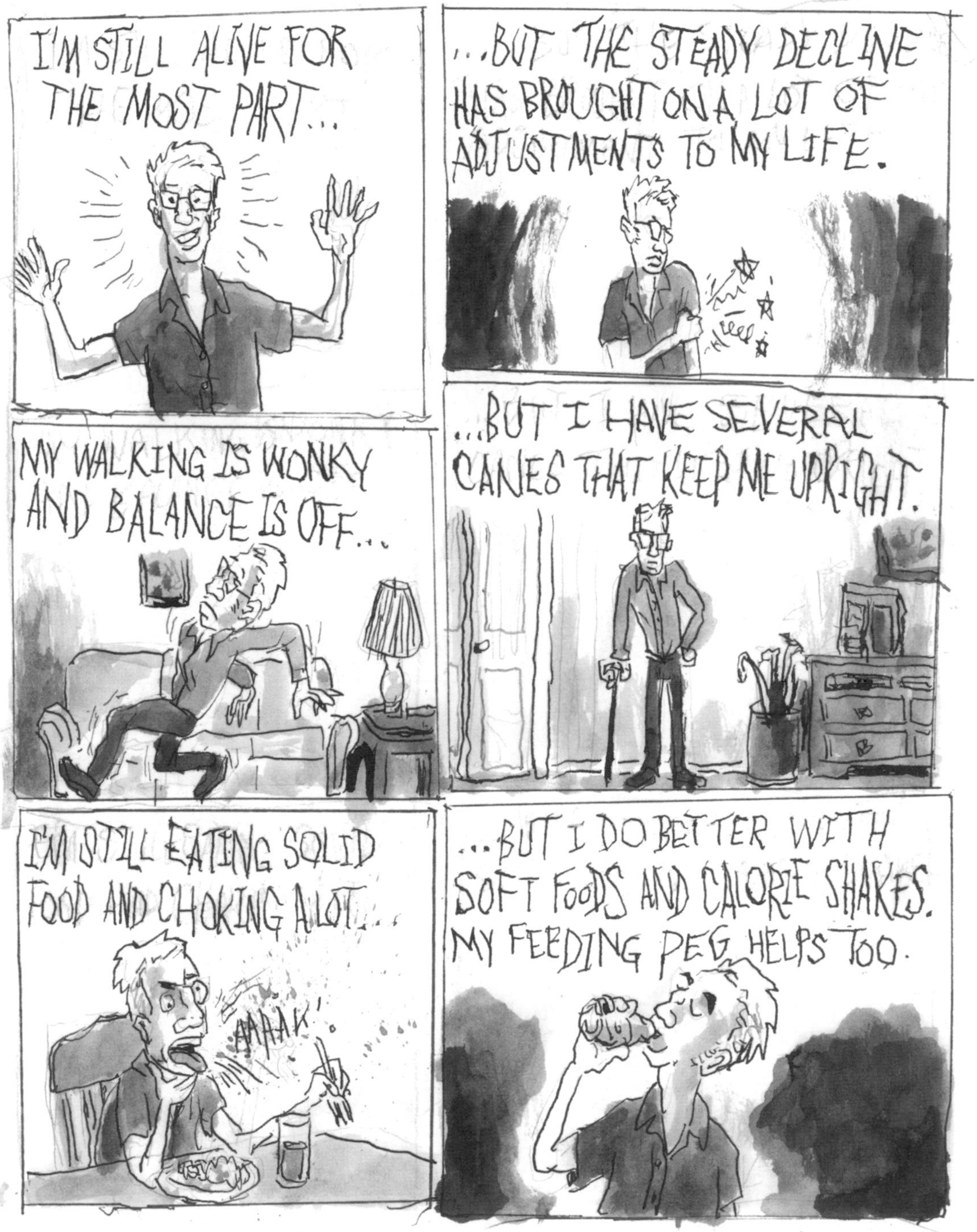

I'M STILL ALIVE FOR THE MOST PART...
...BUT THE STEADY DECLINE HAS BROUGHT ON A LOT OF ADJUSTMENTS TO MY LIFE.
MY WALKING IS WONKY AND BALANCE IS OFF...
...BUT I HAVE SEVERAL CANES THAT KEEP ME UPRIGHT.
I'M STILL EATING SOLID FOOD AND CHOKING A LOT...
...BUT I DO BETTER WITH SOFT FOODS AND CALORIE SHAKES. MY FEEDING PEG HELPS TOO.

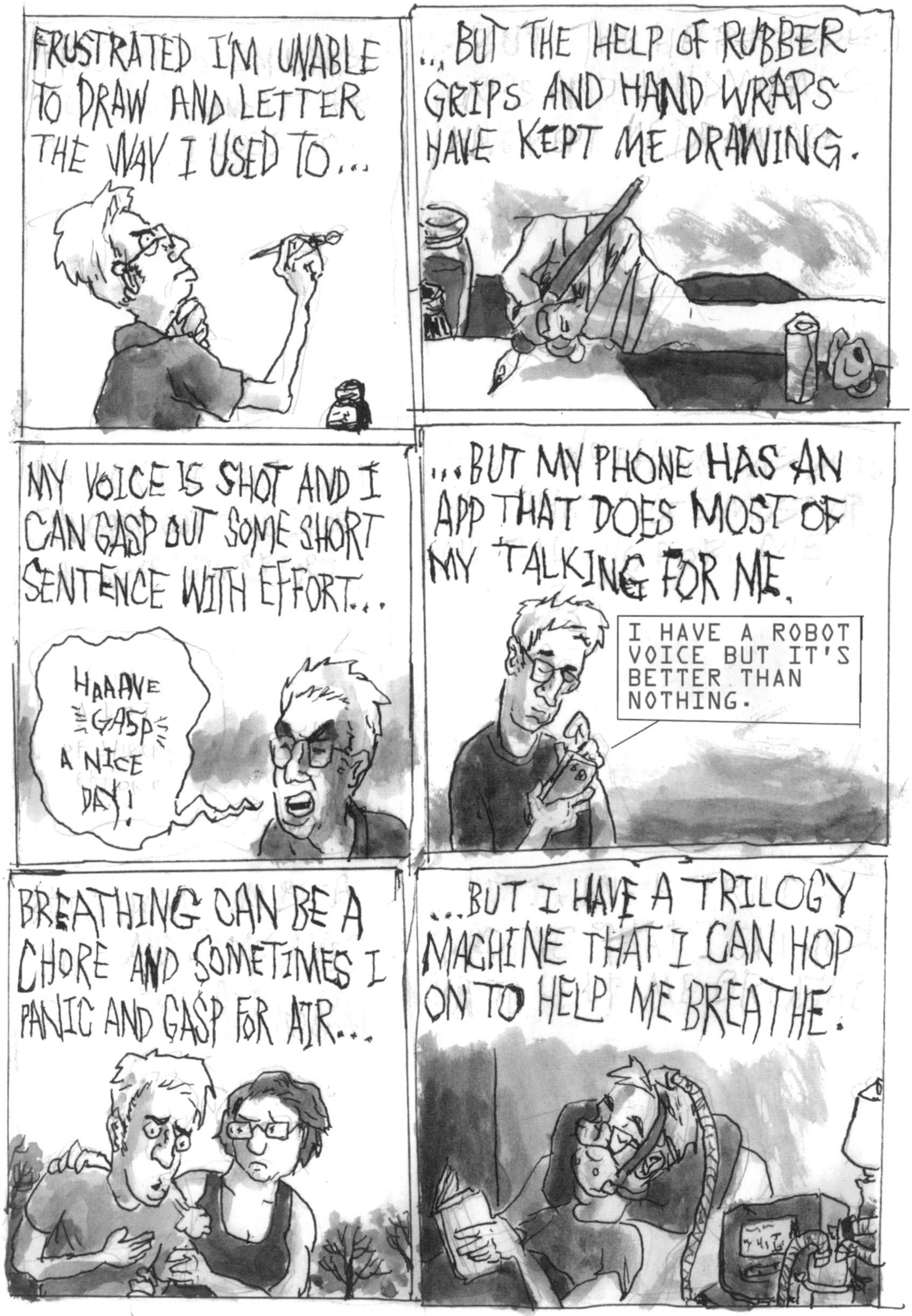
FRUSTRATED I'M UNABLE TO DRAW AND LETTER THE WAY I USED TO...
...BUT THE HELP OF RUBBER GRIPS AND HAND WRAPS HAVE KEPT ME DRAWING.
MY VOICE IS SHOT AND I CAN GASP OUT SOME SHORT SENTENCE WITH EFFORT...
HAAAVE
GASP
A NICE
DAY!
...BUT MY PHONE HAS AN APP THAT DOES MOST OF MY TALKING FOR ME.
I HAVE A ROBOT VOICE BUT IT'S BETTER THAN NOTHING.
BREATHING CAN BE A CHORE AND SOMETIMES I PANIC AND GASP FOR AIR...
...BUT I HAVE A TRILOGY MACHINE THAT I CAN HOP ON TO HELP ME BREATHE.

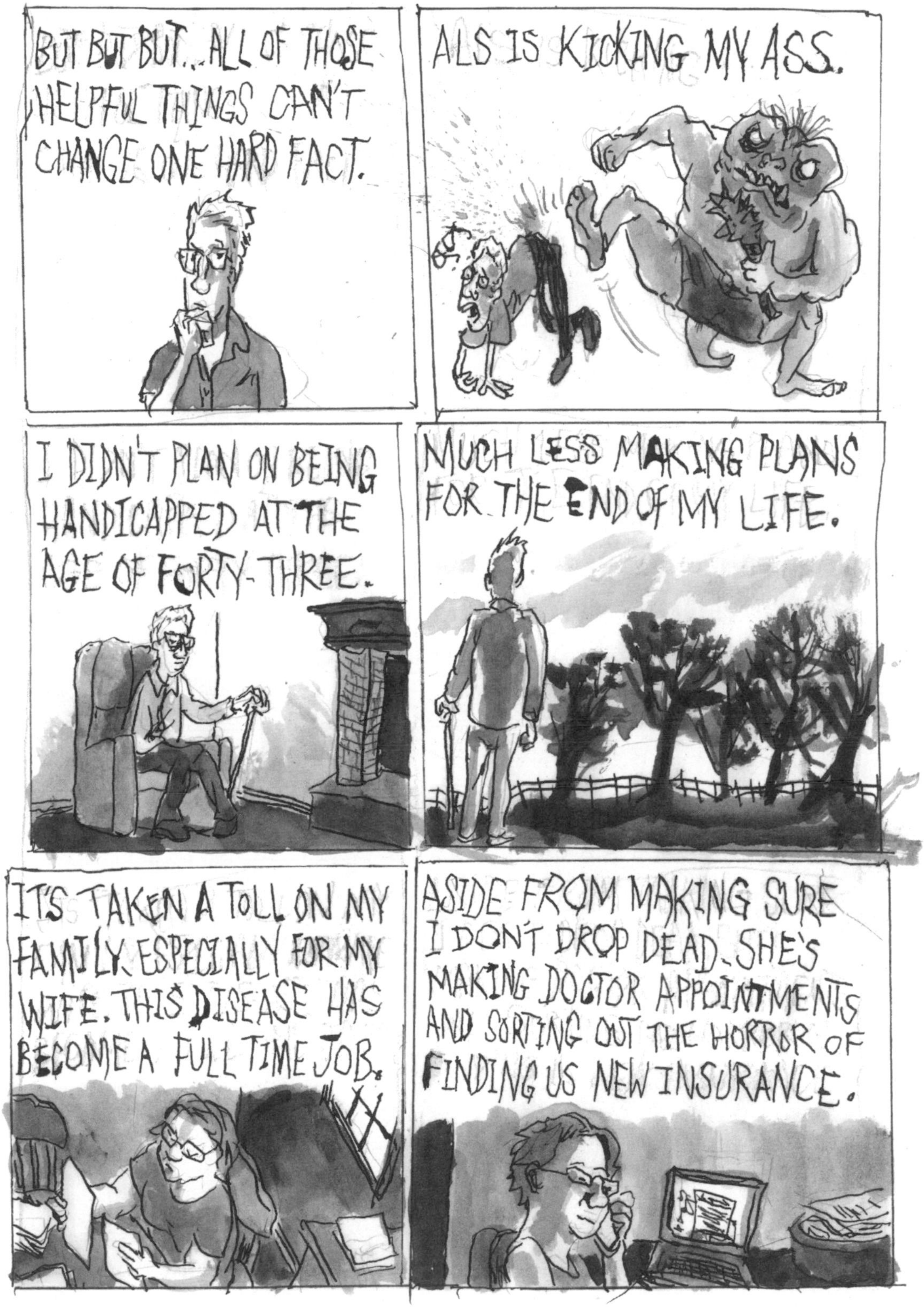
BUT BUT BUT... ALL OF THOSE HELPFUL THINGS CAN'T CHANGE ONE HARD FACT.
ALS IS KICKING MY ASS.
I DIDN'T PLAN ON BEING HANDICAPPED AT THE AGE OF FORTY-THREE.
MUCH LESS MAKING PLANS FOR THE END OF MY LIFE.
IT'S TAKEN A TOLL ON MY FAMILY, ESPECIALLY FOR MY WIFE. THIS DISEASE HAS BECOME A FULL TIME JOB.
ASIDE FROM MAKING SURE I DON'T DROP DEAD, SHE'S MAKING DOCTOR APPOINTMENTS AND SORTING OUT THE HORROR OF FINDING US NEW INSURANCE.

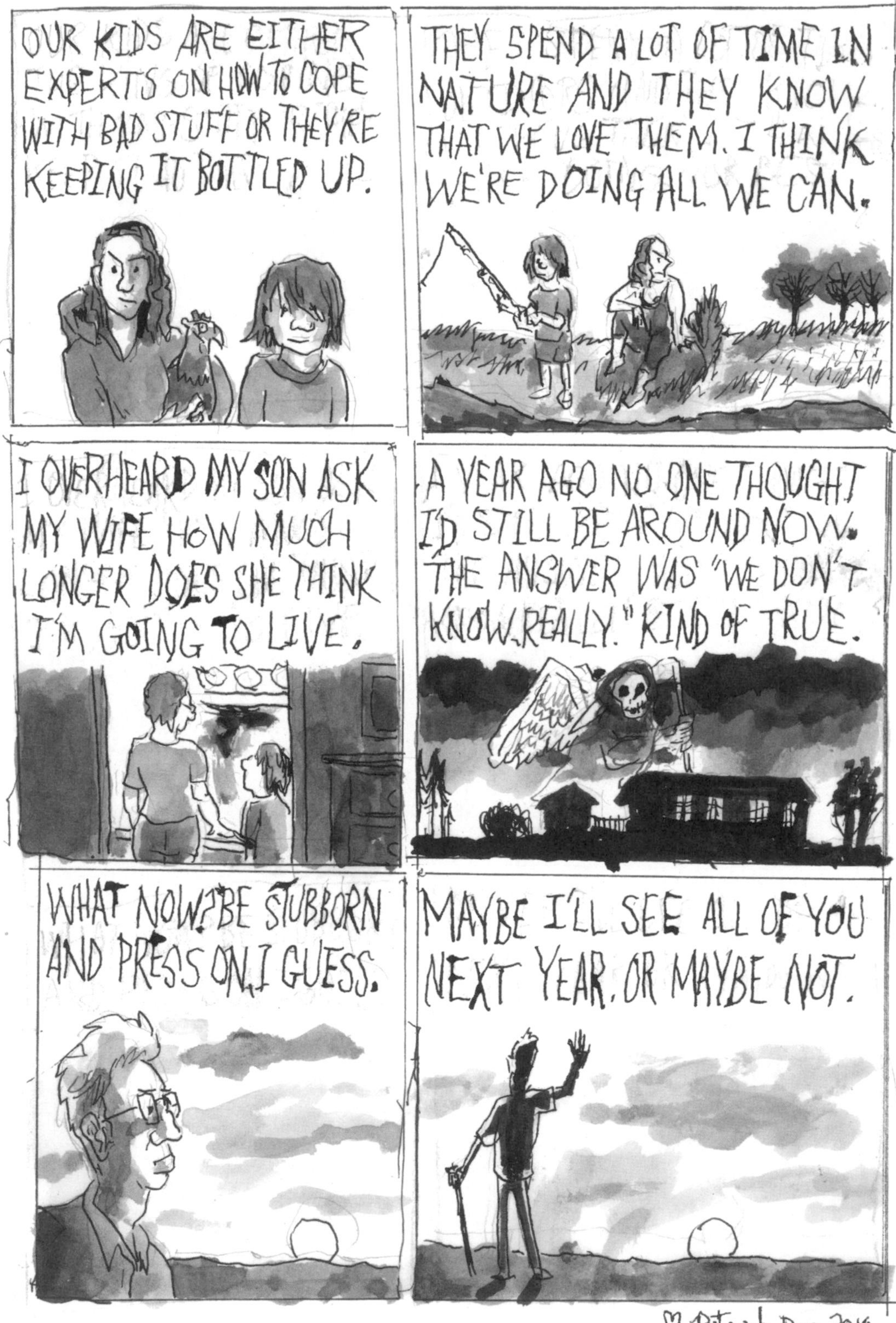
OUR KIDS ARE EITHER EXPERTS ON HOW TO COPE WITH BAD STUFF OR THEY'RE KEEPING IT BOTTLED UP.
THEY SPEND A LOT OF TIME IN NATURE AND THEY KNOW THAT WE LOVE THEM. I THINK WE'RE DOING ALL WE CAN.
I OVERHEARD MY SON ASK MY WIFE HOW MUCH LONGER DOES SHE THINK I'M GOING TO LIVE.
A YEAR AGO NO ONE THOUGHT I'D STILL BE AROUND NOW. THE ANSWER WAS "WE DON'T KNOW, REALLY." KIND OF TRUE.
WHAT NOW? BE STUBBORN AND PRESS ON, I GUESS.
MAYBE I'LL SEE ALL OF YOU NEXT YEAR, OR MAYBE NOT.
♡ - Patrick Dean 2019

FANTAGRAPHICS
ICONIC COMICS COLLECTIONS
World-Class Reprints For Readers From The Casual To The Completist

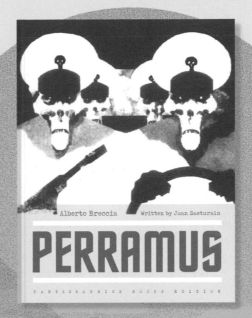

Perramus
By Alberto Breccia
and Juan Sasturain

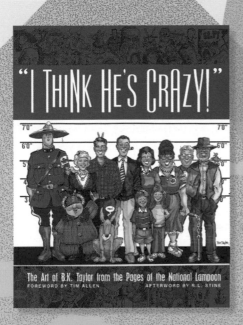

"I Think He's Crazy": The Art
of B.K. Taylor from the Pages
of *the National Lampoon*
By B.K. Taylor

Streets of Paris, Streets of Murder:
The Complete Noir Stories
of Manchette & Tardi Vol. 1
By Jean-Patrick Manchette and Tardi

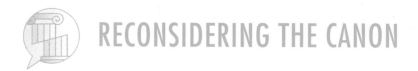

Blankets and *Late Bloomer*

Sloane Leong

WHENEVER CRAIG THOMPSON'S *Blankets* is mentioned in critical conversation, it's often with an especially reverent and knowing nod. Praise ensues, full of words like "masterpiece" and "real literature." The spot *Blankets* has maintained in the Western comics canon has always been confusing to me. Of course, there's lovely, lush ink work and nicely flowing compositions at play — but not nearly enough to compensate for how surface-y and saccharine this fall-from-grace teen romance narrative is. For a 582-page book, it feels like I've read the same four scenes over and over again: sad in the snow, horny in the snow, horny in (someone's) parents' house, religious repression. Maybe I'm being an ungenerous reader, but the praise that continues to be lavished on this 16-year-old memoir feels unstinting to the point of absurdity.

One of the biggest problems I have with the comic is Thompson's shifting point of view and the voice he uses to talk to the reader. This is a 20-something adult's memoir, but it lacks the richness and depth of matured retrospection and often falls back into a child's perspective when convenient. *Blankets* doesn't feel like a meditation on the past but a rosy abbreviation, sanded smooth of actual introspection. When we follow Thompson as a young adult visiting or writing to his first girlfriend, Raina, his inner thoughts are simple surface connections, strangely basic and childlike, as if we're still stuck with the adolescent Thompson on the first page. This could be how he really is, or it could be just be a lack of honesty. Fiction and truth aside, *Blankets* is painfully thin, repetitive and worse, without reflection. Narrating over a childhood memory of learning about heaven, adult Thompson tells the reader, "At that moment I knew what I wanted ... I wanted Heaven."

That's the revelation? You want a good thing and not a bad thing? Even if this was your actual thought as a child, can I at least get a picture painted of how you felt? No, we just get some anemic, puffy clouds.

At that moment,
I knew what I wanted...
I wanted Heaven.

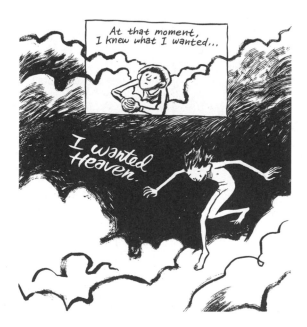

ABOVE: from Craig Thompson's 2003 graphic memoir, *Blankets*.

OPPOSITE: The protagonist's vision of Raina, as depicted in *Blankets*.

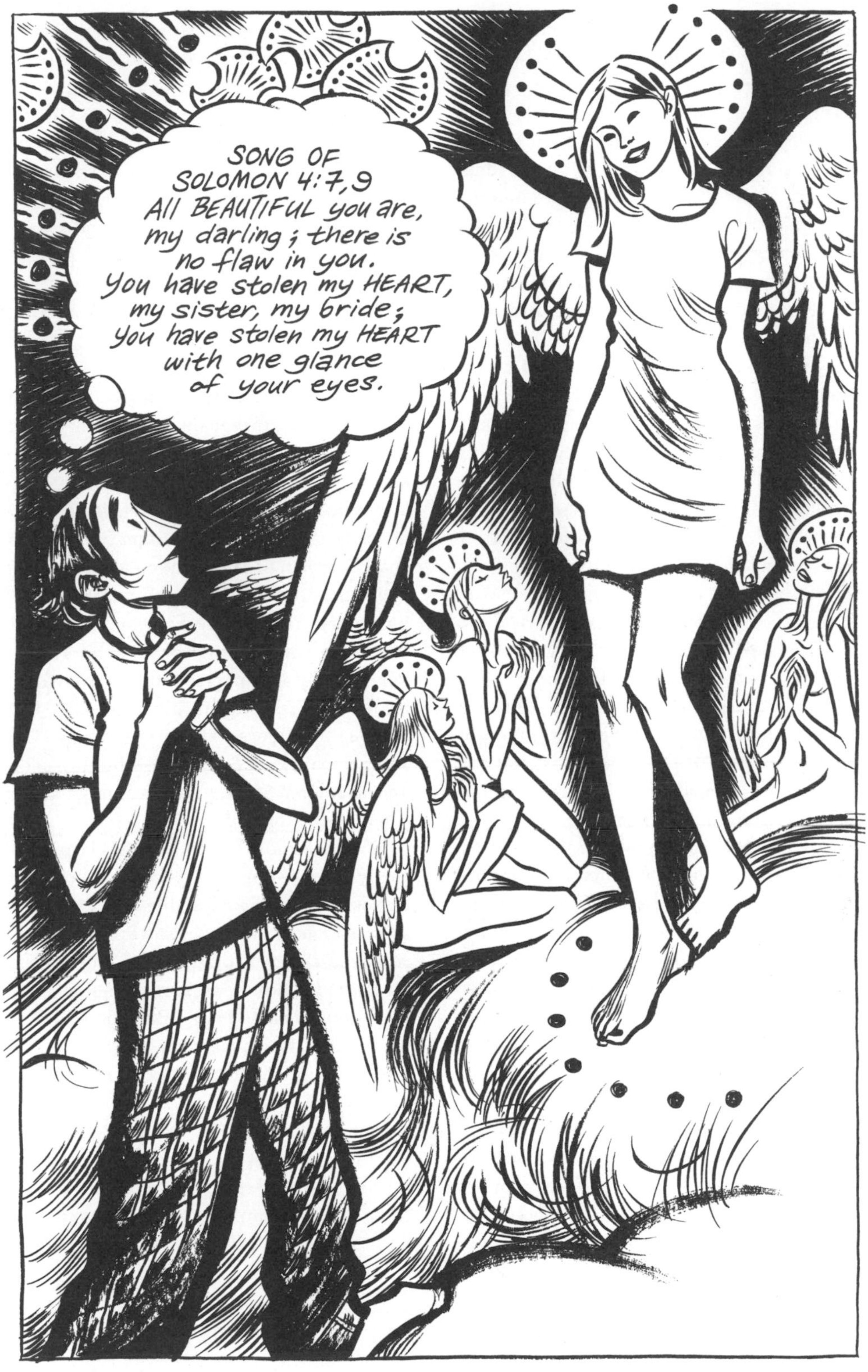
SONG OF SOLOMON 4:7,9 All BEAUTIFUL you are, my darling; there is no flaw in you. You have stolen my HEART, my sister, my bride; You have stolen my HEART with one glance of your eyes.

Well, can I get some narrated insight reflecting on this pivotal moment that shaped him? No? O...K? This pretense of introspection gradually gets worse. Later in the story, Thompson's character whips out Plato's cave allegory when confronted with Raina's autonomy as a human being and not as his personal romantic object — and it's pathetically ostentatious. There is a lack of connective tissue between incidents. Romance and religion and abuse also come off as unexamined — then are left purposefully ambiguous, especially considering much of the story is overpowered by the comprehensive parallels of his sexual perspective on Raina, their relationship and things he's read in the Bible.

In the first quarter of the book, Thompson tells us he was only "half-committed" to his faith and at this point, he also feels half-committed to telling us the truth of his story, at least a truth not sanded down by ego. One way this is manifested is in the attention he gives to any characters besides himself; it's perfunctory at best. His parents and fellow church attendees are all caricatured cutouts, fanatical terrors or two-dimensional shadows lacking any emotional depth. His schoolmates suffer Thompson's same self-obsessed disinterest, sketching the bare impression of human beings. This depiction might work if this was supposed to be comedic or satirical; but it's meant to be Thompson's life, his truth, and so it comes off egocentric and disingenuous.

Raina's personality is given more intimate attention and her carefully rendered and complex home life breaks the mold, but his pubescent obsession framing her is cloying and obnoxious. "Thus, I found my muse," he tells us as they begin writing to one another until — as is tradition — he guiltily succumbs to masturbating (for the first time!) to one of the letters, his cutely outlined ejaculate drawn in sacred isolation. His obsession with Raina as a maternal angel and romantic savior ("I studied her...aware that she'd been crafted by a DIVINE ARTIST. Sacred. Perfect. Unknowable.") and drawing connections between things in her proximity and scripture is overwrought and banal. After their first topless tryst, Thompson draws a portrait of Jesus cheesily smiling down upon their make-out session. Later we get the same imagery of them making out while small-titted angels hold them aloft from the hungry, grasping demons waiting below them in Hell.

Despite these dramatic but unimaginative compositions of biblical elements constantly in orbit around his teen heartthrob and sexual urges, Thompson denies the potentiality in his own story by vastly overestimating the profundity of his own teenage horniness. Over and over, the story shies away from sharing the real meat of his experiences and pulls away from sharing reaction or understanding the current narrator has now. We don't get insight into why he burns everything Raina gives him. We don't get insight into his sexual abuse and how that affected his view of his parents, his sexuality, or his spirituality even though it's depicted as life-altering for him ("I wanted to burn my memories"). Not to mention how the abuse affected his little brother — which was probably the most poignant and impactful memory shared in the book — but is somehow glossed over and ignored for the most part. In fact, Thompson doesn't engage with his younger brother or his abuse at all — except to say he vaguely felt bad for it on one page in a clinical, distanced way ("I neglected my protective role in dangerous situations"). Then the brother disappears until the very end. The only things not clumsily summarized in this sprawling memoir is his overwhelming virginal arousal, so vapidly and thoroughly explored, all to its detriment. Thompson's story remains not just shallow but full of cowardice, and no amount of competent technique and creativity can make up for that.

There're many memoir comics I can think of that easily deserve *Blankets*' place in the canon that haven't been given their full due, like long-form comics *A Chinese Life* by Li Kunwu and Philippe Ôtié, or *Disappearance Diary* by Hideo Azuma. This goes especially for short-form memoir comics (some existing only digitally), by cartoonists like Jane Mai, Annie Mok, Kris Mukai, Laura Park, Sophia Foster-Dimino and Carta Monir, which are often overlooked due to their brevity and format.

For my money, I'd love to see *Late Bloomer* by Maré Odomo take a spot in the comics canon. Maré Odomo is a Seattle-based cartoonist probably best known for their series of comic strips *Letters to an Absent Father*, and their comic collections *Internet Comics 1* and *2*.

OPPOSITE: From Maré Odomo's 2016 book of comics/poetry, *Late Bloomer*.

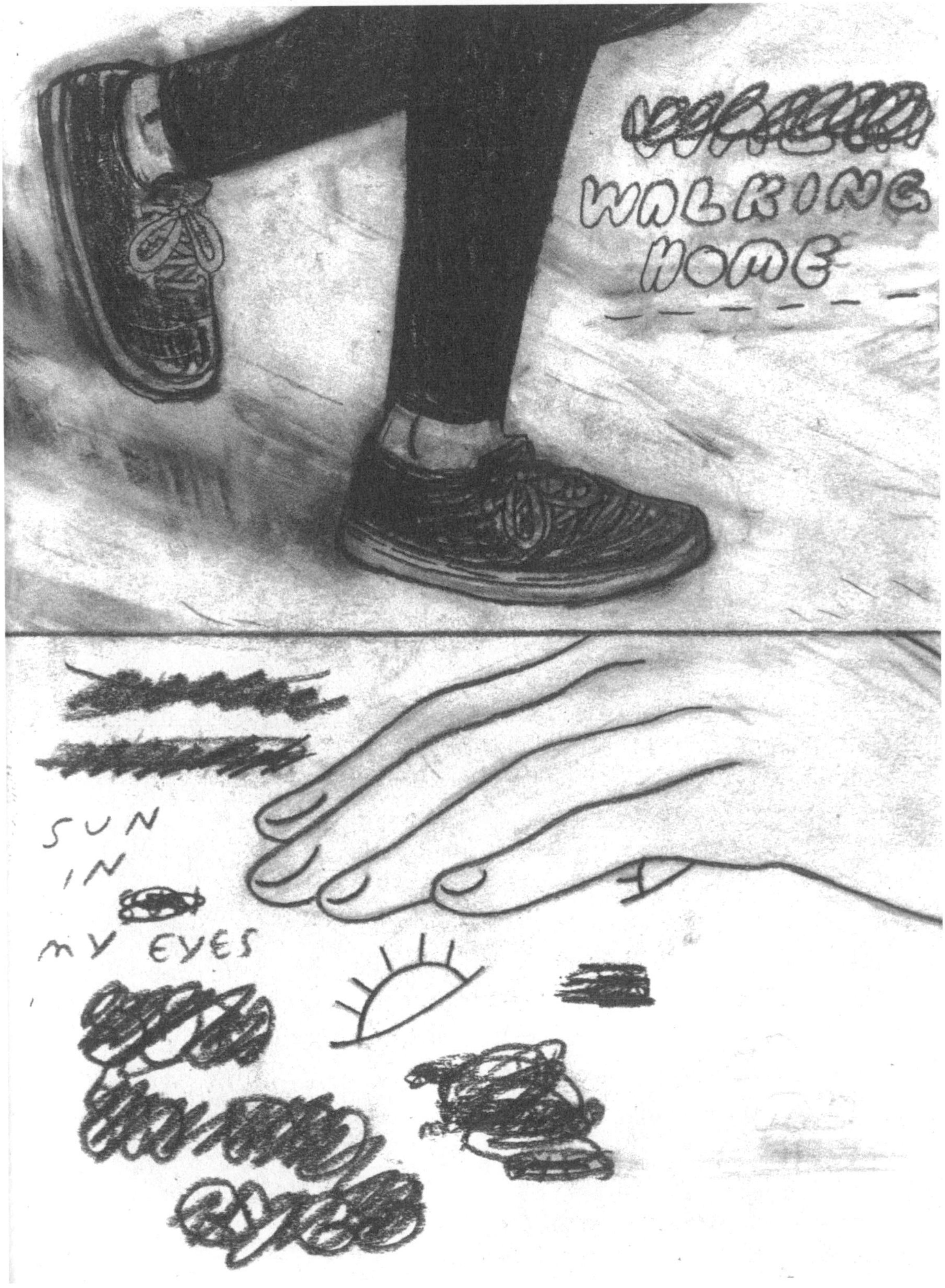
WALKING
HOME
SUN
IN
MY EYES

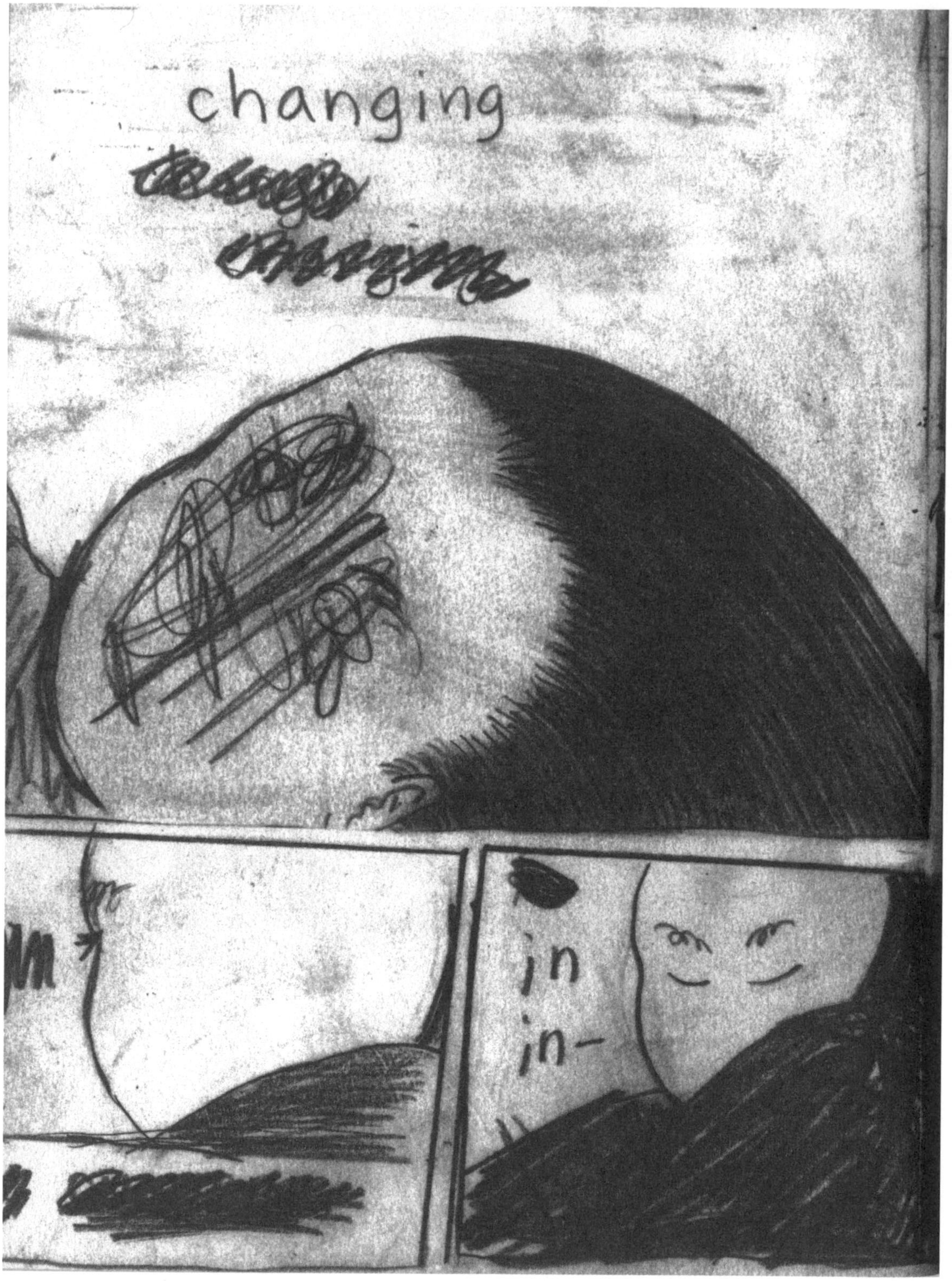
changing
in
in-

Late Bloomer is an understated, 104-page black-and-white comics/poetry book that fits neatly into my back pocket but delivers 1,000 times its weight in silly, solemn pathos. The raw pencil work displayed here is so rich and lustrous, it feels as if it's going to rub off onto your fingers. The tactility of the pages harmonizes with Odomo's penchant for concise narration, sometimes jotted down, scribbled into unreadable black blotches, blown up and outlined or scratched into the page with such passion that even the shortest phrase arrests the eye and demands the weight of your inner voice as you read.

    Late Bloomer is romantically elliptical but not obtuse. Melancholic imagery fragments and melts into dreamy metaphor while the words remain earnest, a touch self-deprecating and a touch mocking. There is no pretension here, just a raw eye, critical of indulgence but still compassionate to former selves. We're drawn into memories of the past and see Odomo caricatured down into the most basic of shapes or rendered with a careful, unsatisfied hand. Every mark and smudge is a crucial blueprint to Odomo's process, mapping out the messy work of introspection and guiding us through a tangle of sensation and memory. There is also a distance created by the erasures, the succinct imagery and compositions, and the terse narration that I find becomes a healthy boundary, a structure that bypasses pretension while maintaining whatever privacy is needed for the author. Those boundaries say more than the artifice of a self-absorbed author ever could. ❀

OPPOSITE: From Maré Odomo's 2016 book of comics/poetry, *Late Bloomer.*

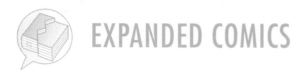

Comics / Collage / Appropriation

Kim Jooha

LONG BEFORE LICHTENSTEIN, the relationships among fine art, appropriation, collage and comics were deeply rooted. In fact, the superhero genre is inherently a work of appropriation — not only "swipes," but the same characters are rebooted again and again by different creators. It is their basic mode of production. Some of the best comics/fine artists' practices are based on these techniques. Across the Pacific Ocean, cartoonist Shigeru Sugiura played with not only iconographies of American mainstream comics but also his own works, which he redrew and republished. Even before and well after the heyday of pop art, many fine artists with an appreciation for the medium were fascinated by the possibilities, such as Jess, Joe Brainard, Öyvind Fahlström, Guy Debord and the Situationist International, Hypergraphics and Ray Yoshida (who mentored several Hairy Who artists).

I'm not the only one making the argument that collage/appropriation and comics have similarities. In the '70s, the French Bazooka Collectif created collage/appropriation art and published it comics magazines, and made controversial contributions to the newspaper *Liberation*. Fine artists, such as Max Ernst, have been interpolated into the comics canon. In 2013's *The Elements of Painting*, Aidan Koch divides famous paintings into panels and shows that they can be read as comics. Comics can be thought of as collages of images (and often words). They need not be rigidly gridded, like they are in Europe or America. The form can be freer and more expressionistic, like shojo manga.

This is because collage and comics are discrete, discontinuous, heterogeneous, modular and

MEMORIES
SHOOT OFF
LIKE FIREWORKS
IN
MAGUA'S
MIND.

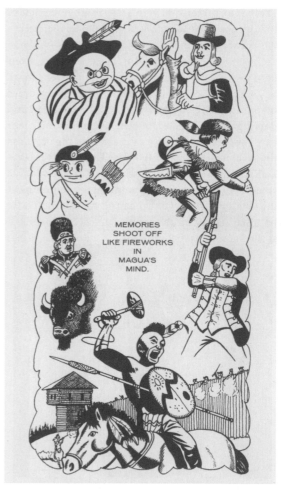

A panel from Shigeru Sugiura's *The Last of the Mohicans*, 1973–1974.

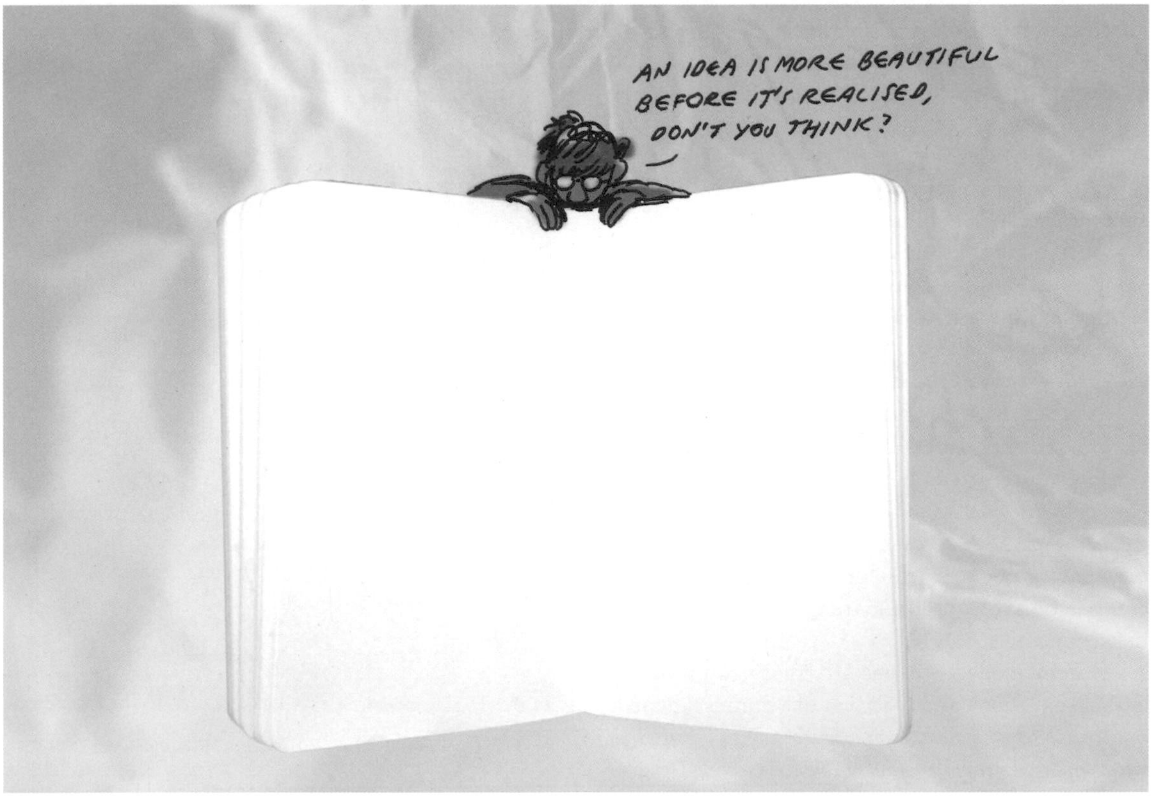
AN IDEA IS MORE BEAUTIFUL
BEFORE IT'S REALISED,
DON'T YOU THINK?

Disa Wallander in *Now: The New Comics Anthology* #6, 2019.

combinatorial. They both have two layers: surface appearance (page) and the underlying source (panel). In both cases, the ontology of the original images, including space, time, medium and method, disappear. As Guy Debord said in *A User's Guide to Détournement*: "When two objects are brought together, no matter how far apart from their original contexts may be, a relationship is always formed." For example, Disa Wallander incorporates different materials and techniques — such as photography, drawing, watercolor and gouache — on the same plane. Marc Bell's "stacked" drawings and comics (for example: "Gustun On These Layers of the Ea_th" from *Hot Potatoe*) translate his mixed media onto the drawing's plane and shows different perspectives of an object.

These two levels of discreteness, modularity, heterogeneity and discontinuity — in addition to the flat space — explains why comics are the medium best suited to collage/appropriation. Patrick Kyle's oeuvre, especially 2018's *Roaming Foliage*, exploits these discrete, modular, heterogeneous, discontinuous and flat spaces perfectly. Kyle's space is "composite," according to digital culture theorist Lev Manovich. Instead of coherent space, a lot of distinct objects composite (are collaged to create) the discrete and heterogeneous space. The narrative is propagated by space, and characters mainly react to space. Space is not just a background, but the character, narrative and conflict. Eli Howey also utilizes this discreteness, modularity, heterogeneity and discontinuity in their 2018 book *Fluorescent Mud*. It represents the sensation of bodily dissociation and mediation with the environment by hybridizing discontinuous and discrete objects and space-times that do not belong to one another.

It is not a coincidence that maturation of newspaper strips occurred around the same time as the dadaist movement and surrealist collages, in addition to cubist and futurist painting and chrono-photography. They were all part of the new Modernist movement that rebelled against the European visual arts tradition of the single viewpoint and continuous space-time.

Drawing inside a panel can also be a collage. The artificial bold lines distinguish every object one another, especially the character and background. Its flatness differentiates it from the three dimensions of cinema and photography, and traditional European paintings. The latter yearns for illusion and simulation of the world, but comics are inherently representational. The latter lives in the continuous space (and time), but comics are the medium of the discontinuous spacetime. Comics artists have been exploiting that since the early days of comics. George Herriman's background in *Krazy Kat*'s dramatically changes every panel, but the reader does not perceive the discrepancy of the space-time.

Another critical development that enabled the birth of comics and collage is mass reproduction. Comics were created for newspapers, which also present their information about different spacetimes in the same plane. We could even argue that the newspaper's graphic design — grids, panels and hybrid compositions of words and images — influenced the birth of comics.

Many collages — especially those composed of databases — look and read just like comics: Eduardo Paolozzi's *Moonstrips Empire News*, *Universal Electronic Vacuum*, *Zero Energy Experiment Pile* and *General Dynamic F.U.N.*; Database-collages like Sol LeWitt's photography, Marcel Broodthaers, Hanne Darboven, Char Esme's *Queasy's*, Sean Tejaratchi's *Craphound*, Jochen Gerner's *Contre la Bande Dessinée*, some *Superstructure* issues and collections of drawings, like Saul Steinberg's books, Al Columbia's *Pim & Francie*, Hokusai and the zines of Ginette Lapalme.

Many talented comics artists are innovating with these forms. d.w. creates recursive comics utilizing the principle; Aeon Mute (of the Canadian micropress ddoogg) works with science's symbolic language and images. Ilan Manouach's use of works like *Maus* and *Tintin* to criticize the ideology behind seemingly apolitical technologies like color and formats of comics production and distribution (see *The Comics Journal* #304 for more); the aforementioned Gerner and Francesc Ruiz employ it to reveal the hidden violence and homoerotic desire respectively in mainstream comics; *Hellberta*, by Michael Comeau, examines contemporary Canadian identity with Wolverine imagery and various narratives and techniques; Finally, Julie Doucet's *Carpet Sweeper Tales* humorously exploits its properties (for example, the repeated use of original image) and subverts the gender dynamics of photo novella/fumetti, itself a medium of collage.

I SURE OF Your Merit
CONSOLIDATED CEMENT,,,,
BU T ...
" "
DONUT ! LOOKING
HERE now , E-Z .

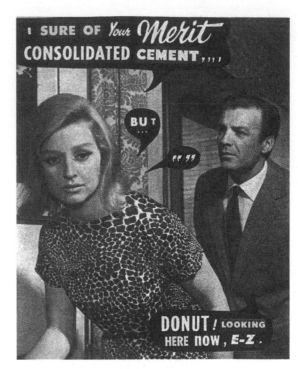

ABOVE: From Julie Doucet's 2016 *Carpet Sweeper Tales*.

OPPOSITE: By Samplerman, circa 2016.

Samplerman's hundreds of collage-comics/pattern of Golden Age comics could only be possible in the time of Tumblr. To have access to gigabytes (or even terabytes) of Golden Age archives online, to download them on one's personal computer, collage them in various patterns with image processing applications like Photoshop, post hundreds of them freely on your website, and have them distributed to a worldwide audience with high-speed bandwidth in their own hands, could not happen until the 2010s. The vernacular comics of the post-digital (i.e., the age of the smartphone and social media), the meme, is appropriation, too. Memes point toward where comics — a medium that's always thrived on technological innovation — can go. These are the comics of the 21st century.

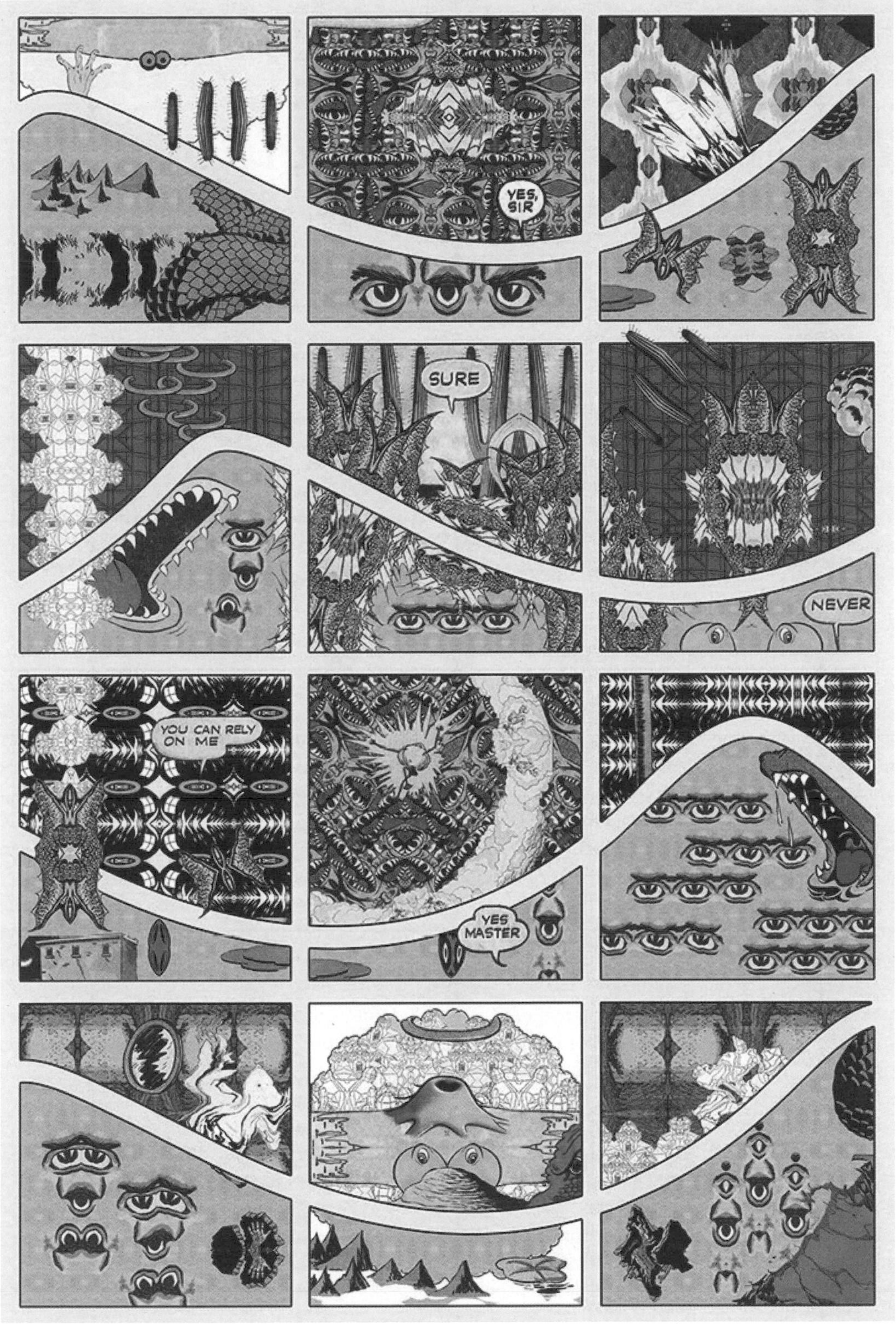
YES, SIR
SURE
NEVER
YOU CAN RELY ON ME
YES MASTER

The Story of the Development of an Independent Political Movement on the County Level

Aaron Dixon

IN THE SUMMER OF 1967, I found myself sitting in the Garfield High School auditorium in Seattle with my friends and brothers, listening to a fiery, inspiring speech. The speaker was none other than Stokely Carmichael, the national coordinator for the Student Nonviolent Coordinating Committee (SNCC). He had been speaking across the country, with H. Rap Brown — also a national coordinator for SNCC — about a new kind of power. A power we black people did not know about. And that power was black power, because black people at that time had no real power over the conditions of their lives. The words "black power" sounded so beautiful, and terrifying at the same time. Carmichael talked about the lies told to us about the history of America and the hypocrisy of the white man, and why it was important for black people to organize and fight back; and most importantly, to create black power so that we could have more determination over our communities and our lives as well as our destiny.

When I left the Garfield auditorium, I was no longer the same person that I was when I came in. I had already been involved in the civil rights movement after meeting Martin Luther King Jr. at the tender age of 13. Now, after Carmichael's speech, my anger and determination had been ignited. Less than a year later Martin Luther King Jr. would be assassinated, and two weeks after King's death I would become the Captain of the Seattle chapter of the Black Panther Party — the first chapter formed outside of the state of California. My daily dress would become the uniform of the Black Panther party, which was a black leather jacket, a powder blue shirt, black pants and a black beret. From that

point on, the Black Panther Party spread across the country like wildfire. We read and studied two hours a day, armed ourselves for protection, distributed the Black Panther newspaper and organized our community. And in the summer of 1969, the U.S. government stated that we were the No. 1 threat to the security of America. Secretly, the U.S. government began to implement a plan to destroy the Black Panther Party within a year. Many Panther offices would be raided, and often there were gun battles with the police.

Many Panthers would be killed — some who were very important leaders — and many Panthers would be imprisoned. Despite the attacks, we created programs to help the community — programs like free breakfast for school children, which spread across the country. We also opened 13 free medical clinics and started a free ambulance program. We gave away thousands of bags of groceries to families in need. In all, we implemented more than 35 different community-based programs. We became the saviors and the protectors of our communities. We also worked with and developed coalitions with many different communities, and groups of all colors. Our purpose was to work toward creating a more humane and just society for all people and all genders. We also had many allies across the world, as well. Black Panther affiliates were in places like India, New Zealand and Australia. There was even a group in Israel that called themselves the Israeli Panthers. We had support organizations throughout Europe, as well as in Japan.

The symbol of the Black Panther Party and some of its educational ideas actually came from the SNCC

VOTE
NOV 8

LOWNDES COUNTY
FREEDOM
ORGANIZATION

The Story of the Development of an
Independent Political Movement
on the County Level   50¢

The cover of *The Story of Development of an Independent Political Movement on the Country Level* pamphlet.

Lowndes County organizing efforts — they too called themselves the Black Panther Party. In 1967, they created a comic book-like pamphlet that explained, in detail, how the sheriff and other public officials were elected and what their duties and responsibilities were.

The pamphlet was done as a "picture story" because many people in rural Alabama were somewhat illiterate and could not read or write. This comic book pamphlet had a great, empowering effect on the people. The Black Panther Party newspaper was put together in much the same way, with pictures and cartoons and drawings, because we understood that many people in the black community were people who responded to and understood pictures and drawings better than words. In 1968, the Sacramento chapter put out a comic book on the free breakfast for school children program. For us, who grew up in the '50s and '60s, the comic book was almost an everyday part of life. Most of us purchased and read comic books almost daily. They captured our minds and sent us into a world of adventure that we could escape to merely by reading and looking at the graphic pictures. The Black Panther Party owes its beginnings to the Lowndes County Organizing Committee, and its graphic, cartoon-like pamphlet reprinted here.

You can read more about my story and the Black Panther Party in my book, *My People Are Rising.* ✺

THE ORGANIZER'S LIBRARY SERIES
of the
SOUTHERN CONFERENCE EDUCATIONAL FUND
3210 West Broadway
Louisville, Kentucky 40211

(Bulk Rates to Movement Groups)

LOWNDES COUNTY FREEDOM ORGANIZATION

THE STORY OF THE DEVELOPMENT OF AN INDEPENDENT

POLITICAL MOVEMENT ON THE COUNTY LEVEL

In the fall of 1965 the Negroes of Lowndes County, Alabama, decided they would have to start their own political party. They called it the Black Panther Party of the Lowndes County Freedom Organization. This is the story of how that party got started.

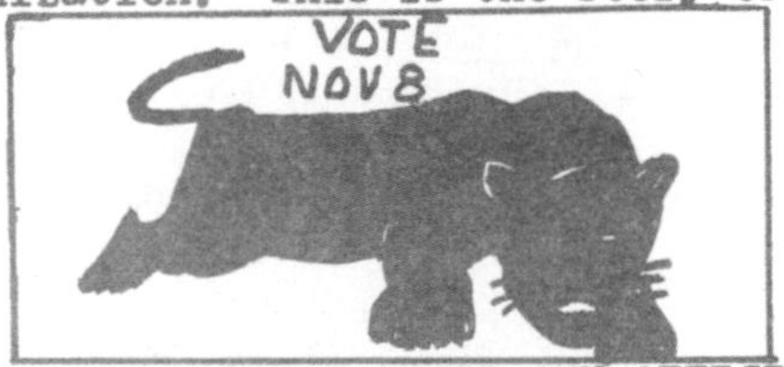
VOTE
NOV 8

THE PEOPLE DECIDE TO ELECT THEIR OWN OFFICIALS

In the early Spring of 1965 a civil rights organization called the Lowndes County Christian Movement for Human Rights was organized. But the people of Lowndes County found out that its politicians wouldn't listen to them when they were acting through the civil rights organization. The people discovered that unless they had political power, all they could do was just ask for their rights.

So the people decided to form their own political organization. They would elect their own public officials. If they could take over the County government, they'd no longer have to ask for what they needed. They could then take it.

So the Lowndes County people asked the Student Nonviolent Coordinating Committee (SNCC) to show them how to start their own political party. SNCC's researchers got a copy of the Alabama Code of Laws (a 12-book set) and began studying all the laws about County governments. When they knew all about how Alabama Counties were set up, SNCC scheduled a series of workshops, beginning in December of 1965. The purpose of the workshops was to help the Lowndes County people learn everything they needed to know about the political laws of Alabama as they applied to County government.

THE ATLANTA WORKSHOPS

The first 3 workshops were held in the SNCC building in Atlanta. At the first one, about 25 Lowndes County people were there. It lasted for four days. When the people went back to Lowndes and began talking about what they had learned, their friends wanted to come to the next one. So by the last workshop held in Atlanta in February of 1966, about 50 people were present.

By this time, a great number of people in Lowndes County knew about the workshops and about the movement to start a new political party. But most of them were unable to come to Atlanta for the four-day workshops.

So SNCC began began holding workshops in Lowndes County. They were held regularly, every two weeks, between February and May of 1966. Hundreds of people attended the workshops by the time the nominating convention was held in May, 1966.

WHAT WENT ON AT THE WORKSHOPS?

The workshops started off by discussing the Alabama laws which say how persons can become candidates for public office. In other words, how a person could be nominated for office.

When everyone knew how you could get nominated, they discussed the laws about how elections must be held in Alabama.

Then the workshops took up the actual offices which were up for election in the Fall of 1966. They were sheriff, tax assessor, tax collector, coroner, and 3 members of the 5-member school board.

SNCC researchers got complete descriptions of the duties, responsibilities and authority of each of these offices from the Alabama laws. They mimeographed these descriptions and distributed them throughout Lowndes County, so that everyone who was interested could find out as much about each office as he felt he needed to know.

The workshops which were held in Lowndes then began to center around the questions people would have after reading the job-description sheets. By the time the May Nominating Convention came around, hundreds of people had read and discussed the duties of the different County offices.

THE PICTURE STORIES

Since many people in the County could not read and write, SNCC drew up picture-stories about each office. They showed what each official was supposed to do, and what the people could do if they controlled those offices.

Here are 3 pages from the Sheriff and 3 pages from the Tax Assessor picture stories.

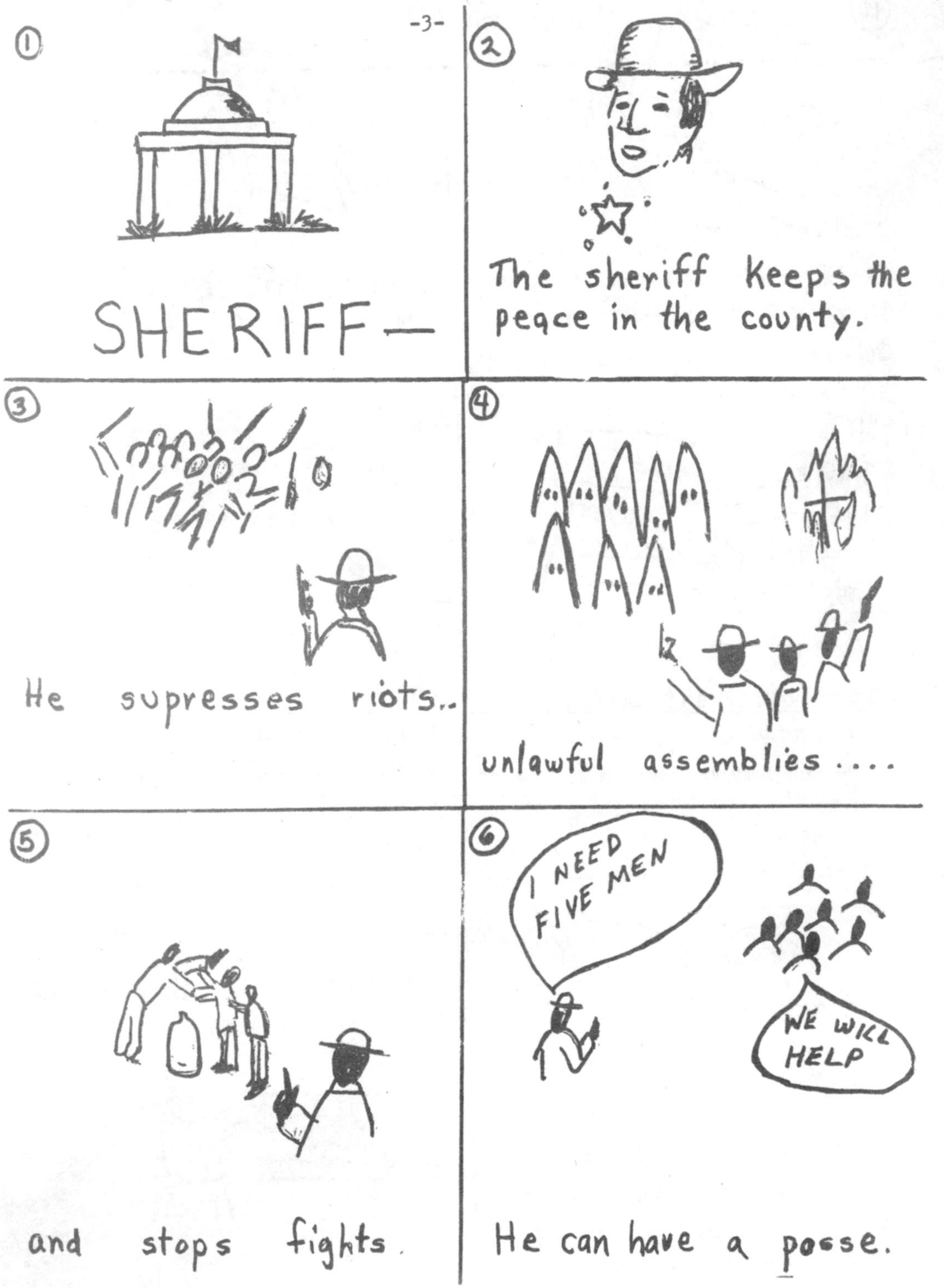
-3-
SHERIFF—
The sheriff keeps the peace in the county.
He supresses riots..
unlawful assemblies ....
and stops fights.
I NEED FIVE MEN
WE WILL HELP
He can have a posse.

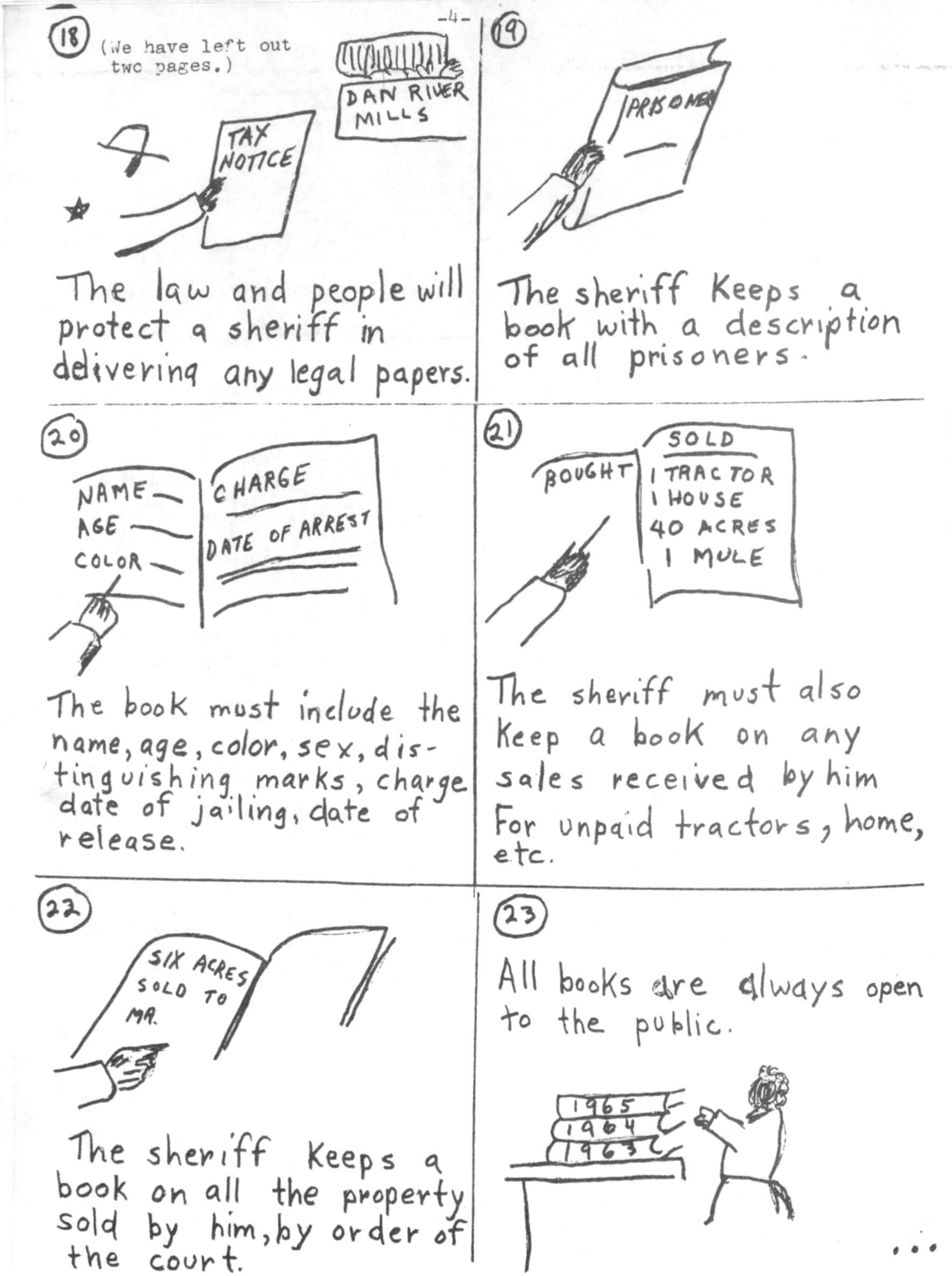
-4-
18
(We have left out two pages.)
DAN RIVER MILLS
TAX NOTICE
The law and people will protect a sheriff in delivering any legal papers.
19
PRISONER
The sheriff Keeps a book with a description of all prisoners.
20
NAME
AGE
COLOR
CHARGE
DATE OF ARREST
The book must include the name, age, color, sex, distinguishing marks, charge date of jailing, date of release.
21
BOUGHT
SOLD
1 TRACTOR
1 HOUSE
40 ACRES
1 MULE
The sheriff must also Keep a book on any sales received by him For unpaid tractors, home, etc.
22
SIX ACRES SOLD TO MR.
The sheriff Keeps a book on all the property sold by him, by order of the court.
23
All books are always open to the public.
1965
1964
1963
...

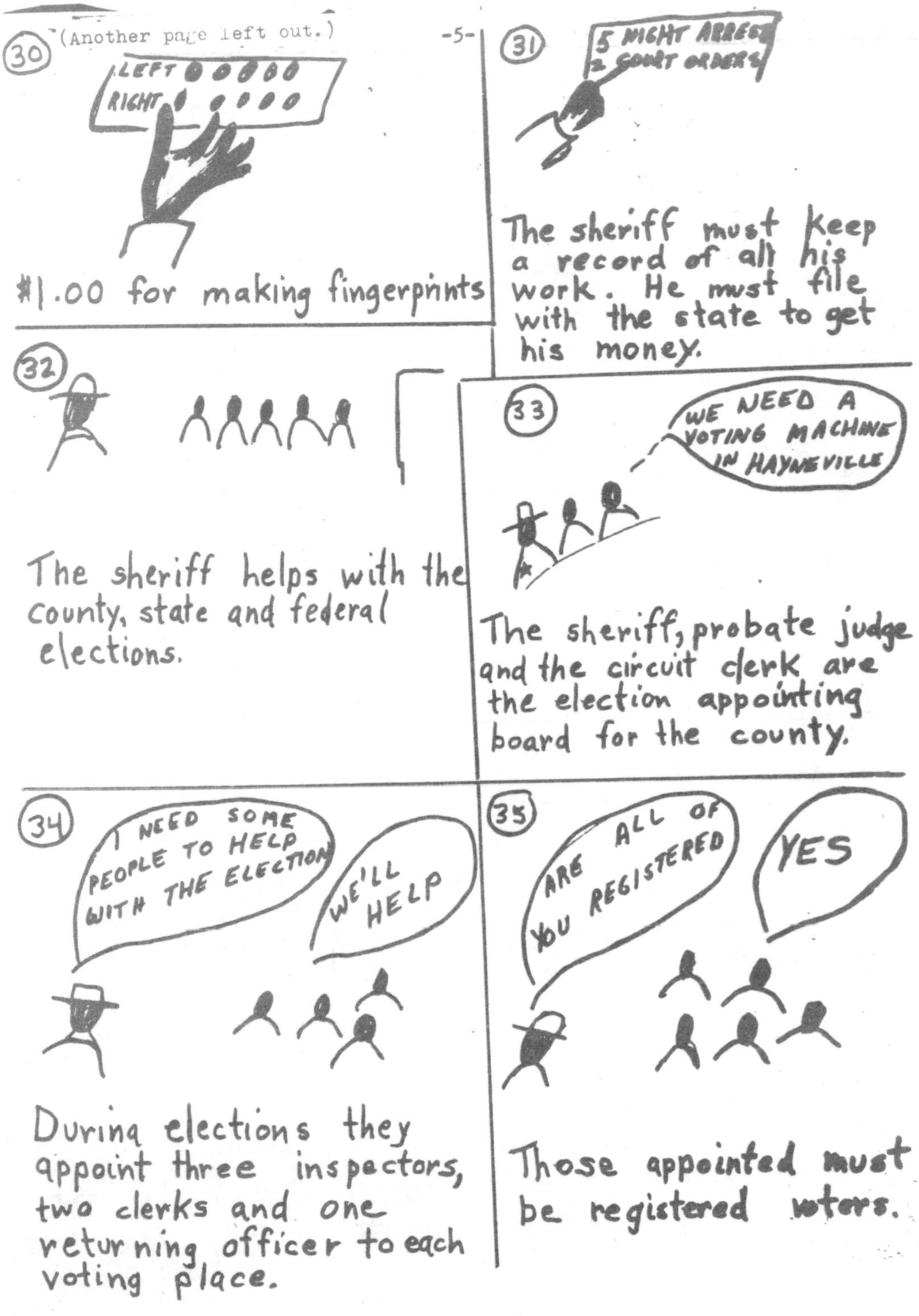
(Another page left out.)
-5-
30
LEFT
RIGHT
$1.00 for making fingerprints
31
5 NIGHT ARRES
2 COURT ORDERS
The sheriff must keep a record of all his work. He must file with the state to get his money.
32
The sheriff helps with the county, state and federal elections.
33
WE NEED A VOTING MACHINE IN HAYNEVILLE
The sheriff, probate judge and the circuit clerk are the election appointing board for the county.
34
I NEED SOME PEOPLE TO HELP WITH THE ELECTION
WE'LL HELP
During elections they appoint three inspectors, two clerks and one returning officer to each voting place.
35
ARE ALL OF YOU REGISTERED
YES
Those appointed must be registered voters.

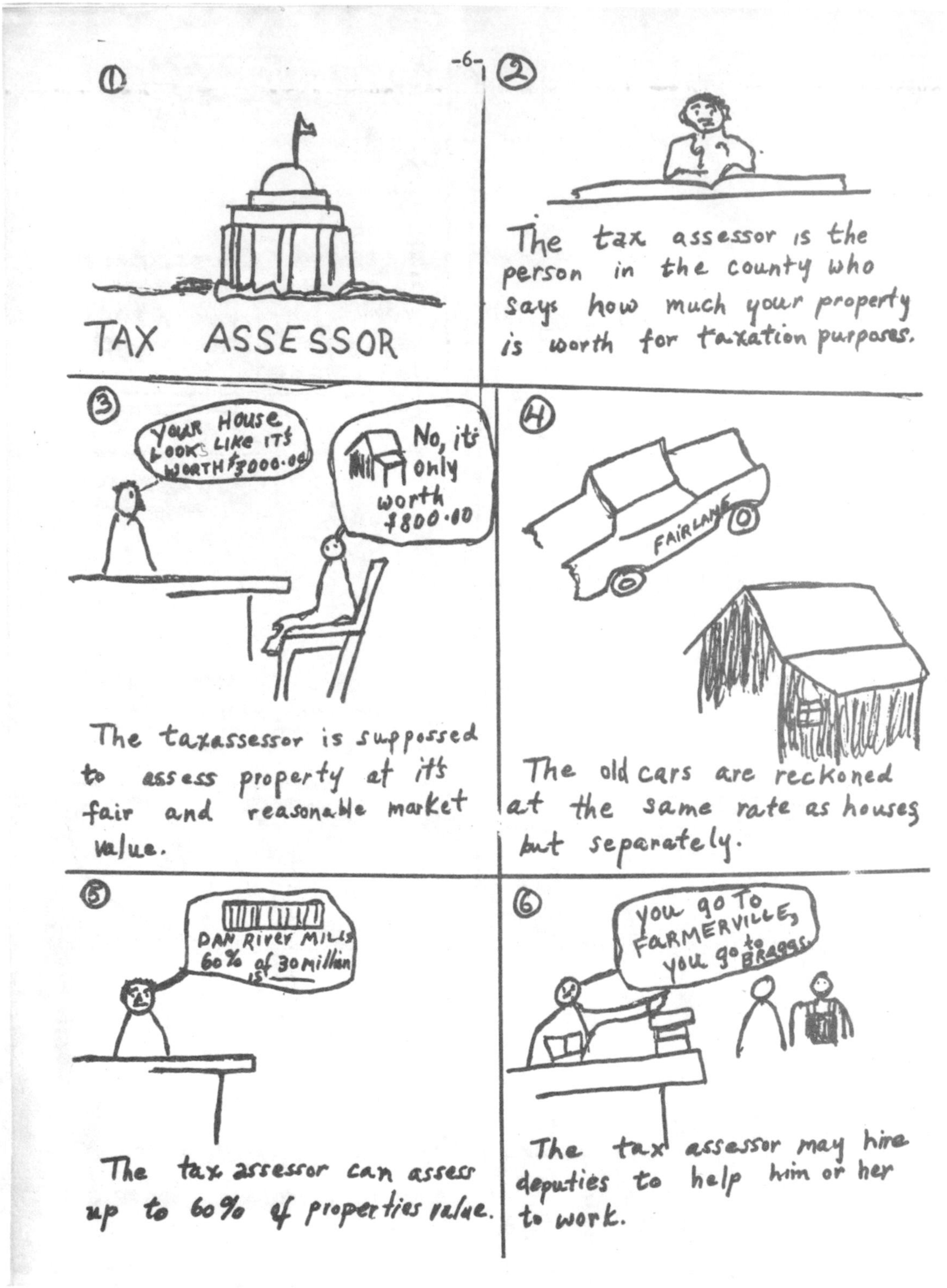
-6-
①
TAX ASSESSOR
②
The tax assessor is the person in the county who says how much your property is worth for taxation purposes.
③
YOUR HOUSE LOOKS LIKE IT'S WORTH $3000.00
No, it's only worth $800.00
The taxassessor is suppossed to assess property at it's fair and reasonable market value.
④
FAIRLANE
The old cars are reckoned at the same rate as houses but separately.
⑤
DAN RIVER MILLS 60% of 30 million is
The tax assessor can assess up to 60% of properties value.
⑥
You go to FARMERVILLE, you go to BRAGGS.
The tax assessor may hire deputies to help him or her to work.

⑦

The tax assessor makes his assessments between October 1st and Janurary 1st.

OCTOBER		JANUARY

⑧

Every person should come before the tax assessor to state how much property he owns.

⑨

Before going into a community the tax assessor must give atleast ten days notice in the county newspaper.

⑩

Before the taxpayer makes his return to the assessor he takes oath about the value of his property.

⑪

A person who lives outside of the county can mail his return to the tax assessor.

⑫

After Dec. 31st the tax assessor or his deputy can demand a return from thee who have not reported their taxes

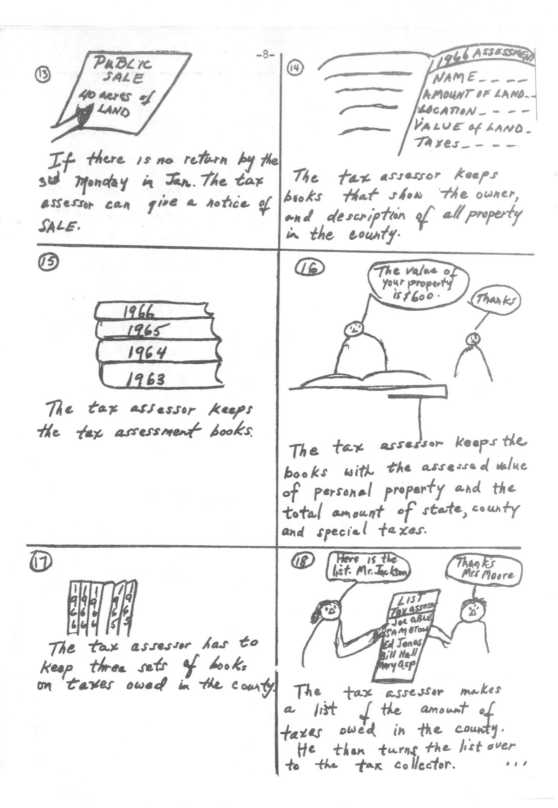

⑬ PUBLIC SALE 40 acres of LAND

If there is no return by the 3rd Monday in Jan. The tax assessor can give a notice of SALE.

⑭ 1966 ASSESSMENT
NAME____
AMOUNT OF LAND__
LOCATION____
VALUE OF LAND_
TAXES____

The tax assessor keeps books that show the owner, and description of all property in the county.

⑮ 1966 1965 1964 1963

The tax assessor keeps the tax assessment books.

⑯ The value of your property is $600. Thanks

The tax assessor keeps the books with the assessed value of personal property and the total amount of state, county and special taxes.

⑰ The tax assessor has to keep three sets of books on taxes owed in the county.

⑱ Here is the list. Mr. Jackson   Thanks Mrs Moore

LIST Tax Assessor Joe Able Sam Brown Ed Jones Bill Hall Mary Gap

The tax assessor makes a list of the amount of taxes owed in the county. He then turns the list over to the tax collector. ...

These picture stories were mimeographed and widely distributed throughout the County. They not only taught the people what the duties of the various County officials were, but also what the rights of the private citizen were.

THE NOMINATING CONVENTION

On May 2, after much difficulty with the white County officials, including the threat of bringing their guns to the Court House to break up any meetings held there, the people got an opinion from the Alabama Attorney General which said it would be legal for them to hold their Nominating Convention in a local church.

So on May 3rd the Convention was held. It was wide open. Anyone in the County who wanted to could run for nomination to any of the offices that were open. There were at least two candidates for each of the offices.

Voting in the Nominating Convention was by secret paper ballot. A regular registration procedure was set up, to make sure that only persons who were qualified to vote under Alabama law could vote in the Convention.

All of the Convention rules and procedures were set up by the Lowndes County people, themselves. The SNCC organizers only helped the people determine whether the procedures met all the requirements of the law.

Another picture story was mimeographed, which told the story of the beginning of the Black Panther Party. Here are some of the pictures from this too.

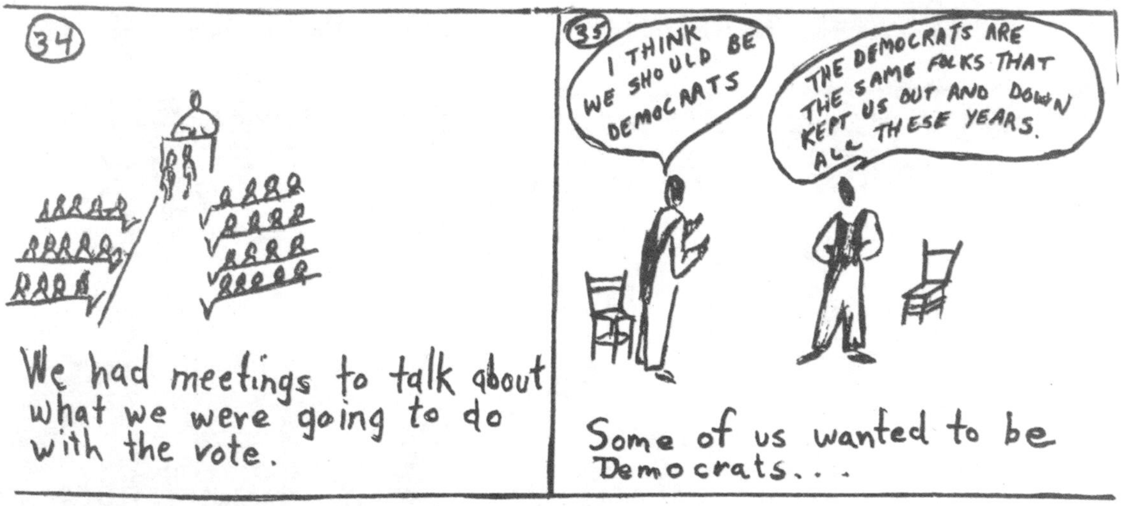
34
We had meetings to talk about what we were going to do with the vote.
35
I THINK WE SHOULD BE DEMOCRATS
THE DEMOCRATS ARE THE SAME FOLKS THAT KEPT US OUT AND DOWN ALL THESE YEARS.
Some of us wanted to be Democrats...

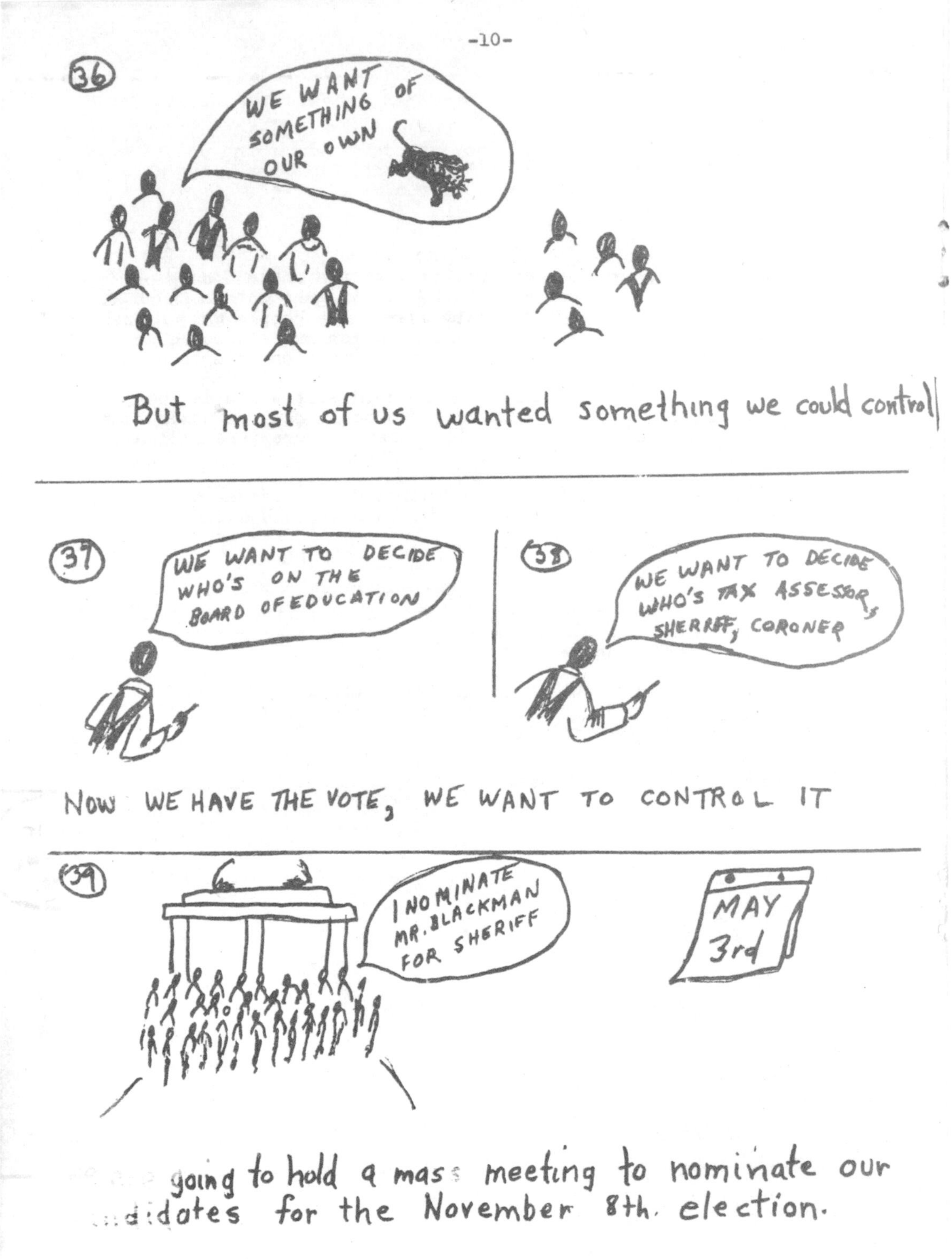
-10-
36
WE WANT SOMETHING OF OUR OWN
But most of us wanted something we could control
37
WE WANT TO DECIDE WHO'S ON THE BOARD OF EDUCATION
38
WE WANT TO DECIDE WHO'S TAX ASSESSOR, SHERIFF, CORONER
NOW WE HAVE THE VOTE, WE WANT TO CONTROL IT
39
I NOMINATE MR. BLACKMAN FOR SHERIFF
MAY 3rd
going to hold a mass meeting to nominate our
didates for the November 8th. election.

THE SUMMER WORKSHOPS

After the Nominating Convention, where there was one nominee picked for each office, the workshops continued throughout the summer. They were aimed toward preparing the candidates to do a good job in the offices they were running for. Many of the people who were not running for office continued to come to the workshops.

These workshops dealt with the ways in which people with money pay off elected officials and get them to sell-out ordinary folks. The way a "bag man," or pay-off man operates was described. The people in the workshops learned that many times the rich people will act like the friends of elected officials. They will invite the officials into their homes for dinner and parties, let them join their clubs, and will almost treat them as equals. Many times this is all that's necessary to get the official to favor them. Sometimes the rich people will actually give money to the official, or help him buy a piece of valuable property real cheap, or get some of his relatives a good job. There are many ways open to the rich person to gain favors from the elected official.

Little by little, the official is made to feel better than the people who elected him, and he begins to see himself as the friend of the rich and powerful.

By the time several such workshops had been held, people in Lowndes County began to see what they had to watch for in a candidate they elected to public office. But, more important, they began to see that the people do not have to put up with such sell-outs. They began to see that officials whom they elect to office, when they sell out this way, can be removed by impeachment, prosecution for not doing their jobs properly, special elections, and so forth.

During the summer there was a lot of hard work too, spreading the word to all the people in the County about the November elections.

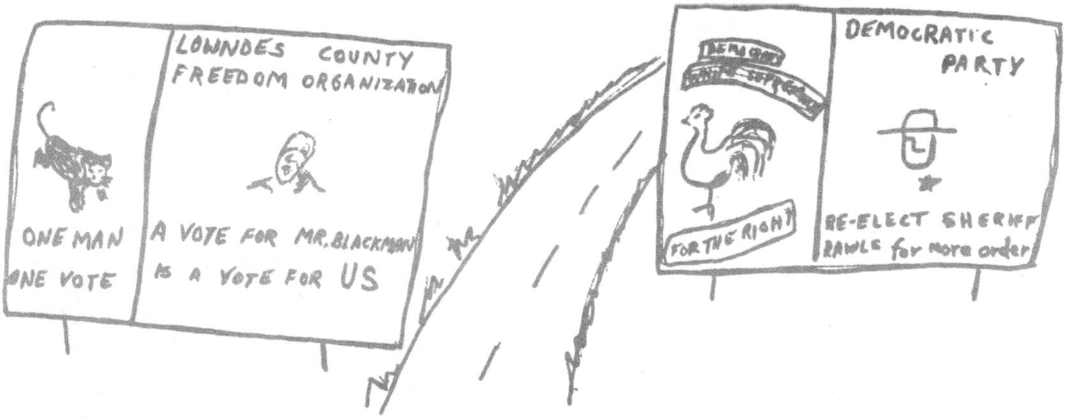
LOWNDES COUNTY
FREEDOM ORGANIZATION
ONE MAN
ONE VOTE
A VOTE FOR MR. BLACKMAN
IS A VOTE FOR US
FOR THE RIGHT
DEMOCRATIC
PARTY
RE-ELECT SHERIFF
RAWLE for more order

ELECTION DAY

On election day, November 8, the Black Panther Party organized
car pools and set up pick-up points to get people to the polls.
There were only 10 hours to be sure everyone got their long-
awaited chance to vote for their own candidates.

The Freedom Organization assigned poll watchers to each polling
place, to challenge any voter who was not who he claimed to be.
At some polls, the Black Panther poll watchers were ordered to
leave by officials, and at a few polls there were no poll watchers.

Black Panther Party workers were fired upon by shotguns and
one of the strongest workers was beaten on the head with a
rifle butt and tire chains by members of a mob near one polling
place, just as it was closing.

Final Returns

Sheriff		School Board #3	
Sydney Logan, Jr. (LCFO)	--1643	Robert Logan (LCFO)	--1664
Frank Ryals (Dem.)	--2320	David M. Lyon (Rep.)	--1937
Coroner		**School Board #4**	
Emory Ross (LCFO)	--1640	John Hinson (LCFO)	--1666
Jack Golson (Dem.)	--2265	Tommy Coleman (Rep.)	--1966
Tax Assessor		**School Board #5**	
Alice L. Moore (LCFO)	--1604	Willie M. Strickland (LCFO)	--1600
Charlie Sullivan (Dem)	--2265	C. B. Haigler (Dem.)	--2170

Tax Collector

Frank Miles, Jr. (LCFO) --1603
Iva D. Sullivan (Dem.) --2268

ELECTION RESULTS

The Lowndes County Freedom Organization candidates captured 43%
of the vote. Over 1600 people voted for each of the seven Black
Panther candidates. The fear, the trick of assigning people to
vote in precincts across the county from their home (only about
half the people were allowed to vote in their home precinct), the
votes of dead people and people who had moved away, and the
misleading help of "poll officials" for some people who could
not read nor write had combined to defeat the Black Panther
Party--this time.

LESSONS FROM THE ELECTIONS

This was the first election in which Negroes of Lowndes County, Alabama, had ever voted. They learned deeply several lessons from it.

---

1. Poor people can nominate their own candidates. They do not have to vote for candidates named by rich people.

2. If poor people controlled the tax assessor's office, the rich could be taxed fairly. The money the County could collect from the rich people could be used for much-needed schools, roads, waters, sewers and other services.

3. If poor people controlled the sheriff's office, he could become a protector of the people, not a protector of the power structure.

4. There are ways of dealing with most of the tricks in the power structure's bag. The most common tricks are:

     *physical violence
     *eviction
     *firing from jobs
     *buying out people with poverty war
         programs, money and jobs
     *election day cheating

5. The best way of dealing with these tricks is for poor people to stick together. Only by sticking together through physical violence, getting kicked out of your home or job, being tricked on election day, and the tempting lure of Government money can the poor people gain power—and hold it.

Once these lessons are learned, they are hard to forget.

Special thanks to comics historian Ryan Holmberg for alerting the *Journal* to this important artifact.

INTERVIEW

Holding Pattern

A Kevin Huizenga Interview

Alec Berry

THE WAITER BRINGS A THIRD ROUND. Some local shit they serve in a place like this, where artisan pizza is for sale and the walls scream regional pride. It's all right. Kevin Huizenga knows him. They met at the Minneapolis College of Art and Design (MCAD), right up the street, where he spent the last three years teaching, and where this waiter went to school.

In the past hour, Huizenga has mentioned feeling old. How he's experienced a shift, and how he's now one of those aged cartoonists all the young guns ignore. He's 42, but this exchange doesn't convince me. Huizenga bought a piece of this waiter's art, and this waiter isn't pushing the chatter to the grave. There's a real exchange happening, and maybe I hold a limited perspective, but I feel it's seldom that the middle-aged and the 20-something come in contact on common ground.

When the waiter leaves, I get the story of the last few years. Huizenga moved to Minneapolis in 2015 for the MCAD job. The job is temporary and about to wrap — he relocated here in the wake of a divorce, leaving his home of 15 years in St. Louis. He says right now might not be the best time for an "official interview," as so many things aren't settled, but I disagree. It seems like some weird in-between worth recording.

He's recently finished his comic book series *Ganges*, or what has become *The River at Night*, a 200-plus page book published by Drawn and Quarterly. In it, Glenn Ganges can't fall asleep, so his mind wanders, ruminating on geology, relationships, video games and time. It's a book that really feels like an achievement, versus someone's latest release.

From 2006 to 2017, the six issues of *Ganges*, some published in a joint effort by Fantagraphics and Coconino Press and some published by the cartoonist himself, landed Huizenga recognition, such as a 2010 Ignatz Award for Outstanding Series, as well as critical acclaim in places like *The New York Times*, where writer and actor John Hodgman wrote: "Huizenga reminds us in a way many novelists cannot, never mind lesser comics writers, that as long as we are mortal, the mundane shall always be a life-and-death struggle."

All that aside, Huizenga doesn't really know what to think or say about *The River at Night* right now. Which is fair. From where we're sitting, it's July 2018. The full book isn't due out till September 2019, and he still has to design the thing. It isn't really done. Huizenga's just living with a mantra, a note hung in

THERE IS NO WAY YOU CAN READ ALL THESE! TRUST ME!
TRUST ME.

ABOVE: From *Ganges* #4, 2011.

OPPOSITE: Illustration of Huizenga by Sammy Harkham, 2019.

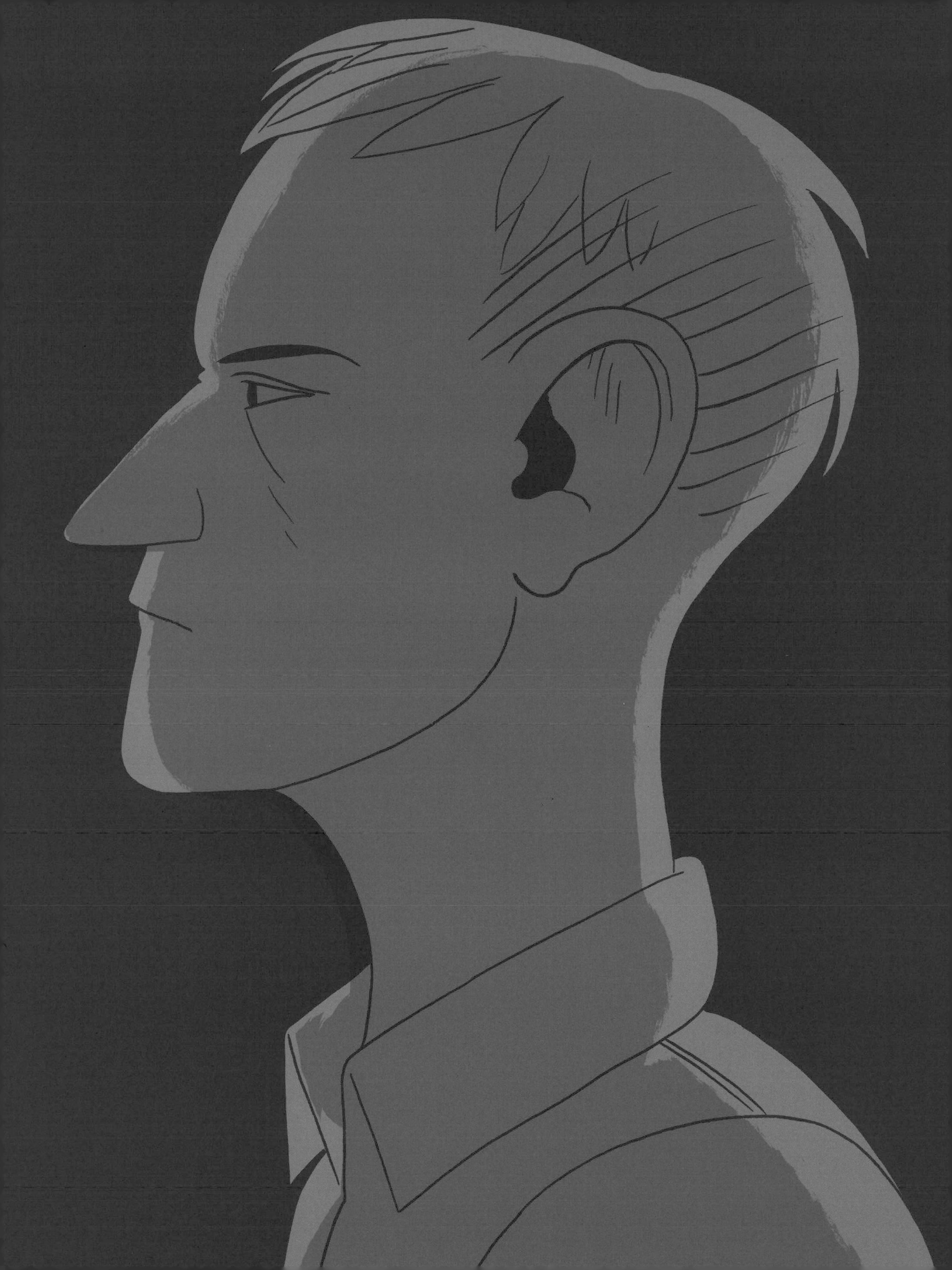

SEEMS LIKE A MILLION YEARS SINCE I CRAWLED INTO BED!
ZZZ
ONE MILLION YEARS
ONE HUNDRED MILLION YEARS
WHAT DO I DO NOW?
SHOULD I GET UP AND DO SOMETHING? OR JUST KEEP LYING HERE?
I GUESS MY BODY IS GETTING SOME REST...
@#!%

From *Ganges* #4, 2011.

his studio that reads: "Hold the book in your hand." A tangible goal, removed of any fluff, that at times summons insanity.

The following conversation has been condensed and edited for reading purposes.

ALEX BERRY: How do you feel that it's done?

KEVEN HUIZENGA: [*Long silence, followed by a laugh.*] How do I feel? I'm very happy with it. I'm very proud of it. But I don't know. I haven't looked too closely at it, and I still have to do the book, you know? It doesn't feel done. The last couple of years have been weird. My marriage ended. I moved to Minneapolis. I started teaching. That was all very stressful and difficult, and throughout that I tried to finish *Ganges* #5 and #6. I wrote it before all that happened, but then I needed to draw it all. I don't know... I worked very hard on it. Now it's done. I mean, obviously, it's a big deal for me. I worked on it for over 10 years. I think I laugh because that's an obvious question, but I haven't even asked myself that question.

I ask this question sometimes of other authors I talk to — I say, "How do you feel about the way the book came out?" What I'm really asking is, "How did it get messed up?" Trying to sympathize and let them know it happens to everyone. Authors, when they think about their books, are mostly disappointed in themselves, how far short they fell, and by disagreements with publishers, by bad covers, blurbs or descriptions, etcetera and by the inevitable printing mistakes, the typos and spelling mistakes. But we don't talk about that kind of thing in interviews, because it doesn't help sell books, of course. Don't call attention to it. I just saw a book the other day with a spelling mistake on the back cover. It can be a rough business. You move on quickly to the new thing, after the heartbreak, to the next heartbreak.

I honestly don't have an answer, because it's not something I have feelings about. It's too big and complicated. I suppose I could give you a list of many different feelings. Obviously, I hope people like it. The

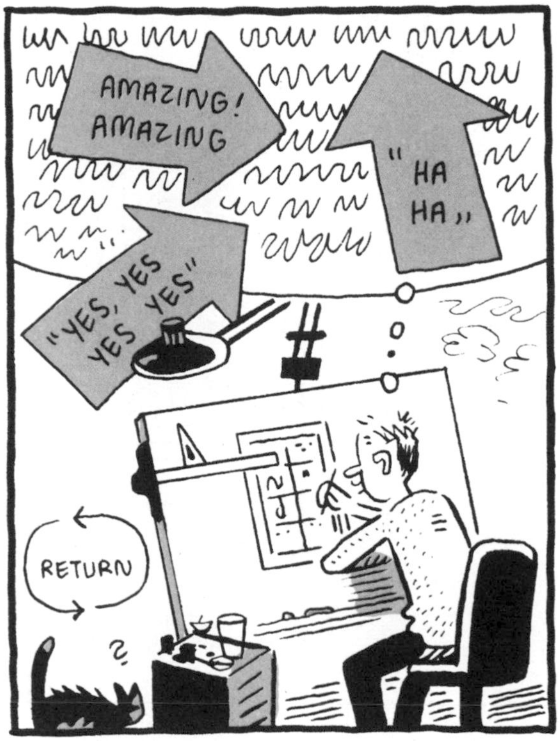
AMAZING! AMAZING
"HA HA"
"YES, YES YES YES"
RETURN

From *Ganges* #6, 2017.

real answer is I don't know how I feel. It's kind of an emotionally blank area taken up by a lot of details and impressions. It's too complex. This is sounding overly dramatic.

I'm grateful to everyone who has helped bring it into the world. Drawn and Quarterly, of course, let me do amazing things with the book design, and was very patient with my slow — I guess it was slow — obsessive approach to it.

The whole thing is outside of normal scales of calculation. I don't have the book in my hands yet. It's different when you hold it in your hands, and come to terms with the actual thing. My whole approach to designing the book was to actually hold the thing in my hand, at size, with all the mistakes fixed and every space, every margin, everything correct, before going to the printer — which doesn't seem like too difficult a thing to do, especially with all the tools at the college I was working at — but that turned out to be incredibly challenging. I had a note hanging up in my studio: "Hold the book in your hand." Every day I started with trying to make that happen, and adjusting it until it was done, and it took a long time and a lot of frustratingly slow progress. I spent a fair amount of money trying to do it. I felt insane at times.

Do you think you've accomplished something?

I don't know. I don't know. I don't know! ... When I started drawing comics early on, it was deeply, deeply pleasurable. I think I just decided to keep doing it. I don't think I have a lot of natural talent for drawing or writing or anything, and I sort of just did the best I possibly could and surprised myself by pushing harder or doing trickier things. That's really all it comes down to. I worked really hard on it, and I surprised myself by what I could pull off. I was telling someone the other day ... I'm very rational, and I'm always thinking hard and worrying and thinking about what's in my life — except for my comics which I just let unfold. I don't try to steer it closely. I just let it go. In my comics, I feel like I'm free. I can make mistakes and try different things out. There's no stakes at all. I just do whatever I want. I don't have a lot of expectations for them at all.

I think what happened was the first issue was pretty well-received. I obviously was going to do a second issue, and then sometime early on I was just like, "Wouldn't it be funny if it all took place in the same night, and it was all about Glenn not being able to fall asleep and I just kept coming back to that over and over?" That idea was enough. At a certain point, I thought, "Well, I should end this." So, the challenge became, "How do I end this?" That's where I lost a few years.

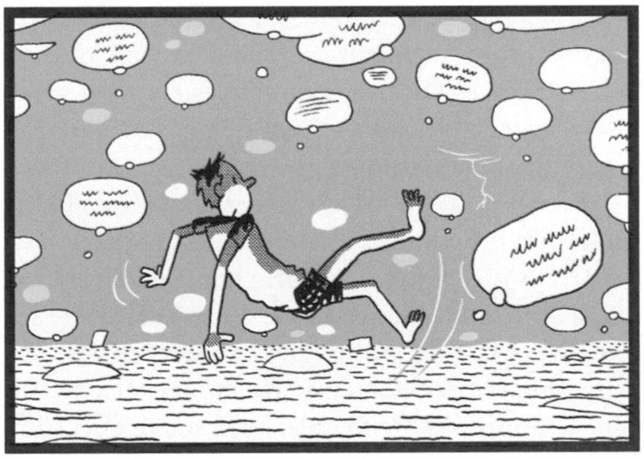

From *Ganges* #3, 2009.

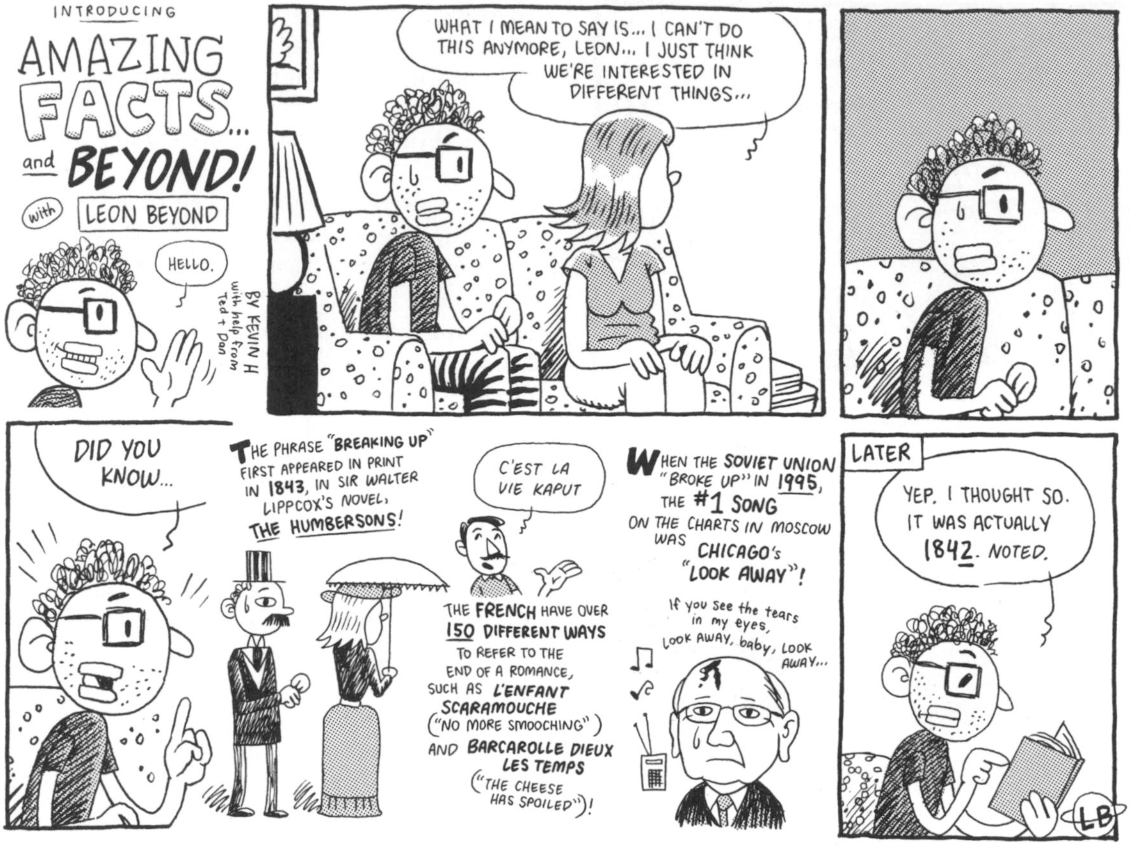
INTRODUCING
AMAZING FACTS... and BEYOND!
with LEON BEYOND
HELLO.
BY KEVIN H with help from Ted + Dan
WHAT I MEAN TO SAY IS... I CAN'T DO THIS ANYMORE, LEON... I JUST THINK WE'RE INTERESTED IN DIFFERENT THINGS...
DID YOU KNOW...
THE PHRASE "BREAKING UP" FIRST APPEARED IN PRINT IN 1843, IN SIR WALTER LIPPCOX'S NOVEL, THE HUMBERSONS!
C'EST LA VIE KAPUT
THE FRENCH HAVE OVER 150 DIFFERENT WAYS TO REFER TO THE END OF A ROMANCE, SUCH AS L'ENFANT SCARAMOUCHE ("NO MORE SMOOCHING") AND BARCAROLLE DIEUX LES TEMPS ("THE CHEESE HAS SPOILED")!
WHEN THE SOVIET UNION "BROKE UP" IN 1995, THE #1 SONG ON THE CHARTS IN MOSCOW WAS CHICAGO'S "LOOK AWAY"!
If you see the tears in my eyes, LOOK AWAY, baby, LOOK AWAY...
LATER
YEP. I THOUGHT SO. IT WAS ACTUALLY 1842. NOTED.
LB

A strip by Huizenga, Dan Zettwoch and Ted May that appears in the collected *Amazing Facts ... & Beyond! with Leon Beyond*, 2013.

Did your divorce play a role in the delay?

It took as long as it took. Of course, the divorce played a role. The divorce, the moving and the new job — teaching three college classes, no less — were like a storm of the most stressful things in life. It was a combination of things.

Especially *Ganges* #5, which, the amount of work that went into that issue. A book about endlessness, it's tricky to find the right form for. Also, it's not like it was the only thing I was doing — I did make several other comics and bodies of work in that time. Also, the *Leon Beyond* strips, which paid better, in the short term, anyhow. I researched and drew a short graphic novel about American painters in Florence. I drifted into other work, and there's also the thing of, when people pay you to do things, and there's real deadlines, it's hard to turn down that work, especially when there's not a day job anymore. As often happens, you do something for its own sake, for yourself, for little or no money, and then people respond to it, and then they ask you to make them a poster or a story for a magazine, or interviews, or reprint things, and that stuff takes days and weeks and months, and maybe even pays better — per page, per hour — than the comic books, which don't get done, and then people ask why is it taking so long? These are good problems, anyhow. It's tough to turn down also because you wonder if you turn it down if anyone will ever ask again. That kind of thing. It's normal.

I did have a time figuring out how to finish the book, and it was mostly a problem of figuring out how to incorporate the geology material from John McPhee's book, which Glenn is reading in issue one, and which I hoped to make part of the story. Once I

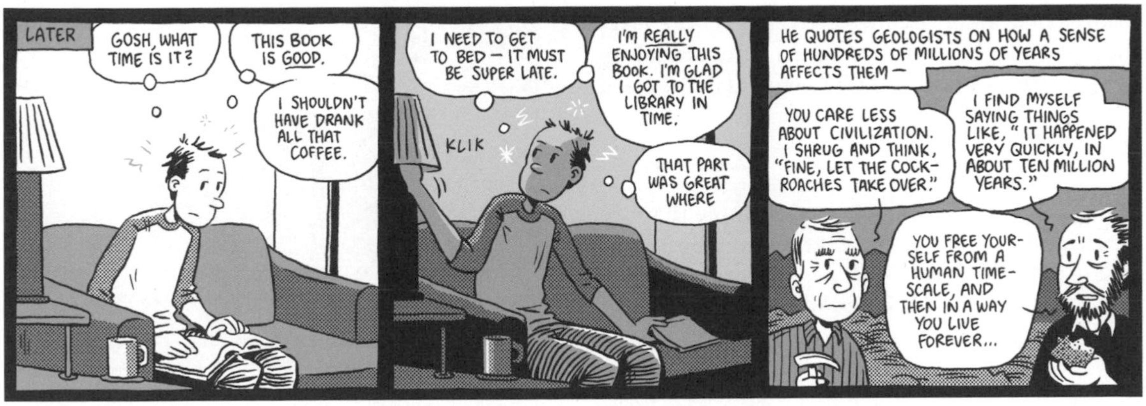
LATER
GOSH, WHAT TIME IS IT?
THIS BOOK IS GOOD.
I SHOULDN'T HAVE DRANK ALL THAT COFFEE.
I NEED TO GET TO BED — IT MUST BE SUPER LATE.
KLIK
I'M REALLY ENJOYING THIS BOOK. I'M GLAD I GOT TO THE LIBRARY IN TIME.
THAT PART WAS GREAT WHERE
HE QUOTES GEOLOGISTS ON HOW A SENSE OF HUNDREDS OF MILLIONS OF YEARS AFFECTS THEM —
YOU CARE LESS ABOUT CIVILIZATION. I SHRUG AND THINK, "FINE, LET THE COCKROACHES TAKE OVER."
I FIND MYSELF SAYING THINGS LIKE, "IT HAPPENED VERY QUICKLY, IN ABOUT TEN MILLION YEARS."
YOU FREE YOURSELF FROM A HUMAN TIME-SCALE, AND THEN IN A WAY YOU LIVE FOREVER...

From *Ganges* #1, 2005.

started working on that section and began researching and reading other books about geology and the age of the earth, I ended up finding books which either contradicted some of what I read in other books, which lead to having to read further, etc. That really took the book into the wilderness for a few years. I would sit at the St. Louis University library and read stacks of books about geology, and the history of geology, the changes over time to how people understood how things changed over time. I loved it, but progress was slow. I read philosophy of science, about neuroscience, and on and on. It was the best, and I was also reading about physics, too, and language, and I had ideas of how it all could be woven together, but it would also fall apart or get boring as comics, and I struggled with the patterns and implications of things, and how to put it on a comics page. Twice, I had built a kind of structure that I ended up dismantling.

I ended up cutting it down for the comic book even from what I had drawn because I realized it was getting too complicated. And then I even cut it down further for the book. So, I did a lot of work for about eight pages in the book. Four pages, really, represent years of thinking and reading.

In some other interview, you said your ideal scenario for a project is to print 50 copies of a minicomic or zine and just mail those to friends. What's the thought there?

I think when I approach a project I think about it in those terms. And that's about it.

Then why do *Ganges* as a book?

I don't know. I ask myself that sometimes. I mean, it doesn't matter. It really doesn't matter. [*Huizenga pauses, starts talking, backtracks, asks himself the question: "Why do it as a book?"*]

I really don't know. I mean, at this point, I have a lot of work in notebooks and folders that I don't think I'll ever publish. I mean, I'm proud of it. But sometimes I feel like ... I mean, some of the shine of publishing has worn off. I have published a few books now, and I understand that you publish a book and life goes on. Nothing changes that much. There's been a few essays written about why it's not a good idea to

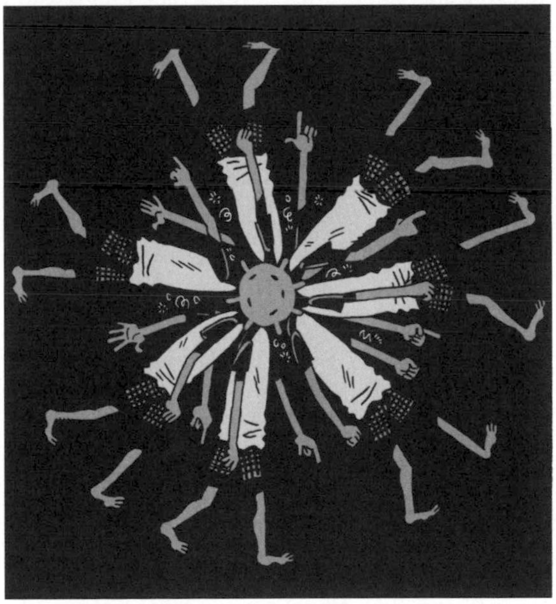

From *Ganges* #4, 2011.

write a book, and I've collected them over the years, and I've thought about making a little anthology because they're usually pretty funny and well written.

How so?

Just the usual jokes of "It's more trouble than it's worth" and "Nobody cares." Like we're going down a dark path here ... but I love books. I'm obsessed with books and making beautiful books. I'm interested in doing it for its own sake. When I say, "It doesn't matter," that's not an argument against doing it. It's just saying there aren't a lot of big expectations. The book *Ganges* is, in a way, a lot about time. And there's this motif about time, and in some ways the process of working on the book and still working on the book, I feel like I'm lost in some sort of time warp. I can't really tell if I'm going slow or fast anymore. It's been a long time, but at the same time it doesn't feel like a long time. From another perspective, I'm not really in any hurry.

You mentioned that some of the shine of publishing has worn off. That nothing changes that much. Life moves on. Is that OK? Is that a challenge after spending more than 10 years on something?

It's all a challenge. If it's not OK, then I don't know. Again, the question of spending 10-plus years on something — as if that's strange or significant. It seems normal to me. The worst thing about it is people asking about it. I wanted to draw these comics, and that's how long it took. I guess most people don't do this kind of thing, but too bad for them.

Is Glenn Ganges simply a vehicle for you to pursue various kinds of stories?

Yeah, I mean he's a vehicle, but all characters are like that. It's more like ... in comics there's this whole idea of continuity, and I guess in writing in general and in fiction in general, a character has a life: a beginning, middle and end. I just thought I could use Glenn in a lot of different scenarios, and it wouldn't matter. I could just restart him. I guess at some point I learned the one rule of art is to not reinvent the wheel. Sometimes, if you have something and it's working, just keep using it.

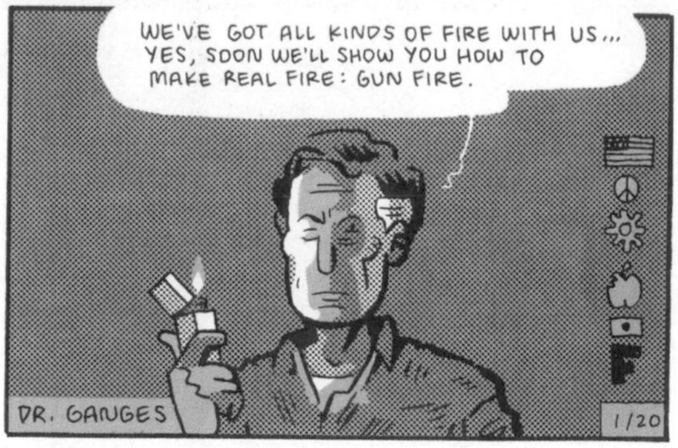
WE'VE GOT ALL KINDS OF FIRE WITH US... YES, SOON WE'LL SHOW YOU HOW TO MAKE REAL FIRE: GUN FIRE.
DR. GANGES
1/20

From *Fielder* #1, 2018.

But I don't think of all of it being the same character. In the new issue [*Fielder* #1], there's a Dr. Ganges, who's Glenn, but he's older and he has gray hair. He's got a daughter and grandkids. Dr. Ganges ... but it's not necessarily Glenn in the future. If anything, it's in the past. It takes place in the 1950s.

I like the idea of Mickey Mouse. I like the idea of this iconic form, who's also your iconic character. But at the same time, I want to do different stories. Mickey Mouse is the sorcerer's apprentice. He's also Goofy's friend or whatever. By design, he's supposed to be generic as possible. I really like the idea of a character that the reader can use as an avatar to experience the world. I mean, so much of writing and making art is trying out different things and going, "Yeah, I guess that works," and you just keep moving. You can't really plan. But if you come across something and it works, then you can think, "Oh, this'll work in other scenarios as well. That's a good thing to speak with."

My friend, Ted May, once described writing, for him, as like a slot machine. You keep pulling the lever and all the symbols come up, and sometimes it's a jackpot. Working on anything, like when I was putting *Fielder* #1 together, as I was finishing it, sending the files off, I was going through my pile of papers and trying to figure out what to save and what to throw away. I had forgotten how, while I was working on the stories, they went through so many different changes. So many panels I drew and redrew and changed. George Saunders wrote this piece recently where he described having a little meter on your forehead. That as your writing you're trying to keep it in the green instead of going into the red. That's really what it's

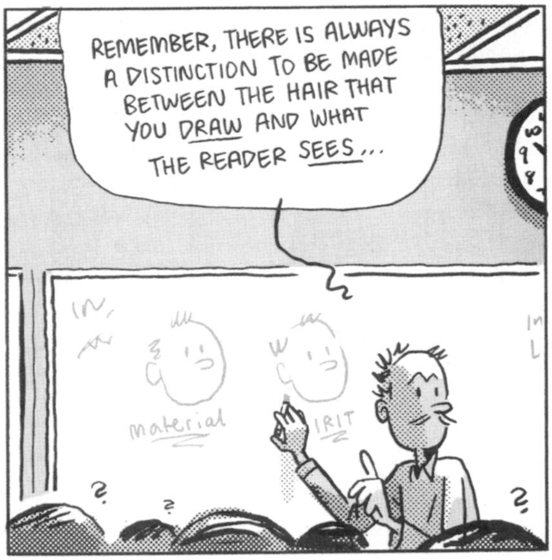
REMEMBER, THERE IS ALWAYS A DISTINCTION TO BE MADE BETWEEN THE HAIR THAT YOU DRAW AND WHAT THE READER SEES...
material
IRIT

From *Fielder* #1, 2018.

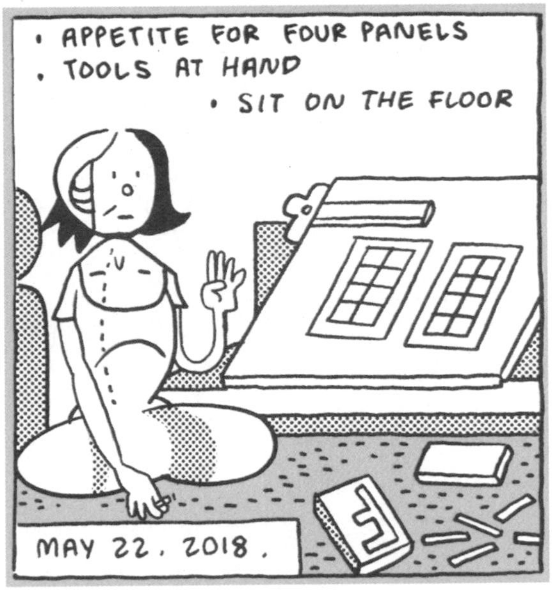
• APPETITE FOR FOUR PANELS
• TOOLS AT HAND
• SIT ON THE FLOOR
MAY 22. 2018.

From *Fielder* #1, 2018.

like. It's just stabbing in the dark, and hopefully you find enough paths through the thicket that you eventually end up with something you're happy with. Once I get down the path of working on something, I don't abandon the whole thing. I usually get it so it's good enough to publish or do something with.

Did you move to Minneapolis for the job at MCAD or did you just move here?

For the job. After my marriage ended, I moved around for a while, and went up to stay at Anders Nilsen's apartment while he traveled, and the job opened up at MCAD so I moved up here in 2015.

Teaching has forced me to re-engineer my own process and look at other peoples' processes, and I love it. I love all that stuff. In some ways, I think of comics as part of a larger thing, which in general is that human beings like to work on something that they can concentrate on — and lose a sense of ego and find a flow of working. Comics is the thing that I found that in. I use that as a guide as to how I should arrange my process. It should be a regular practice that I can concentrate on. If it's too frustrating, it's not working right.

When it's not, how do you bring it back to a good place?

Right now, I sit on the floor to work. Like I concentrate on just sitting. I sit cross legged, which makes it difficult to get up and move around. After 45 minutes of sitting, you just naturally get more concentrated on what you're doing. In my experience, that's a fact. Or using a timer to trick yourself into sticking with something, instead of getting frustrated and saying, "Screw this, I'm going to do something else." More and more lately, I do what I call the pen test, where I take out a bunch of my pens and make geometric designs with them and see if they're still worth keeping. But then, after a while of just mark-making, I remember that it's fun to make marks and draw.

Do you like drawing?

I don't know. Not really. But I usually do when I trick myself into doing it. I think what I like is listening to music. I like listening to podcasts, and then drawing is a way to do those things. And then sometimes when all that stuff is working together I'm enjoying myself.

More and more in the last couple years, I've been listening to metal: black metal, doom metal, death metal. Bands like Yob, Inter Arma, Wode. It's just a new thing in the last few years. I suppose it has a lot of energy. It's cathartic. All the growling and screaming. I like a good metal drummer. I'm not into the darkness

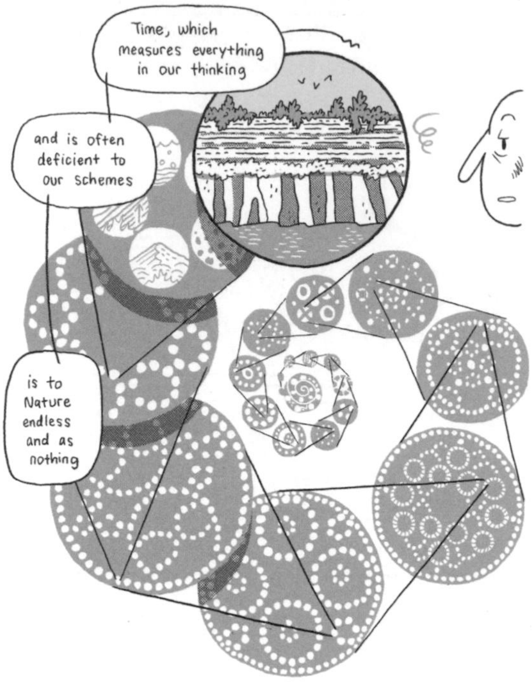
Time, which measures everything in our thinking
and is often deficient to our schemes
is to Nature endless and as nothing

From *Ganges #5*, 2016.

of satanic stuff, like I'm very ironic about that. I think it's like gangster rap, where it's a pose to show off artistry. In some ways, realizing that, it was interesting because it opened up a whole new realm of expression I had never really thought of before. Like how well can you create something out of extreme evil darkness. Some bands I like have an almost Lovecraftian demonic vibe. They talk about demons coming out of the stars. I like that kind of cosmic metal.

In your *Comix Skool USA* zines, there's this emphasis on note-taking. Was this a new thing for you while making these zines or has this thought-process-put-to-paper been part of your life longer than that?

I used to spend most of my time at the desk on pages, but starting in like, 2011 or so, I started using small notebooks in order to focus and concentrate at the desk. Instead of clicking around on the internet, or whatever other distractions. Empty my head, doodle and then deal with whatever needed dealing with, to follow through in a linear way rather than jump around from thing to thing.

Back in the early 2000s, after quitting my day job, I spent a few years very anxious and unfocused. One of the things I settled on was making small sketchbooks out of scrap paper that came from the printer after I printed minicomics, blue paper, and I called these "Focus Books." The idea was that whenever I was feeling unfocused, anxious and unsure what to do, which was often, I'd spend time doodling and writing in these small booklets, and usually after some time I'd settle down and focus enough to turn my attention over to a page of comics. They were a mixture of warm-up work, journaling, calendar and to-do list, doodling and focus object. And working out things for strips, usual sketchbook stuff. I don't know if this helped or just attacked the symptoms.

Later, I started taking notes on what I was reading. The other focusing exercise that seemed to work reliably was starting the day reading some non-fiction essays, something with clear and complex thinking, and that would get me into a frame of mind to settle in and work and feel like myself again. Hopefully. Then, after 30 or so of those Focus Books I moved back into using notebook sketchbooks.

When I started teaching at MCAD in 2014, the notes turned into thinking through what I would be teaching, the raw material that went into the zines. I think I was trying to get across the idea of thinking on paper, playing on paper, that working in your notebook was part of being a cartoonist and writer, and also, why not publish some of it, spread it around.

What are you thinking about?

A few years ago, I was very interested in ... I had been doing a lot of reading in various subjects like neuroscience and philosophy and Buddhism and meditation. Books about [Theodor] Adorno and critical theory and geology. A lot of that reading started to come together. I started seeing all these connections, and I was taking a lot of notes about these different subjects. That still continues on. I still read a lot about Buddhism, meditation. I think about that stuff a lot. I've practiced it for a few years, now. I often think about that practice. I think about what I should do if ... ways I could get more serious about it. Like formally. I have a loose

GLENN LANDS, GRABS THE ALLSLAYER, SPINS AND FIRES —

From *Ganges* #2, 2008.

collection of topics that I think of as my studies. In some ways, I wish I could just focus on them and not worry about …

Money?

Yeah, money or mundane things.

You mentioned that you like to just let your comics unfold, to not worry too much about steering things. Is that your way of escaping mundane shit?

Well, gee, of course it is. We all have our ways of escape. I used to play video games a lot, too.

But as far as not thinking about that other stuff, it's almost like in my head I have a — I don't know — I've always tried to concentrate on producing work, and having a daily block of time where I sit at my desk and work and process papers and write and draw, and all the rest of it, at a higher level, I try to let happen organically. Even with what we're doing right now, I hesitate sometimes because I don't really have anything interesting to say about it because I don't think about it that much. It feels like, in some ways, that's the wrong career move. You're supposed to sort of

know your projects and know your career and ambitions and all that sort of stuff, and —

I made 12 zines for my students, right? And in some ways, that was sort of what I wanted to do. I just wanted to make a zine. I know how to. I have stuff on paper that I think is interesting. I know how to mail it. Beyond that, the idea of "Oh, should this be a book? Should I edit this into a book? Should I divide it into chapters?" I don't know. Sometimes it feels like if you think about something too much, you kill it because you make it too hard to work on. So, I try to keep things easy to work on. A page at a time. At too high a level, I just don't think about it that much. ❀

A Tribute to Clare Briggs
by Noah Van Sciver

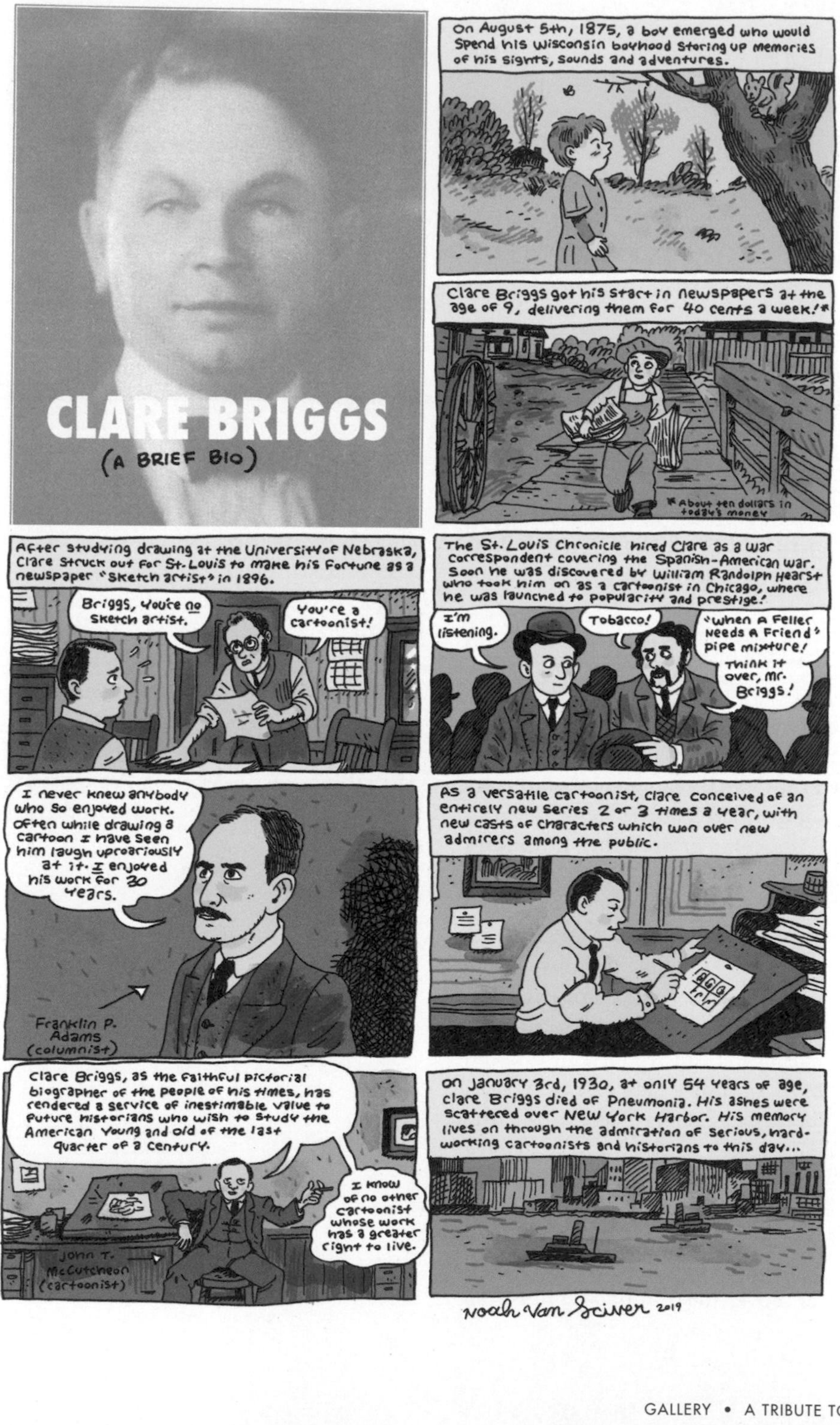
CLARE BRIGGS
(A BRIEF BIO)
On August 5th, 1875, a boy emerged who would spend his Wisconsin boyhood storing up memories of his sights, sounds and adventures.
Clare Briggs got his start in newspapers at the age of 9, delivering them for 40 cents a week!*
*About ten dollars in today's money
After studying drawing at the University of Nebraska, Clare struck out for St. Louis to make his fortune as a newspaper "sketch artist" in 1896.
Briggs, you're no sketch artist.
You're a cartoonist!
The St. Louis Chronicle hired Clare as a war correspondent covering the Spanish-American war. Soon he was discovered by William Randolph Hearst who took him on as a cartoonist in Chicago, where he was launched to popularity and prestige!
I'm listening.
Tobacco!
"When a Feller Needs a Friend" pipe mixture!
Think it over, Mr. Briggs!
I never knew anybody who so enjoyed work. Often while drawing a cartoon I have seen him laugh uproariously at it. I enjoyed his work for 30 years.
Franklin P. Adams (columnist)
As a versatile cartoonist, Clare conceived of an entirely new series 2 or 3 times a year, with new casts of characters which won over new admirers among the public.
Clare Briggs, as the faithful pictorial biographer of the people of his times, has rendered a service of inestimable value to future historians who wish to study the American young and old of the last quarter of a century.
I know of no other cartoonist whose work has a greater right to live.
John T. McCutcheon (cartoonist)
On January 3rd, 1930, at only 54 years of age, Clare Briggs died of pneumonia. His ashes were scattered over New York Harbor. His memory lives on through the admiration of serious, hard-working cartoonists and historians to this day...
Noah Van Sciver 2019

Cartoonist Noah Van Sciver has colored a selection of Briggs' turn-of-the-20th-century gags for this gallery.

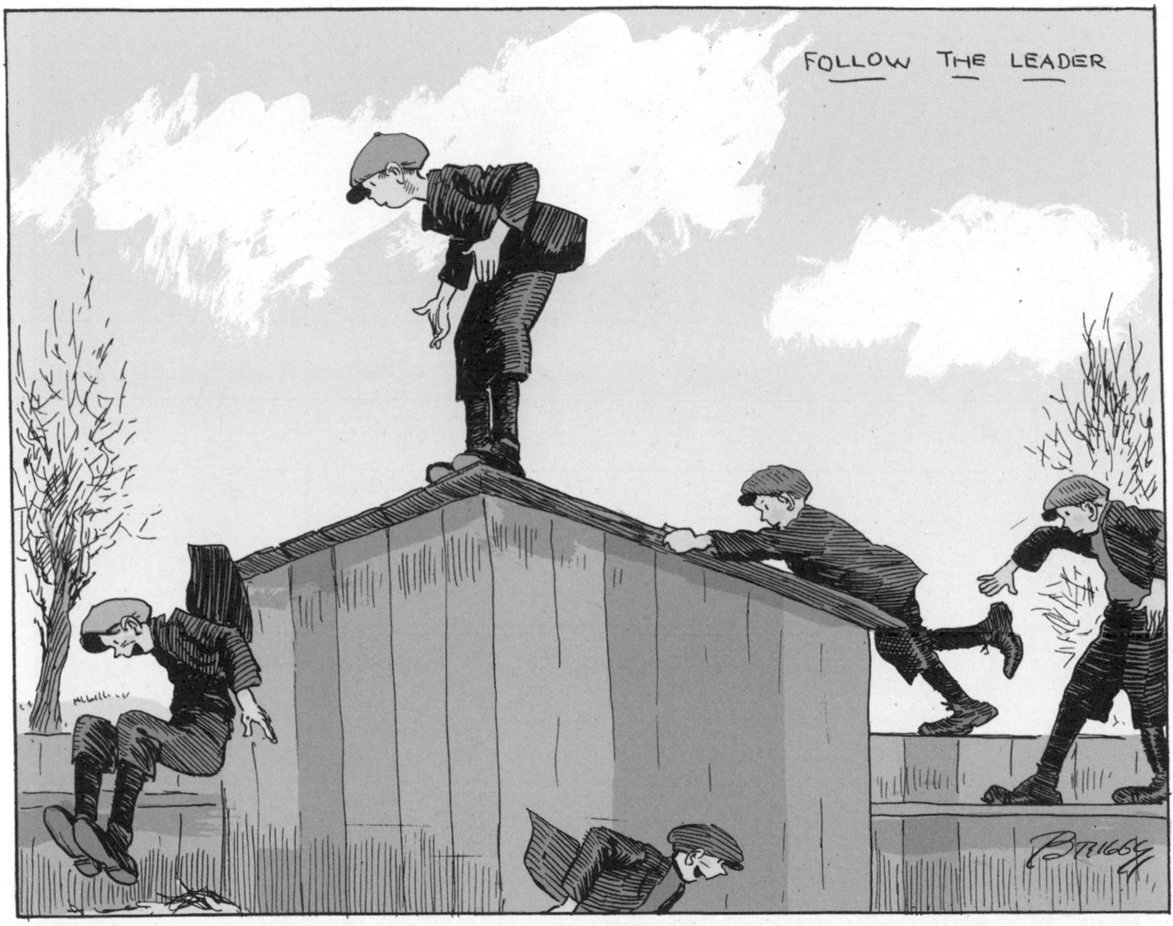
FOLLOW THE LEADER
BRIGGS

WHEN YOU'RE TWO MILES FROM HOME --- OUT OF GASOLINE ----ONLY ONE OAR --CHILLED THROUGH -- DENSE FOG COMING UP -- WIND AND WAVES RISING AND AGAINST YOU --UNFAMILIAR WITH CHANNEL --ETC. ETC.

BRIGGS

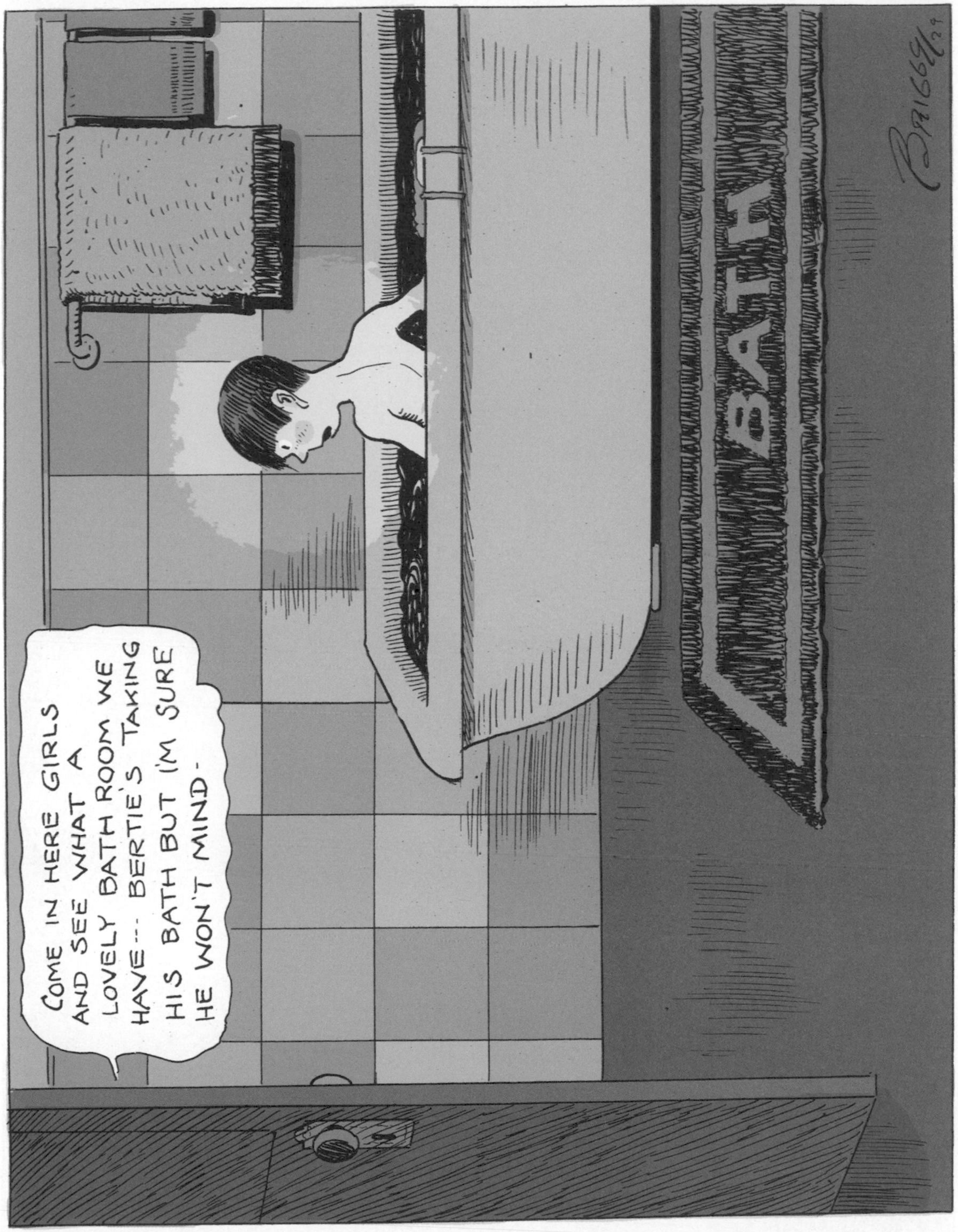
COME IN HERE GIRLS AND SEE WHAT A LOVELY BATH ROOM WE HAVE-- BERTIE'S TAKING HIS BATH BUT I'M SURE HE WON'T MIND-
BATH
BRIGGS '29

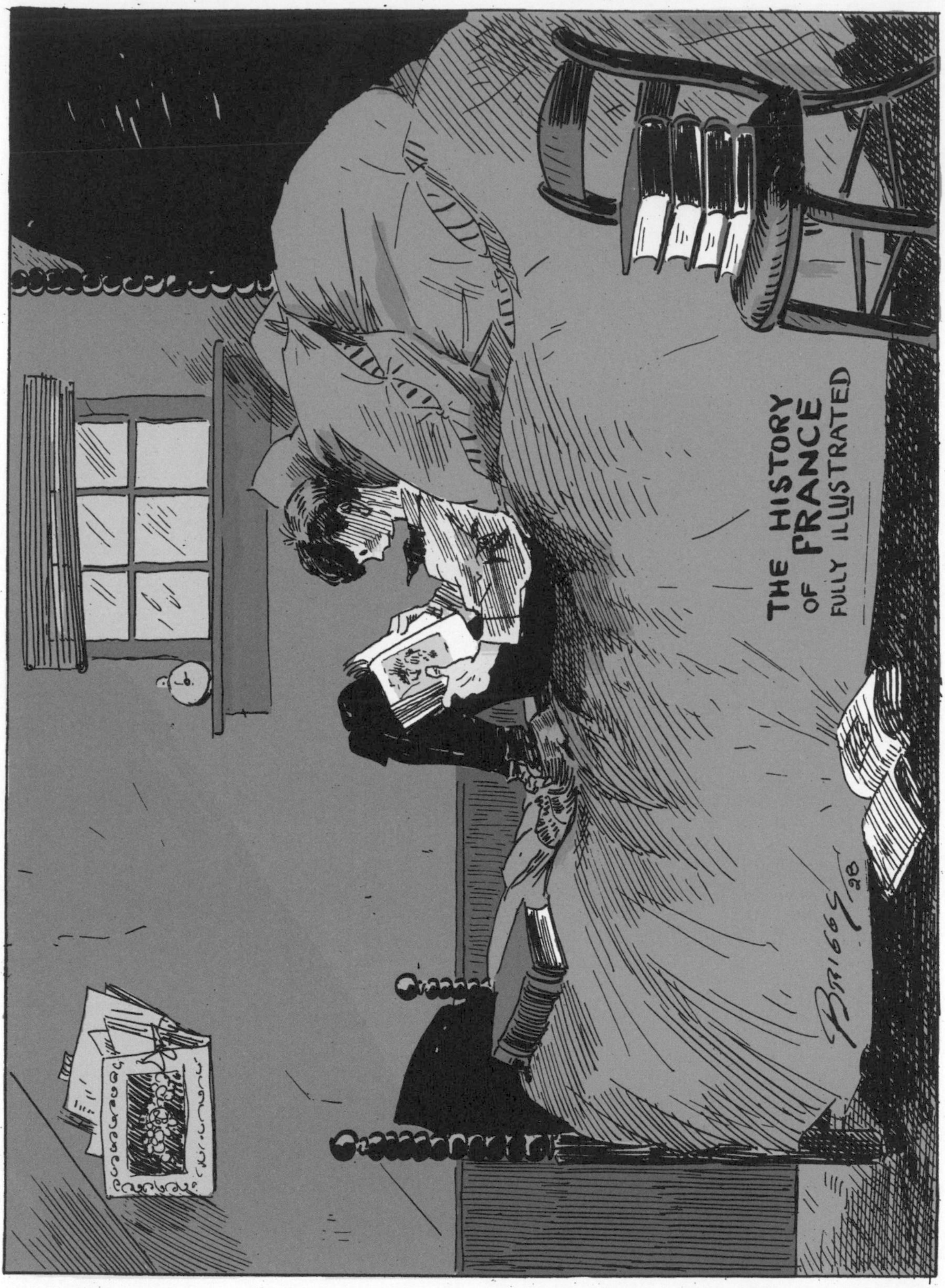
THE HISTORY
OF FRANCE
FULLY ILLUSTRATED
BRIGGS '28

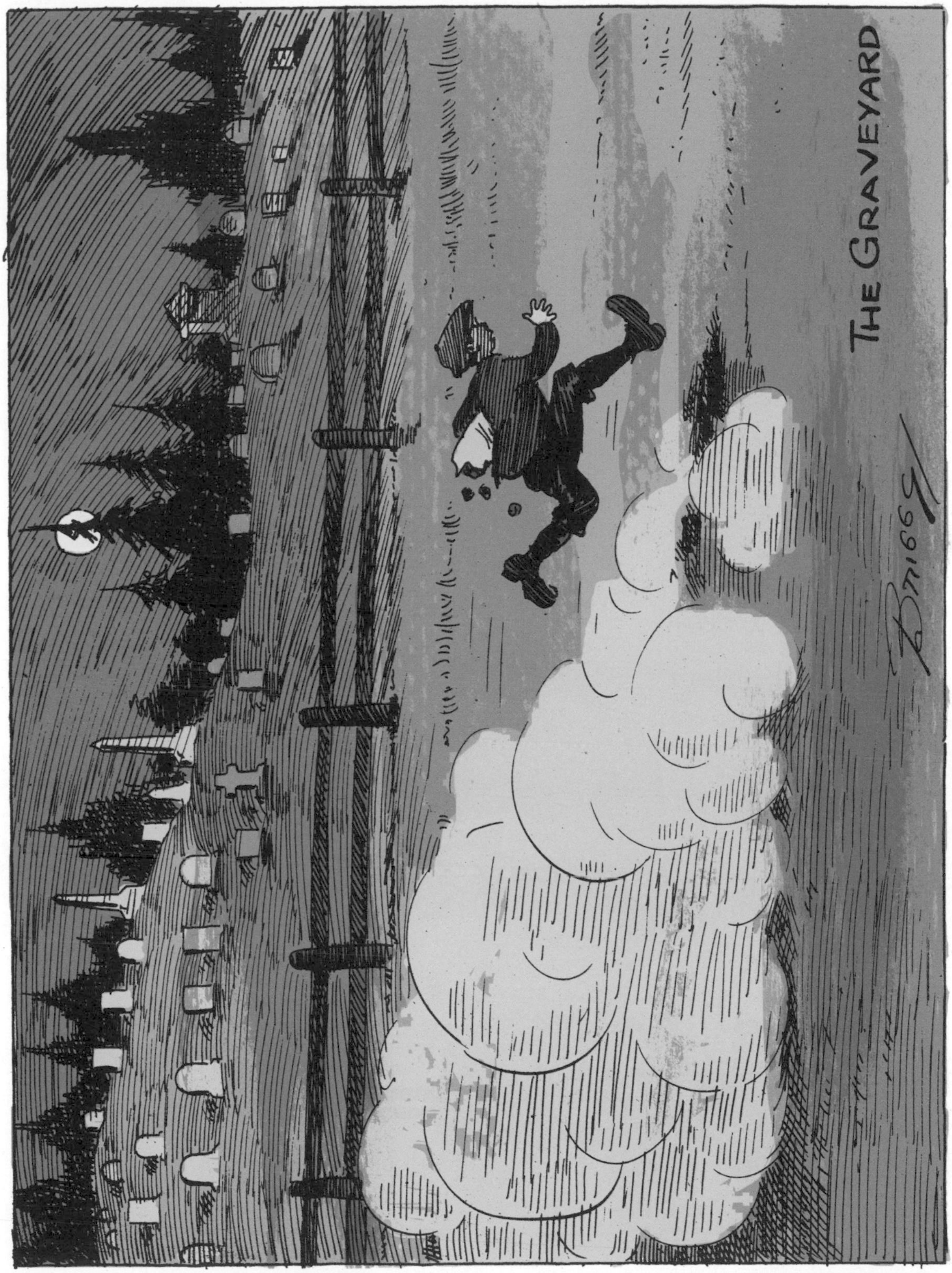
THE GRAVEYARD
Briggs

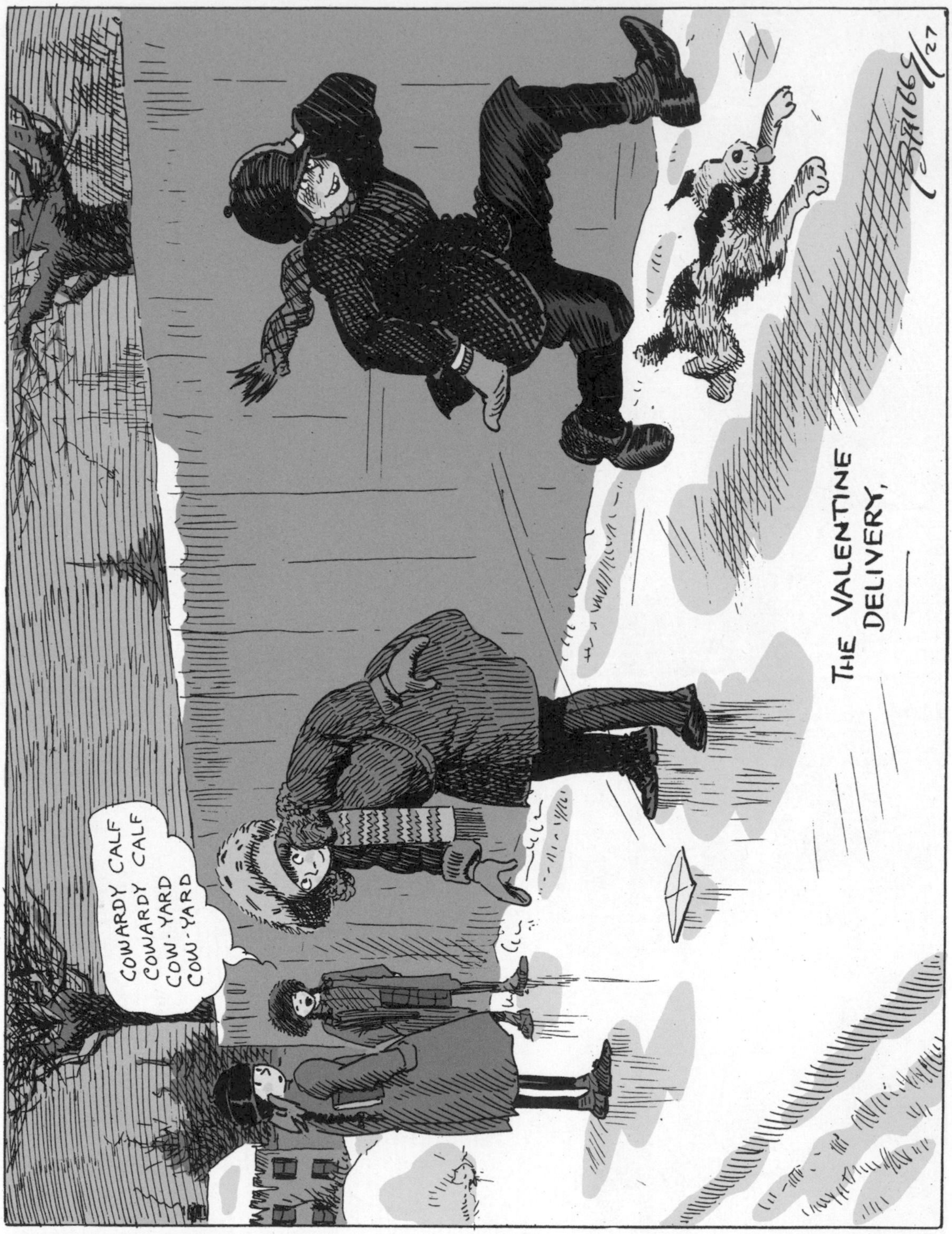
COWARDY CALF
COWARDY CALF
COW-YARD
COW-YARD
THE VALENTINE
DELIVERY,
BRIGGS

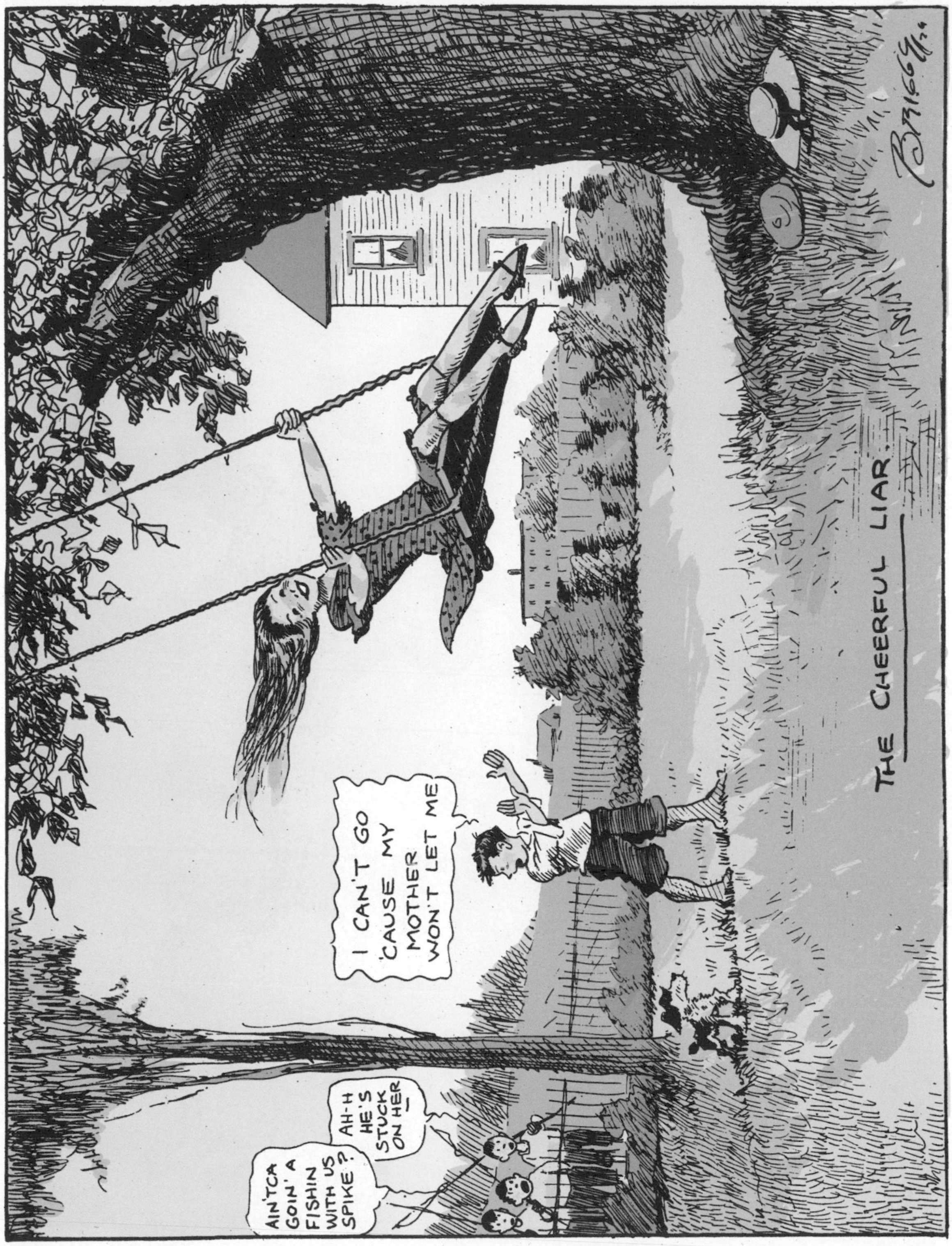
AIN'TCA GOIN' A FISHIN WITH US SPIKE?
AH-H HE'S STUCK ON HER_
I CAN'T GO 'CAUSE MY MOTHER WON'T LET ME
THE CHEERFUL LIAR
BRIGGS

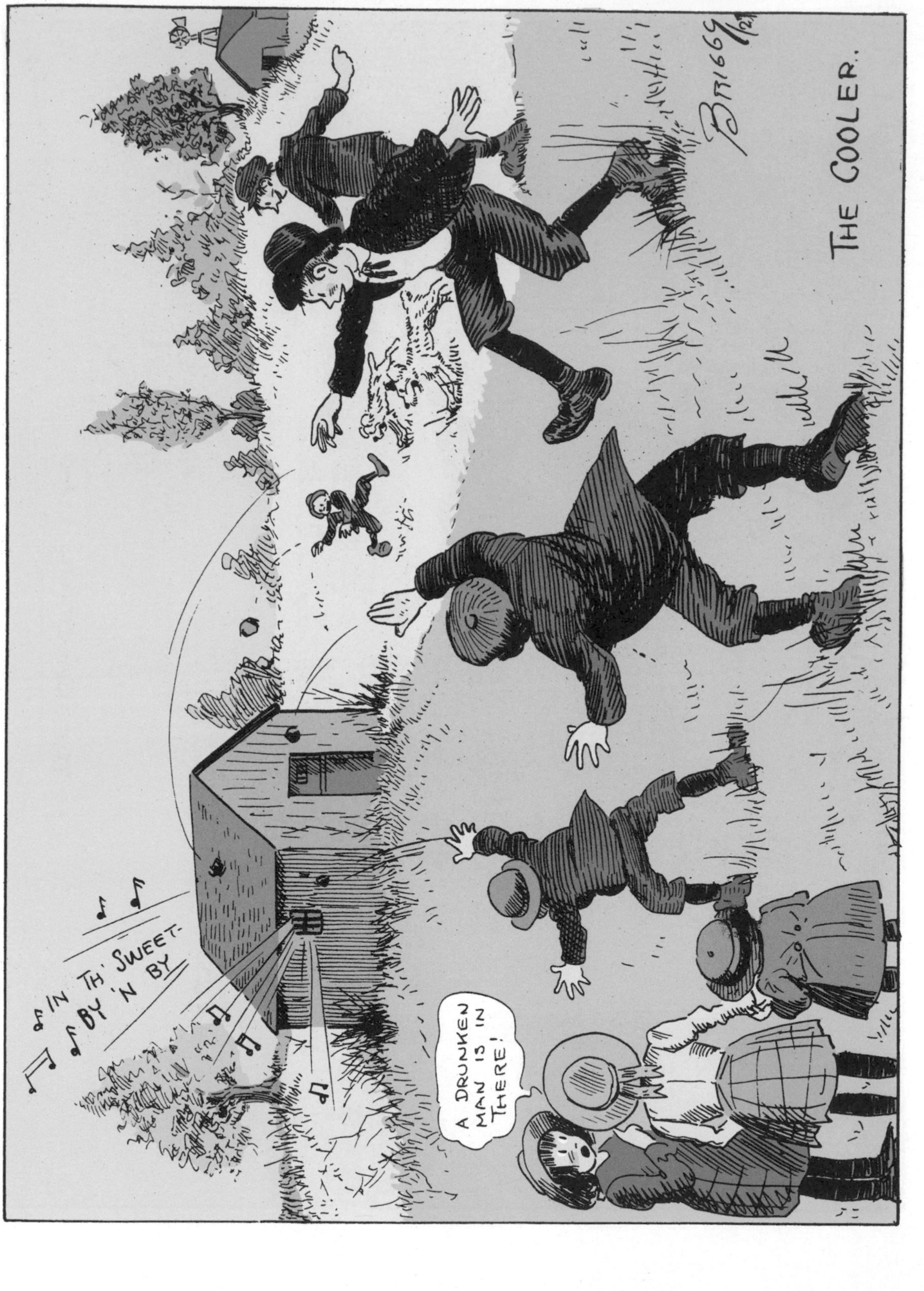
IN TH' SWEET-
BY 'N BY
A DRUNKEN MAN IS IN THERE!
BRIGGS
THE COOLER.

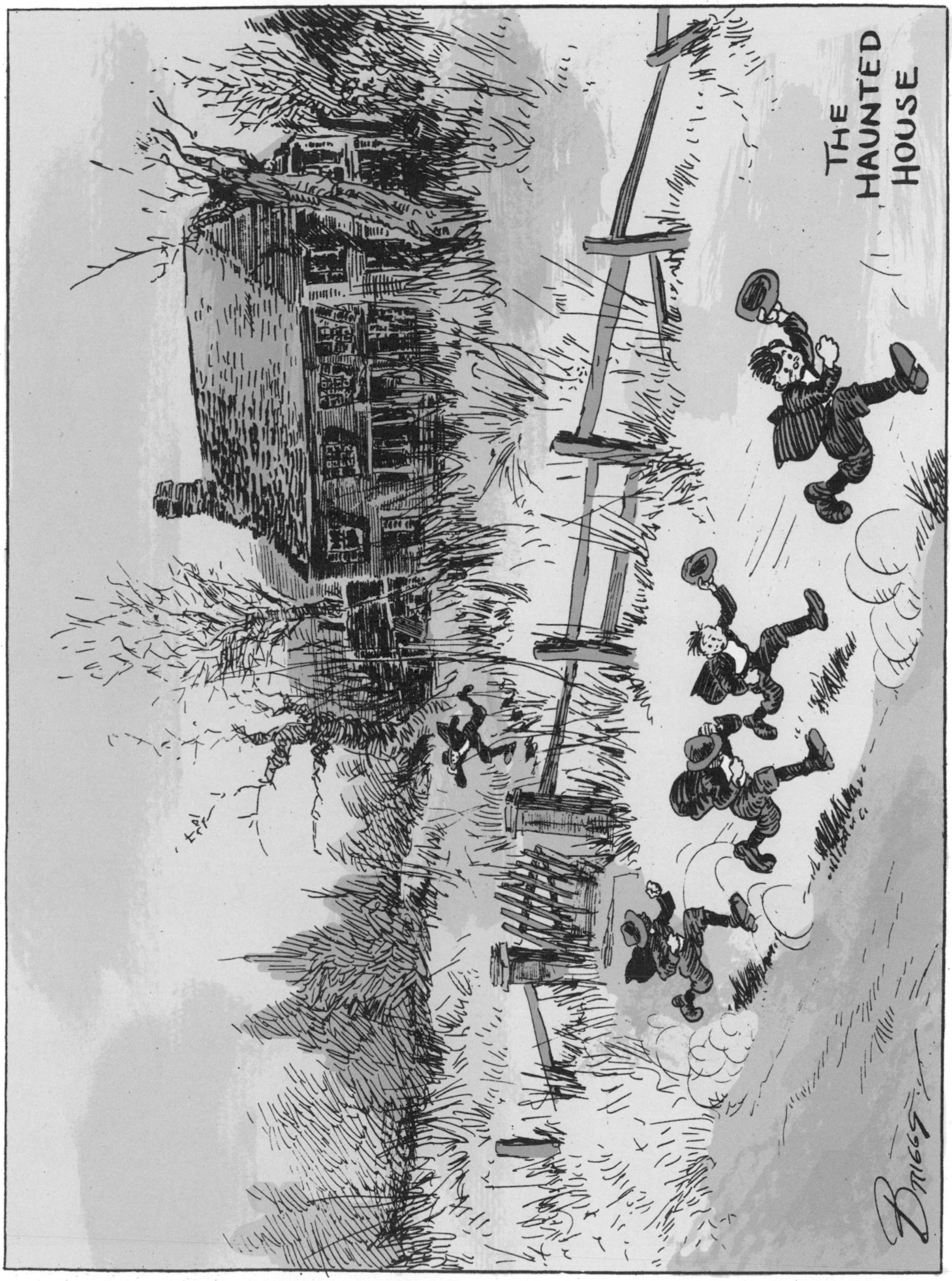
THE HAUNTED HOUSE
BRIGGS

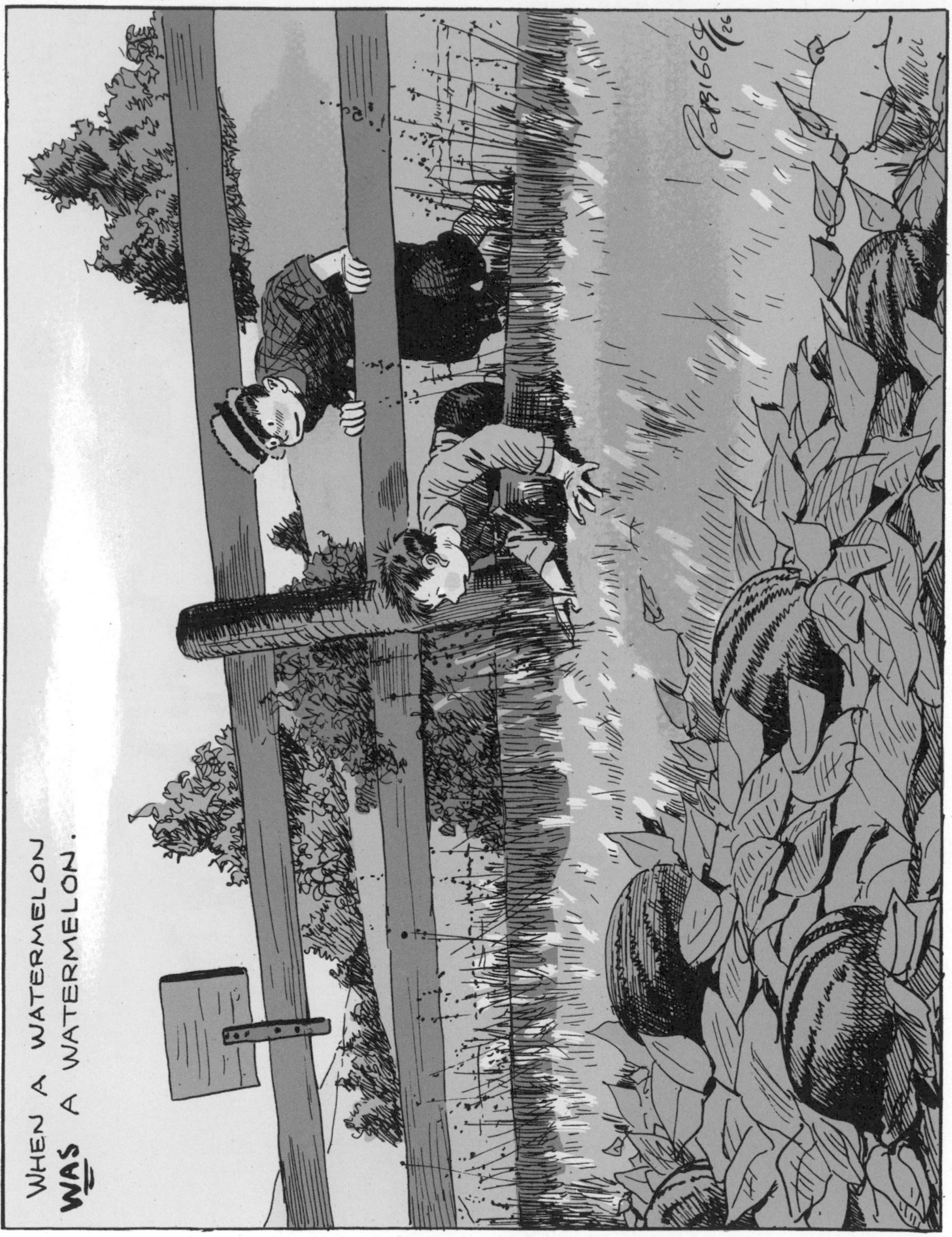
WHEN A WATERMELON
WAS A WATERMELON.
BRIGGS

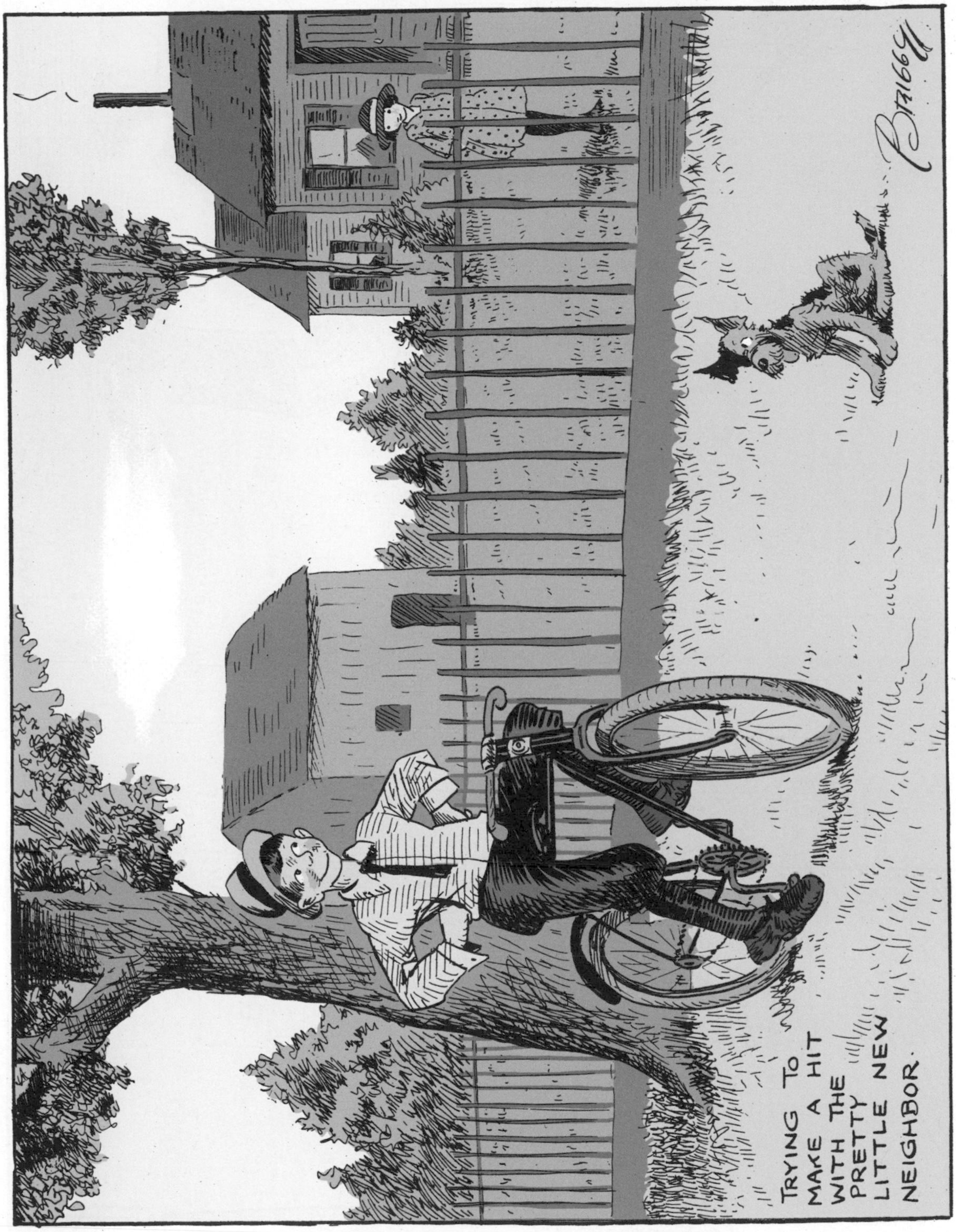
TRYING TO
MAKE A HIT
WITH THE
PRETTY
LITTLE NEW
NEIGHBOR.
BRIGGS

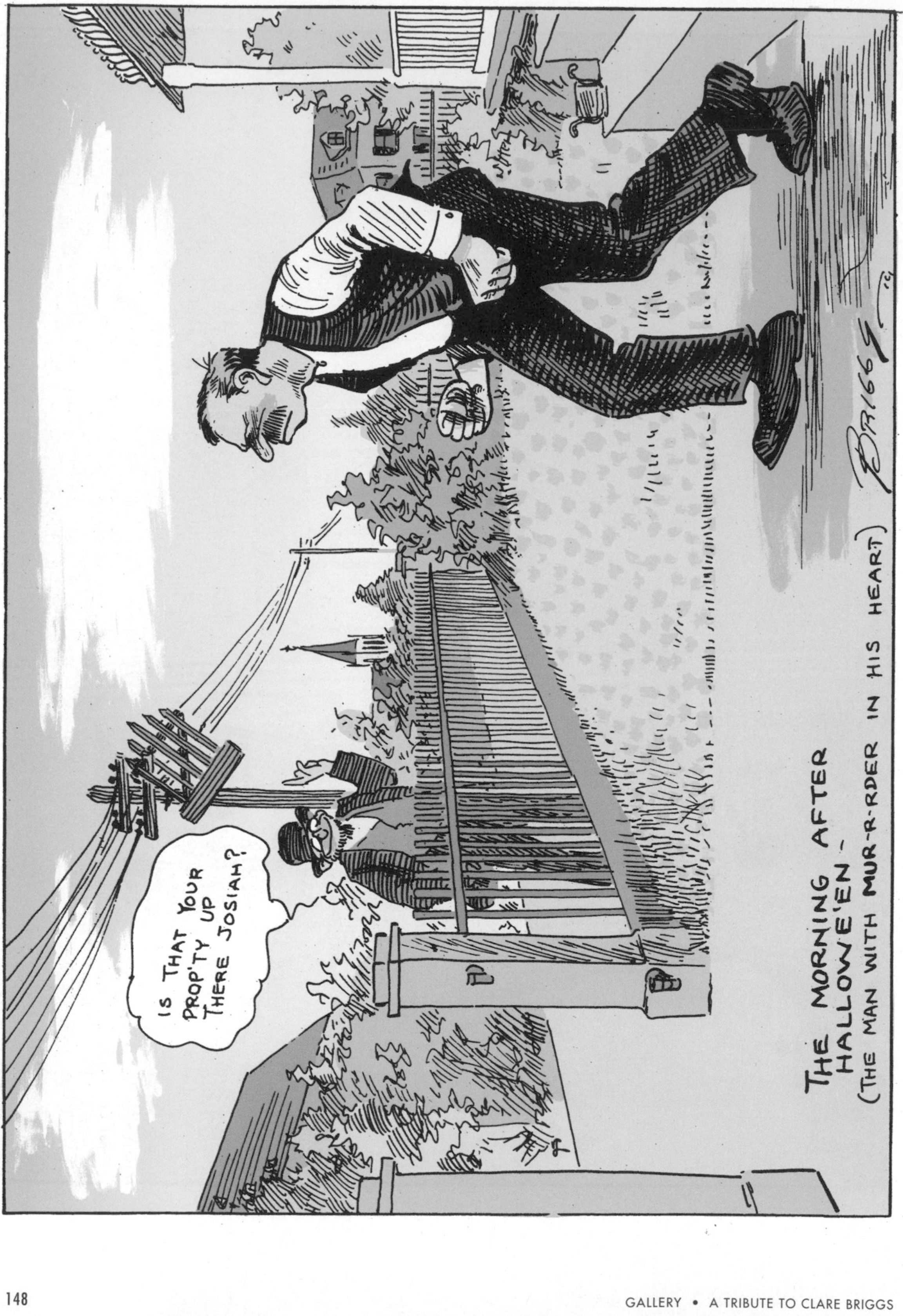
IS THAT YOUR PROP'TY UP THERE JOSIAH?
BRIGGS
THE MORNING AFTER HALLOWE'EN -
(THE MAN WITH MUR-R-RDER IN HIS HEART)

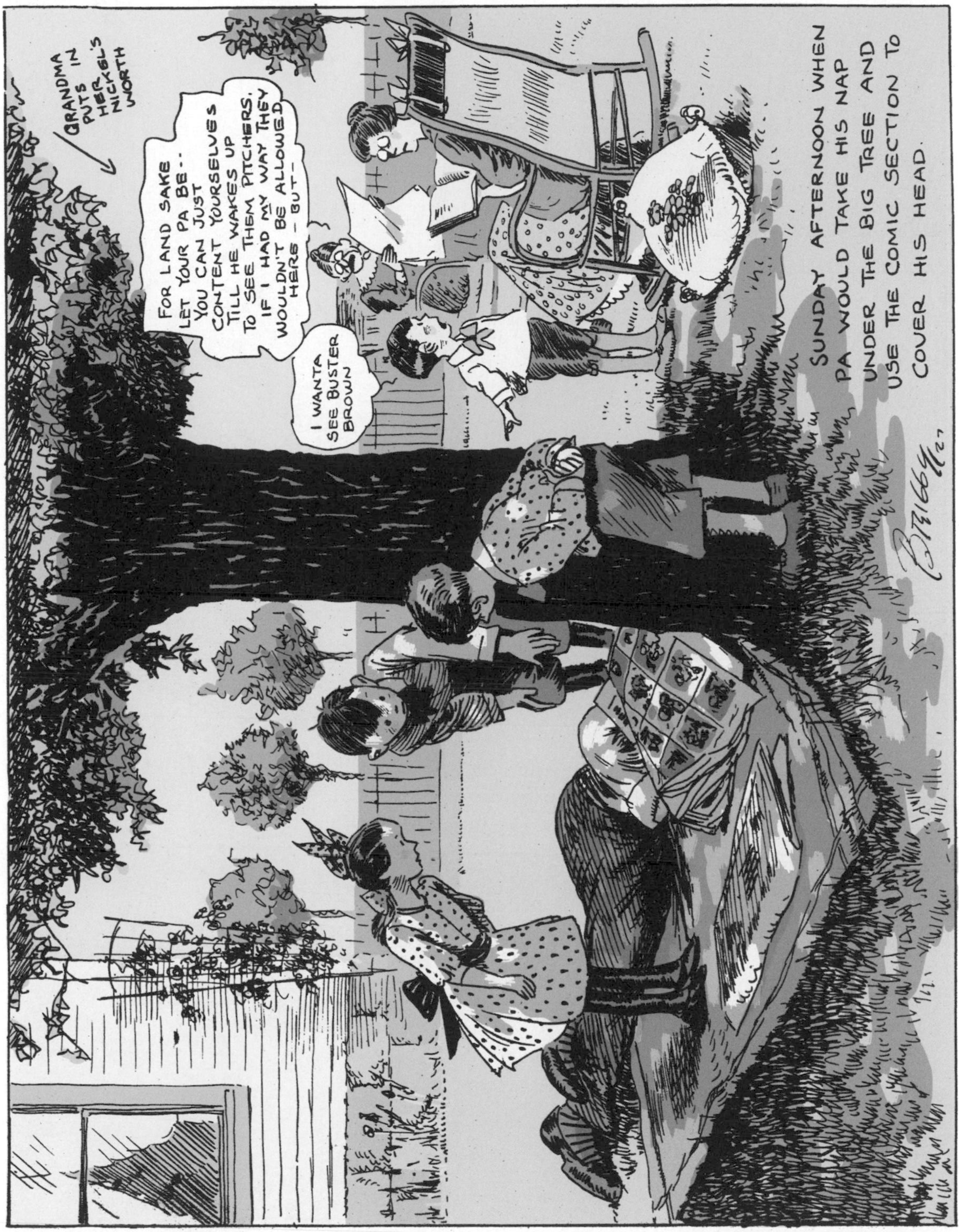
GRANDMA PUTS IN HER NICKEL'S WORTH
FOR LAND SAKE LET YOUR PA BE.. YOU CAN JUST CONTENT YOURSELVES TILL HE WAKES UP TO SEE THEM PITCHERS. IF I HAD MY WAY THEY WOULDN'T BE ALLOWED HERE - BUT-
I WANTA SEE BUSTER BROWN
SUNDAY AFTERNOON WHEN PA WOULD TAKE HIS NAP UNDER THE BIG TREE AND USE THE COMIC SECTION TO COVER HIS HEAD.
BRIGGS

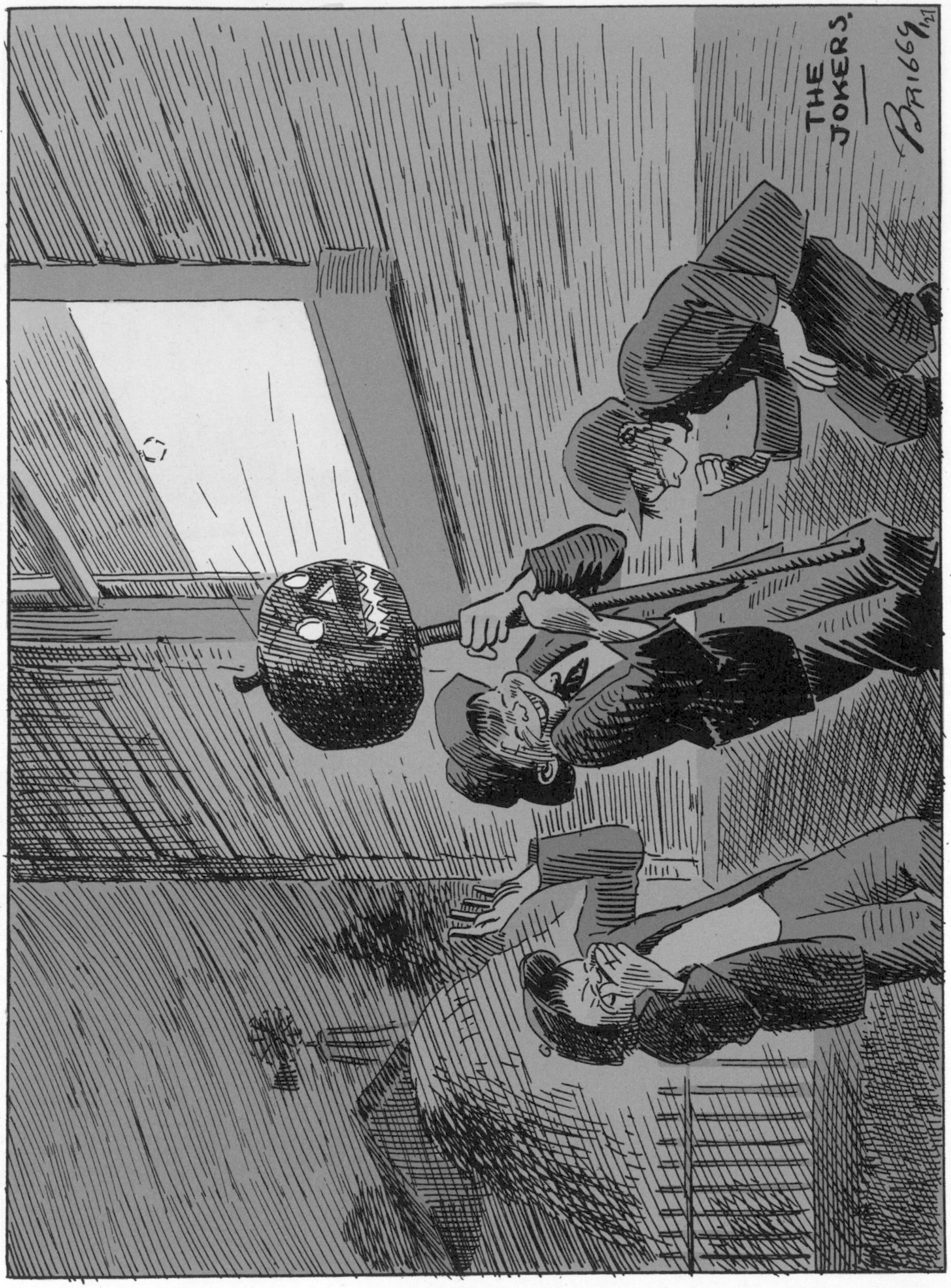
THE JOKERS.

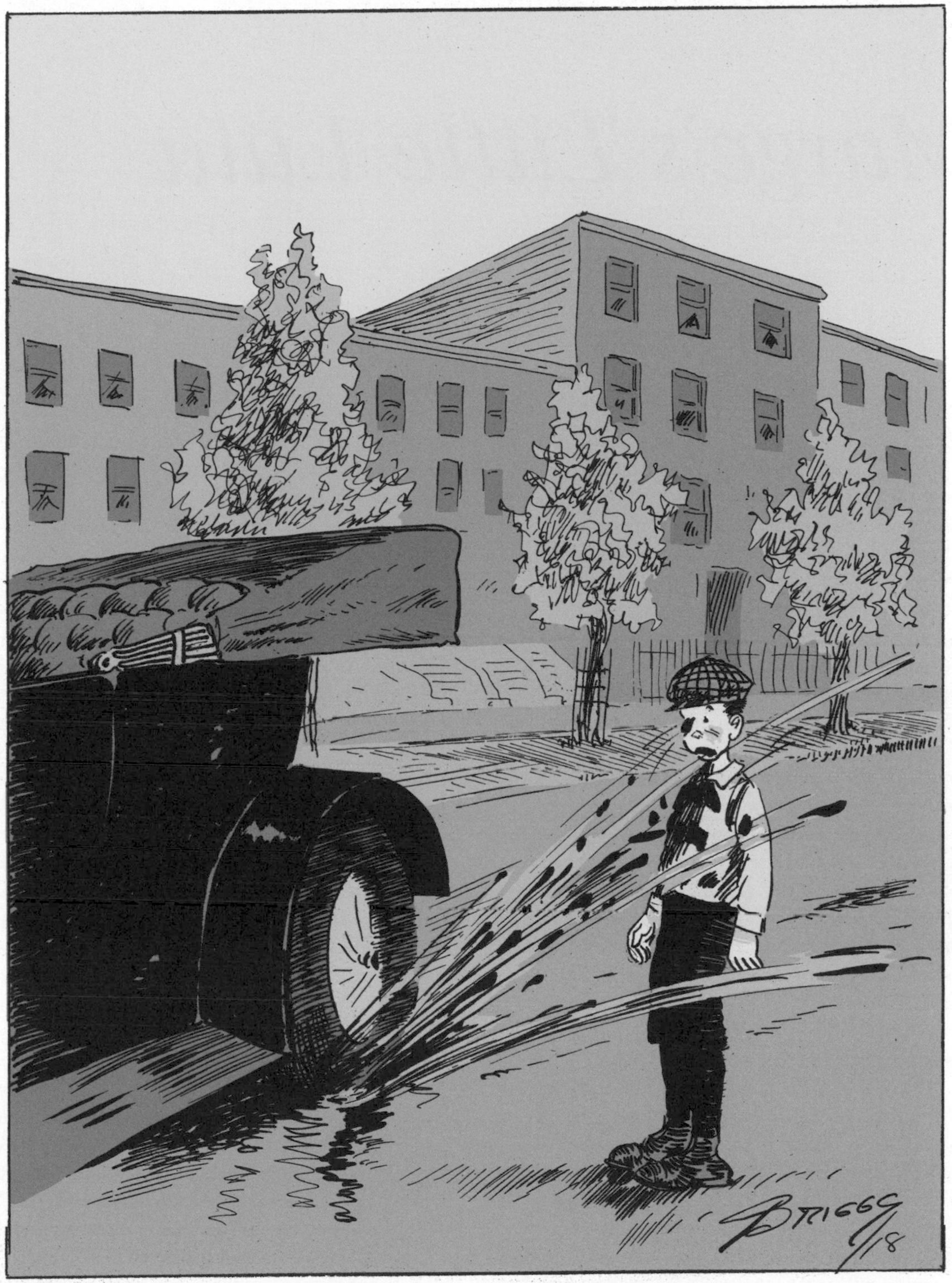
BRIGGS
'18

Marge's Little Lulu

Kayla E.

FOR ALMOST A DECADE, my work has been an attempt at some kind of dialogue with Marjorie Henderson Buell's Little Lulu character. And while the ghost of Marge haunts each panel, it is actually the Lulu as imagined and written by John Stanley and drawn by Irving Tripp with whom I am attempting to communicate most regularly in my work.

I was first drawn to Little Lulu as a child. I was obsessed with mid-century kids' comics — *Archie*, *Casper*, the Harvey horror comics, *Richie Rich* — mostly because I think I found them calming. To be frank, my childhood was chaotic. When you're a kid, it's almost impossible to name abuse — you just don't have the words yet, not unless they've been given to you.

Several years into my current practice, I realized that Little Lulu had given me a context that I was desperate for as a child. I think she named what was happening to me in a way that was palatable, in a way I could handle. In my favorite issues, there was a clear enemy: Tubby Tompkins. The nemesis. And there he was — in gorgeous, simple panels — the perfect little proxy for abuse. It was a visual language that I needed badly.

Michelle Ann Abate, a professor of literature for children and young adults at Ohio State, wrote a captivating paper on Little Lulu in the *Journal of Graphic Novels and Comics* in 2016. She called it "From Battling Adult Authority to Battling the Opposite Sex: Little Lulu as Gag Panel and Comic Book." In it, she chronicles how *Little Lulu* moved from an "ongoing battle with adult authority" in Buell's *Saturday Evening Post* strips from 1935 to 1944, to an "ongoing battle with

her male peers … her sworn enemy and, thus, the target of her pranks," in Stanley and Tripp's comic book series, which ran from 1948 to 1984.

The paper basically makes the case that Little Lulu's new enemies — the boys, generally, and Tubby, specifically — mirrored a 20th-century anxiety around the gendering of children. Where, for most of the 19th century, Americans "thought of children as sexless, in every sense of this word," at the turn of the century, there was a marked transition. "A paradigm shift occurred in the way that both children and childhood were viewed in the United States," explains Abate. "Whereas babies and young children were formerly regarded as 'sexless cherubs,' they were now seen as 'nascent men and women.'"

This paradigm shift was taken to new heights in the 1950s — precisely the moment in which Stanley and Tripp's *Marge's Little Lulu* comics were making their way to shelves across the United States — a time which was, according to Abate, defined by a "rigid adherence to traditional gender roles for men and women, widespread homophobia and booming consumer economy especially in the realm of items for children."

A tectonic event was happening in post-WWII America, a great divergence. Stanley and Tripp's *Little Lulu* was not immune to this sociopolitical upheaval. Abate, quoting literary scholar Janet Horowitz Murray, explains, "There is a full-blown gender war raging in Lulu's neighborhood, and the comics are clear on one point: it's the boys who started it."

Bill Schelly, in conversation with the brilliant Mark Newgarden (for this very magazine's website,

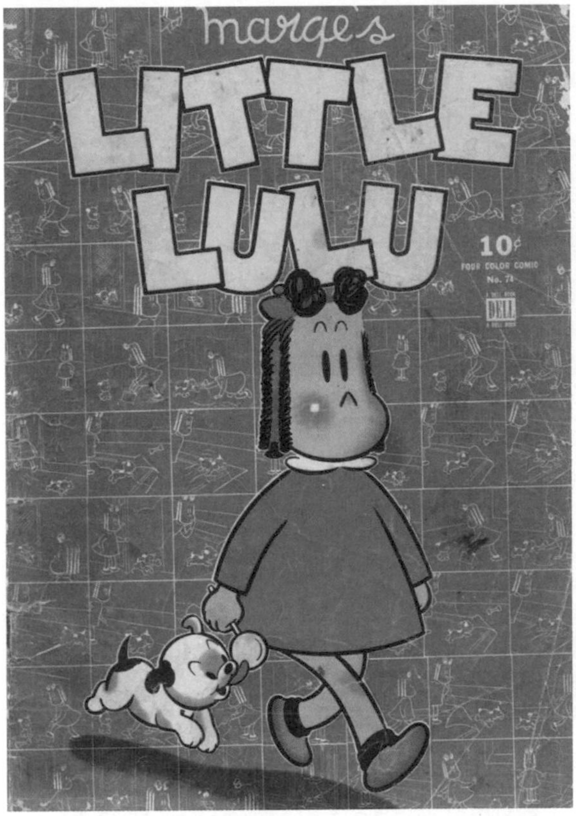
marge's
LITTLE LULU
10¢
FOUR COLOR COMIC
No. 71
DELL
Little Lulu cover, a 1954 John Stanley/Irving Tripp issue.

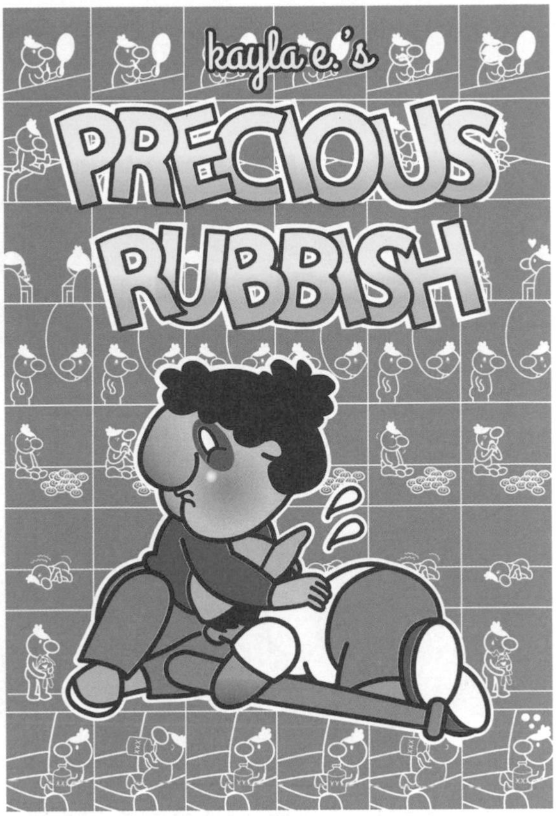
kayla e.'s
PRECIOUS RUBBISH
Precious Rubbish #21 cover, Kayla E.'s homage.

actually), called Tubby "one of the most complex characters to appear in any comic book. Tubby's infuriating narcissism, sexism, arrogance and insensitivity make him a perfect foil. He'd be a monster if he wasn't essentially likable." He then went on to say, "Young readers experienced a 'shock of recognition' when they read those comics. I suspect a lot of older readers liked them, too."

The work that I make is precisely concerned with this shock of recognition, and I am eternally grateful to Schelly for giving me those words. As a cartoonist, I am fascinated by the silliness surrounding depictions of misogyny in 20th-century comics. Oddly, it was this whimsicality in the violence that comforted me as a child — there's a distance there that's only found in the stories, in play. There is a difference between Road Runner dropping an anvil on the head of Wile E. Coyote and watching something heavy crush someone to death in a snuff film. The distance between these situations is the subject of my work.

I've been reappropriating 20th-century comics to tell my own story for the past seven years. (In fact, I did a series based on George McManus' *Bringing Up Father* for tcj.com in 2014.) In 2015, I began writing and drawing *Precious Rubbish*, my current body of work, which is based very much on *Marge's Little Lulu* as written and drawn by Stanley and Tripp. It's the most autobiographical work I've ever done, and it is my first work that deals specifically with childhood trauma and abuse.

Bear with me here, because we're going to do one of those A is to B as C is to D analogies. *Precious Rubbish* is to the snuff film as Marge's *Little Lulu* is to Wile E. Coyote and the anvil. Does that make sense? The space between the slapstick gender war of *Marge's Little Lulu* and the violent reality of misogyny and abuse was a haven for me as a child, but in my work I am collapsing it. According to Abate, "Little Lulu is far from either a pitiable victim or a weak damsel in distress. On the contrary, she retains her signature

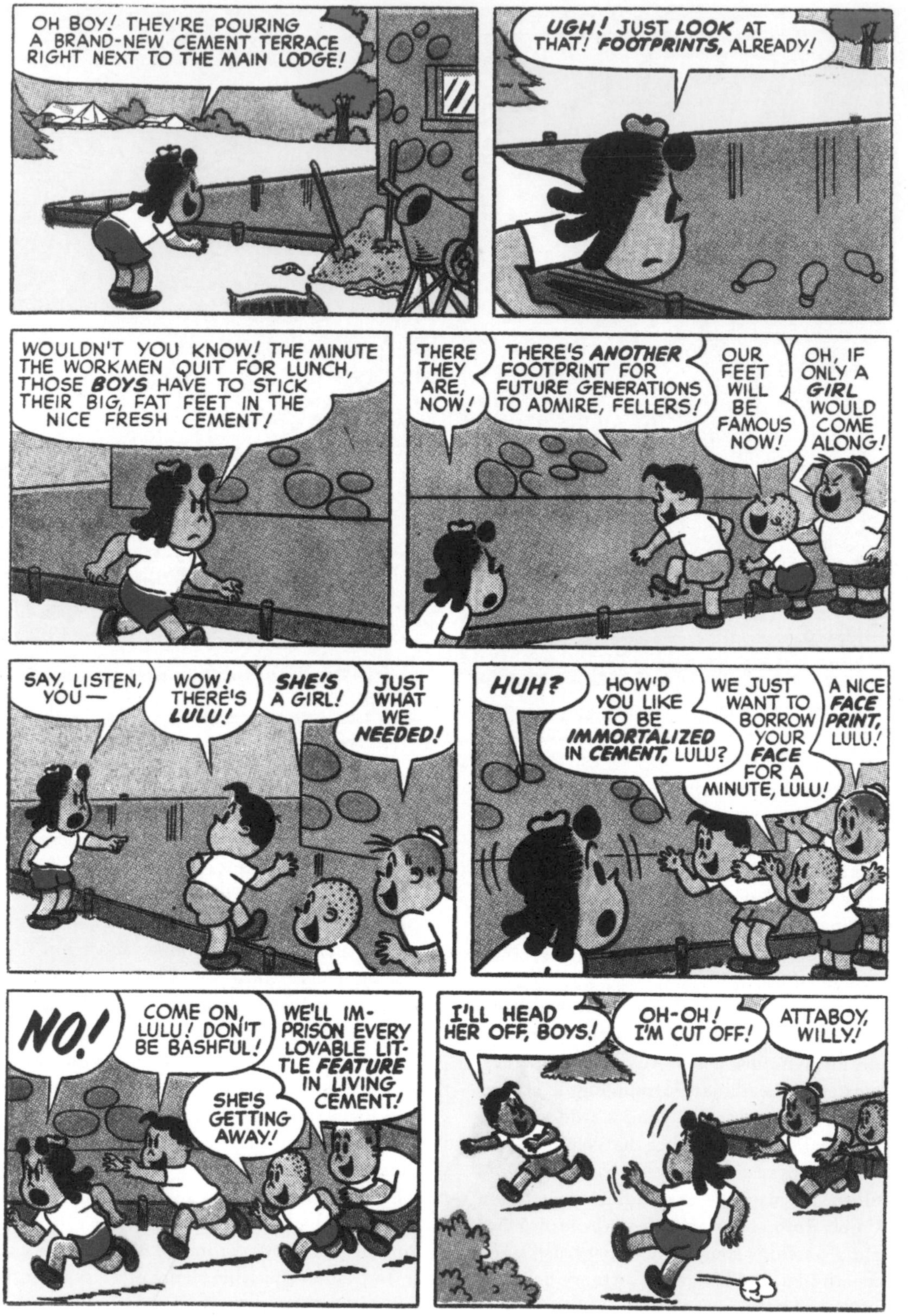
OH BOY! THEY'RE POURING A BRAND-NEW CEMENT TERRACE RIGHT NEXT TO THE MAIN LODGE!
UGH! JUST LOOK AT THAT! FOOTPRINTS, ALREADY!
WOULDN'T YOU KNOW! THE MINUTE THE WORKMEN QUIT FOR LUNCH, THOSE BOYS HAVE TO STICK THEIR BIG, FAT FEET IN THE NICE FRESH CEMENT!
THERE THEY ARE, NOW!
THERE'S ANOTHER FOOTPRINT FOR FUTURE GENERATIONS TO ADMIRE, FELLERS!
OUR FEET WILL BE FAMOUS NOW!
OH, IF ONLY A GIRL WOULD COME ALONG!
SAY, LISTEN, YOU—
WOW! THERE'S LULU!
SHE'S A GIRL!
JUST WHAT WE NEEDED!
HUH?
HOW'D YOU LIKE TO BE IMMORTALIZED IN CEMENT, LULU?
WE JUST WANT TO BORROW YOUR FACE FOR A MINUTE, LULU!
A NICE FACE PRINT, LULU!
NO!
COME ON, LULU! DON'T BE BASHFUL!
WE'LL IMPRISON EVERY LOVABLE LITTLE FEATURE IN LIVING CEMENT!
SHE'S GETTING AWAY!
I'LL HEAD HER OFF, BOYS!
OH-OH! I'M CUT OFF!
ATTABOY, WILLY!

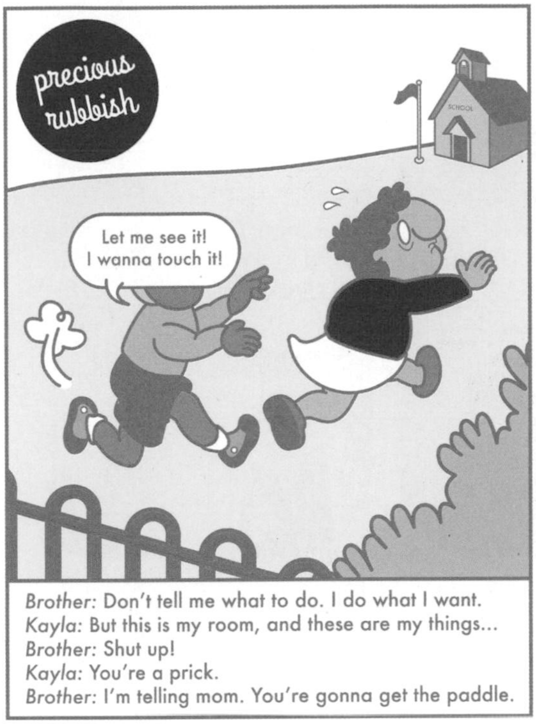
precious rubbish
Let me see it! I wanna touch it!
SCHOOL
Brother: Don't tell me what to do. I do what I want.
Kayla: But this is my room, and these are my things...
Brother: Shut up!
Kayla: You're a prick.
Brother: I'm telling mom. You're gonna get the paddle.

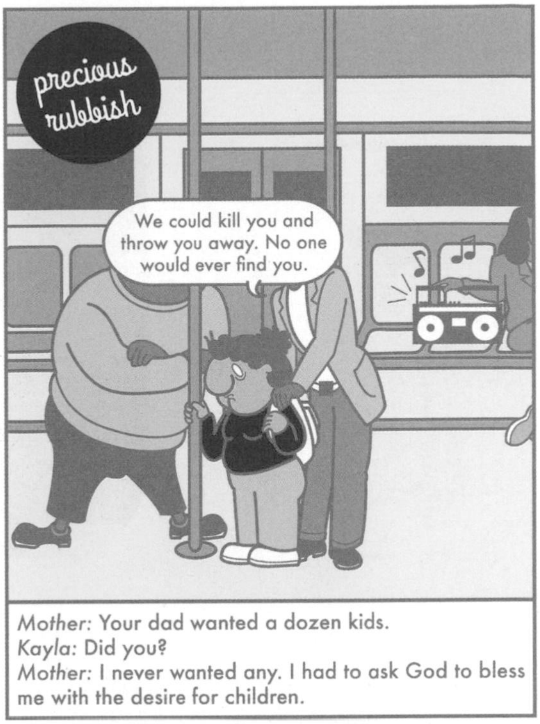
precious rubbish
We could kill you and throw you away. No one would ever find you.
Mother: Your dad wanted a dozen kids.
Kayla: Did you?
Mother: I never wanted any. I had to ask God to bless me with the desire for children.

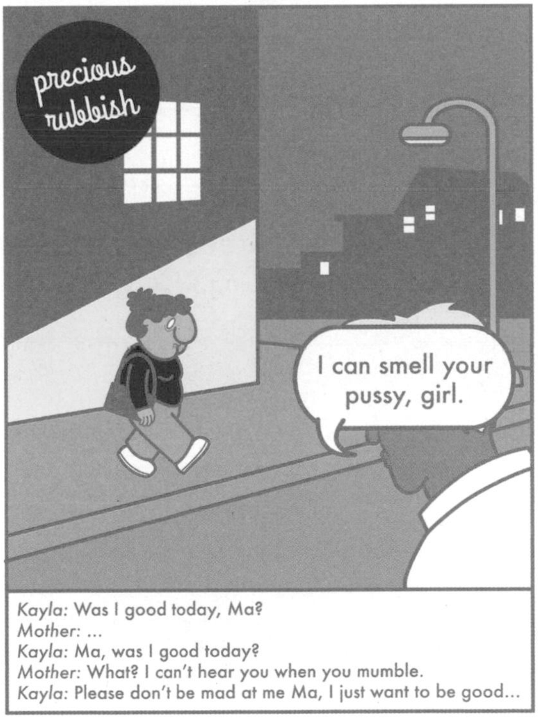
precious rubbish
I can smell your pussy, girl.
Kayla: Was I good today, Ma?
Mother: ...
Kayla: Ma, was I good today?
Mother: What? I can't hear you when you mumble.
Kayla: Please don't be mad at me Ma, I just want to be good...

ABOVE AND RIGHT: Panels from *Precious Rubbish*, by Kayla E.

moxie." Schelly echoes this in his interview by Newgarden: "Lulu wanted nothing more than to show that a girl can do anything a boy can do, and that girls are often smarter than boys."

In *Precious Rubbish*, sometimes a child just no longer has the strength to muster up "signature moxie." Sometimes abuse is inescapable. Sometimes racism is internalized. Sometimes the joke isn't funny. *Precious Rubbish* removes the distance from trauma that *Marge's Little Lulu* gave me as a child, and it imagines a world that looks very similar, but without any of the cartoonish safety. Stanley saw that tension roiling beneath the surface; I am certain. It permeates the entire narrative. It touches every character. *Precious Rubbish* is that tension made manifest. ❀

OPPOSITE: From "Wet Cement" in *Marge's Little Lulu and Tubby at Summer Camp* #2, 1958.

In the next issue...

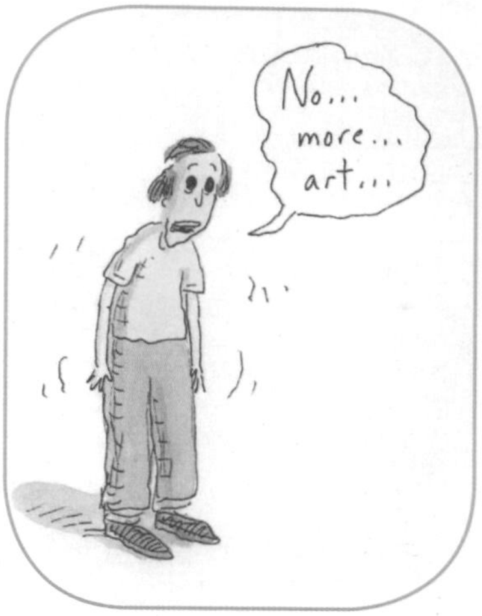

No... more... art...

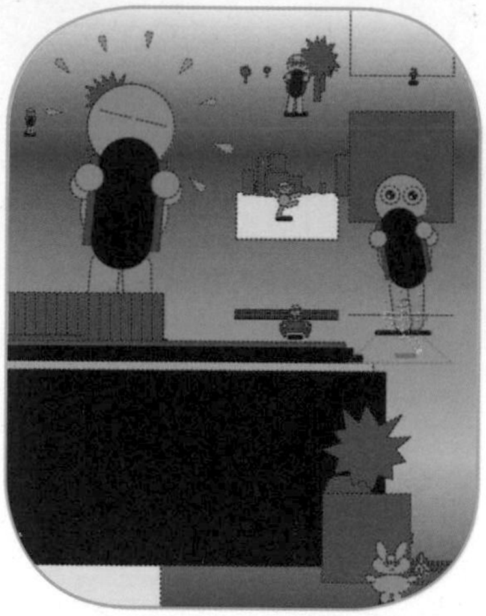

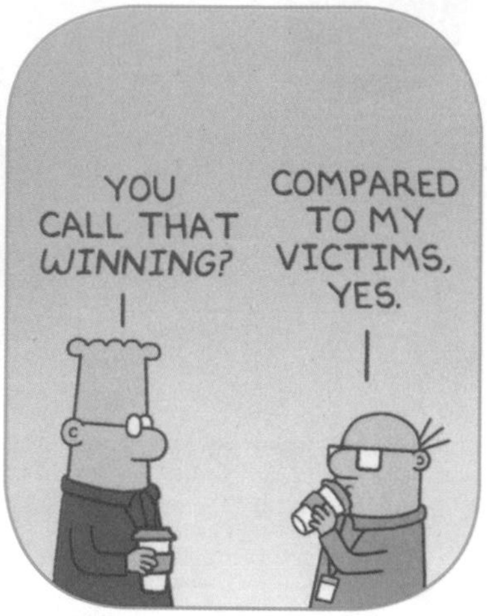

YOU CALL THAT WINNING?
COMPARED TO MY VICTIMS, YES.